D1537581

WITHDRAWN
FROM THE RECORDS OF THE
MID-CONTINENT PUBLIC LIBRARY

910.452 D379
Delgado, James P.
Lost warships
        35.00

MID-CONTINENT PUBLIC LIBRARY
Antioch Branch
6060 N. Chestnut Ave.
Gladstone, Mo. 64119

AN

LOST WARSHIPS

AN ARCHAEOLOGICAL TOUR
OF WAR AT SEA

JAMES P. DELGADO

LOST
WARSHIPS

☑® Checkmark Books®
An imprint of Facts On File, Inc.

MID-CONTINENT PUBLIC LIBRARY
Antioch Branch
6060 N. Chestnut Ave.
Gladstone, Mo. 64119

AN

MID-CONTINENT PUBLIC LIBRARY

3 0002 001148353 6

Lost Warships: An Archaeological Tour of War at Sea
Copyright © 2001 by James P. Delgado

All rights reserved. No part of this book may be reproduced
or utilized in any form or by any means, electronic or
mechanical, including photocopying, recording, or by any
information storage or retrieval systems, without permission
in writing from the publisher. For information contact:

Checkmark Books
An imprint of Facts On File, Inc.
11 Penn Plaza
New York, NY 10001

Library of Congress Cataloging-in-Publication Data
Delgado, James P.
    Lost warships: an archaeological tour of war at sea /
    James P. Delgado   p. cm.

    Includes bibliographical references and index
    ISBN 0-8160-4530-5

    1. Warships. 2. Naval Battles. 3. Shipwrecks.
4. Underwater archaeology. I. Title.
V750 .D45 2001   910.4'52—DC21

Checkmark Books are available at special discounts when
purchased in bulk quantities for businesses, associations,
institutions or sales promotions. Please call our Special Sales
Department in New York at (212) 967-8800 or (800) 322-8755.

You can find Facts On File on the World Wide Web at
    http://www.factsonfile.com

Originally published in Canada by Douglas & McIntyre, Ltd.
Editing by Maureen Nicholson
Design by Gary Blakeley
Maps by Eric Leinberger
Jacket illustrations: *front* montage, USS *Saratoga*'s bow at Bikini
Atoll, 1990. Bill Curtsinger. Sinking of USS *Monitor*. *Harper's
Weekly*, December 6, 1863. Author's collection; *back*
Perspective view of *Vasa*. Gunnar Olofsson, *Vasa* Museum,
Stockholm

Printed and bound in Hong Kong
Printed on acid-free paper

10 9 8 7 6 5 4 3 2 1

**PAGES ii AND iii The engagement between *Quebec* and
Surveillante (copy of 1789) by Auguste Rossel De Cercy
(1736–1804).** Bridgeman Art Library, London

PAGE vi Bow of HMS *Victory*, Portsmouth, England.
James P. Delgado

**PAGE vii Shell fragment recovered from deck of HMS *Prince
of Wales* after battle with *Bismarck*. It is inscribed "From
Bismarck to Prince of Wales."** Vancouver Maritime Museum,
Michael Paris

*For all those who sail in harm's way, and for
those who made the ultimate sacrifice at sea.*

*For my grandparents, Al and Betty Delgado,
whose generation sacrificed much in World War II
to ensure that we would enjoy the freedoms and
benefits of today.*

*And, last but not least, for the two most important
men in my life, my father, Robert Delgado, and
my son, John, and for Richard Goodhart, the
father-in-law I never knew.*

Contents

Preface

Yes, and this was the end of the Admiral Graf Spee, and perhaps it was for this that a pocket ship was she, for in Davy Jones's pocket, scuttled most ingloriously, she rusts beneath the rolling, bowling, she rusts beneath the rolling sea.

—"The Sinking of the Graf Spee" (song)

From space, the view of earth leaves no doubt that ours is a water planet. Water dwarfs the land masses, and one great ocean washes all those shores. Though it bears many names—Mediterranean, Baltic, Indian, Pacific or Atlantic—that ocean covers most of the earth. The sea has defined our history since the beginning of human endeavour, when we first built ships. It is the source of our life and the connective thread of our commerce. It is also our largest battlefield.

Millennia of war at sea have left lasting traces in our collective memory. But the battlefields of the ocean are a vast, unmarked grave. No monuments can stand on waters identifiable only by coordinates on a chart. The sea rarely gives up the dead. Occasionally, we return to those battlefields, to speak of sacrifice and determination, or to toll the bell and toss wreaths into the dark sea. We erect monuments on land: Nelson's Column in Trafalgar Square, the uss *Maine* Memorial at Arlington and a score of other statues and cenotaphs around the world.

We memorialize the surviving ships. By far the greatest number of preserved historic ships are warships: wooden sailing ships like Nelson's *Victory* and the fabled "Old Ironsides," uss *Constitution*; steam sloops like HMS *Warrior*; ironclad "monitors" like the Chilean *Huascar*; armoured pre-dreadnoughts like Dewey's *Olympia* and Togo's *Mikasa*, and many World War II ships. Over a hundred warships from World War II remain, including the Canadian corvette HMCS *Sackville*; the British cruiser HMS *Belfast*; German U-boats; U.S. aircraft carriers such as uss *Yorktown*; battleships like uss *Missouri*, and cruisers, destroyers, PT boats and landing craft from the last great naval war.

Veterans of later conflicts have lobbied to save ships from "their" wars. Today, the Vietnam conflict destroyers uss *Barry* and uss *Turner Joy*, the Cold War veteran submarines uss *Nautilus* and uss *Growler*, and the Falklands campaign veterans HMS *Plymouth* and HMS *Onyx* are all museum ships.

War at sea is a powerful subject rich in history, imagery and emotion. For those who did not serve, some sense of "what it was like" can be conveyed by the reality of the armour, the guns, the cramped quarters and the written or recorded word, the photograph, painting or film of those times. But it should come as no surprise that all of these books, songs and films; those museum ships resting peacefully at the dock; and the displays of paintings and memorabilia in galleries do not satisfy our need to remember, commemorate and touch the past. That is why, over the past five decades, underwater explorers, divers and archaeologists have ventured into the deep in search of lost warships.

I know the allure of that search, for I am one of those adventurers. On the bottom, on a ship that slipped beneath the waves with guns firing, time seems to stand still. I have swum through passageways of ships lost before I was born, overheads smeared with oil, past dark compartments filled with the detritus of war and the presence of the dead.

When we enter those dark compartments, history comes alive. I've felt it, after sharing memories with survivors and then diving to see first-hand what they've talked about. I'm not alone. That is why millions watch televised visits to *Bismarck*, *Yorktown* or the wrecks of Guadalcanal's Ironbottom Sound. That is why archaeologists raise artifacts and entire ships, like the Swedish galleon *Vasa* and Henry VIII's carrack *Mary Rose*, to share with nondiving museum visitors.

This book reviews what archaeologists have learned about lost warships. It is an archaeological tour through an imaginary museum of those ships. Some of the wrecks, and their stories, have been

Loss of uss *Monitor*. *Harper's Weekly*, December 6, 1863.
Author's collection

Port quarter of *Vasa*, gun ports open. *Vasa* Museum, Hans Hammerskiold

featured in the popular media. The stories of *Vasa*, *Hunley*, USS *Monitor*, USS *Arizona*, *Mary Rose*, the Nydam ship or the lost Mongol fleet of Kublai Khan are just a few of the warships to "surface" through television or in magazines like *Naval History* or *National Geographic*. For most people, the stories end there. But for archaeologists and other students of the past, archaeology is more than just the initial discovery.

Archaeology—the scientific recovery and study of the past—is nearly two centuries old, but underwater archaeology dates from only the 1960s. Since then, thousands of shipwrecks have been discovered, and a few hundred have been documented, excavated or recovered. Some sank in storms. Others were sent deliberately to the bottom, blasted to a watery grave with their

crews. The ships range from ancient row galleys that sank each other, pierced by huge bronze "rams" at their wooden bows, to modern steel ships attacked by aircraft, missiles and nuclear weapons. In studying these lost warships, archaeologists learn many things. Older wrecks may provide us with the details of the look of the ships. Newer wrecks may provide a closer picture of a battle.

In the chapters that follow, readers will see how little we know about many warships from ancient times through the medieval period. Archaeologists and naval historians often must "reconstruct" warships from paintings, sculptures, images on coins, models from tombs and descriptions in ancient literature. And that is often not enough. We need the wreck of the

A model of a xebec, a Mediterranean warship of the early eighteenth century and lineal descendant of the row galleys of earlier centuries. Models are often the only three-dimensional evidence, other than wrecks, for early warship design. Vancouver Maritime Museum, Michael Paris

ship. Otherwise, it's guesswork. Nautical archaeology as a result is dominated by many discussions and occasional controversies over the size of ships, the arrangement of oars and decks, and the construction of the hull—not to mention tactics and how battles unfold.

Nautical archaeologists in particular are interested in how warships were built and worked, and specifically how they differed from merchant ships that carried passengers or cargo. The changing technology of armament and propulsion influenced the design of warships, as did the availability of materials. Changes often did not happen progressively and uniformly around the world. Contrary to most history books, the Chinese adopted gunpowder weapons, the rudder, armour and paddlewheels long before Europeans did. While the Mediterranean powers focussed on oar-powered warships, the Northern Europeans were building larger, ocean-going sailing ships that developed platforms for guns—the genesis of the famous galleon.

The evidence from the sea provides a better picture of when certain developments, such as the introduction of guns, occurred. It also gives us a better sense of the sophisticated, often intricately developed methods of construction employed by warship architects. The carefully engineered bow of an ancient warship, built to withstand the shock of ramming another ship, or the methodical reinforcing of a multidecked galleon to carry the weight of the guns, reminds us that our ancestors were at least as clever as we are today. Wrecks like the famous *Vasa* or *Mary Rose*, both of which capsized and sank, killing most of their crews, also remind us that some of those lessons of warship design were learned through harsh example.

Archaeology, generally, can be a tool to study people and their behaviour. Individuals and societies under stress often make choices that are revealing about themselves and their circumstances. The archaeology of warships shows how ships can be built quickly to respond to a crisis. Years of tradition may be discarded in times of

Graf Spee **burns off Montevideo, 1939.** Vancouver Maritime Museum

strategic vulnerability. Technology leaps forward in those moments. Certain types of ships may be found to be more efficient. Hence, World War II saw increased construction of carriers, submarines and destroyers. Shortcuts not acceptable in peacetime—ships built out of green timber, or the rapid "acceptance" of all-welded as opposed to riveted construction—arise from wartime emergencies. There are also dramatic examples of recycling—warships that are practically rebuilt and pressed back into service in wartime. All of these choices speak volumes about human nature.

The response to new technologies—and the misapplication of those technologies—is particularly revealing. The nineteenth-century introduction of armour, steam engines and shell-firing guns changed warships and naval warfare. But in some cases, such as the rise of the battleship, the efforts and energies expended were largely wasted. Battleships did not function, fight or die as the tacticians and designers intended. From the mid-nineteenth to the mid-twentieth century, 650 battleships designed for ship-to-ship battle

were built. Only sixteen were sunk as a result of this type of action. In this, anthropologist Richard A. Gould sees a "consistent misapplication of new technologies to naval tactics." How this happened, and why, is a question he has examined. The answers are complex, perhaps debatable, and may include tactical indecision, confusion over the meaning of a new technology, the need to integrate a new technology before its implications are known or tested, the fascinating difference between theory and practice, and the need to match a foe's developments, weapon for weapon.

The archaeology of the warship, therefore, looks not just at ships, but also at who we are. When we discover how crews lived, ate, fought and died, we examine the human condition on a more intimate scale. The presence of cannabis sticks, probably to brew a narcotic tea for muscle-strained Punic oarsmen, in the Marsala wrecks of two thousand years ago; the striking differences between the fittings and food of Royal Navy officers and their crews found in eighteenth-century British wrecks; the crowded crew accommodations inside a German World War II U-boat wreck; or the large number of personal weapons and items found in the wreck of *Mary Rose*—these details clarify the conditions of the people who lived aboard ship and their times.

As an archaeologist, historian and museum director, much of my career has been entwined with stories of warships and their crews. I have worked to preserve and document warships that are still afloat. I have spent days exploring sealed-off compartments, dark passageways and cold boiler flats, along with long hours in the archives or museum storerooms. And I have enjoyed many conversations with veterans. As well, I have had unique opportunities to explore frigates, submarines, battleships, destroyers, carriers and more.

My experiences on land, in the archives and museums, and aboard surviving warships made distant battles more personal, as did interviewing veterans of the Pacific War, especially American

One of the guns from *Vasa* on a reconstructed gun carriage. Something as simple as the technology for mounting guns could bring victory or defeat, life or death in a sea battle. Four-wheeled gun carriages like *Vasa*'s were more easily moved and reloaded than two-wheeled carriages, but they could also become dangerous "loose cannon" in rough seas unless lashed down. *Vasa* Museum, G. Bauer

Wartime "emergency"-built wooden schooners rise on the ways in North Vancouver, British Columbia, during World War I. Vancouver Maritime Museum

and Japanese survivors of Pearl Harbor. Logbooks, muster rolls, reminiscences and faded photographs brought into focus battles beyond my memory. But by far my most intense experiences came beneath the sea as an archaeologist. Famous and forgotten ships, types of vessels and weapons otherwise only glimpsed in photographs and paintings, or in models, and the reality of the battlefield added to my education and to my enthusiasm.

Diving on these ships and learning their stories carries a responsibility. The responsibility is to bring forth the images and stories and share them. I have been fortunate in meeting and working with many colleagues from around the world who have also explored lost warships. Many of us collaborated to create *The British Museum Encyclopaedia of Underwater and Maritime Archaeology*. At the same time, one of those colleagues, Mensun Bound, assembled papers and articles and published two volumes, *The Archaeology of Ships of War* and *Excavating Ships of War*.

Exchanges with my colleagues, as well as the undeniable fascination of seeing some of these submerged warriors and their battlefields, were the inspiration for *Lost Warships*. My book is not intended to be a comprehensive review of war at sea, nor a detailed accounting of the development of the warship through history. It is not full of the technical specifications for these ships, nor a blow-by-blow accounting of sea battles. A number of exceptional books do just that, including several by scholars who integrate archaeological research, particularly for ancient and medieval ships and the eighteenth-century ships of the line. Many of those books are intended for a specialist audience, be they archaeologists, naval historians or naval architects. *Lost Warships* is instead intended for a wider audience: divers, students of the past and those interested in the saga of war at sea. It offers a three-thousand-year tour of that great, rarely visited museum on the ocean floor, and of many of the warships that lie there. It is also a look at how archaeologists have reconstructed the past, bringing back to the land of air and light remnants from earlier times.

James P. Delgado
Vancouver, British Columbia
October 2000

Rubbing of a battle scene from Angkor Wat, Cambodia, c. A.D. 1152. George Belcher

Acknowledgements

THE GENESIS OF THIS book was a four-year project to assemble and edit *The British Museum Encyclopaedia of Underwater and Maritime Archaeology*. My first debt is to that editorial board and contributors, all of whom worked very hard to create that five-hundred–page tome and demonstrated that an impressive body of work already existed on warships both ancient and modern. This book would not have been possible had not so many colleagues graciously shared their research and images from the encyclopedia.

Lost Warships would also not be possible were it not for the support of the board of trustees of the Vancouver Maritime Museum, who have actively encouraged my research and writing since I joined the museum in 1991. As always, the museum's exceptional W. B. and M. H. Chung Library was an invaluable resource.

Friends and colleagues provided assistance, advice, and books and shared their own research. I am grateful to Kathy Abbass, Chris Amer, Dan Bailey, Bob Ballard, George Bass, George Belcher, Mensun Bound, Burl Burlingame, John Broadwater, John Brooks, Arne Emil Christensen, Art Cohn, Kevin Crisman, Chris Dobbs, Bill Dudley, Lars Einarsson, Andrew Elkerton, Honor Frost, William H. Garzke Jr., Peter Gesner, Captain Max Guérout, Rachel Grant, Edward C. Harris, Alex Hildred, Olaf Hockmann, Robert Holcombe Jr., Paul Johnston, Don Keith, Roger Knight, Lars Ake Kvarning, Richard Lawrence, Dan Lenihan, Colin J. M. Martin, Daniel A. Martinez, Bob Mealings, Torao Mozai, Larry Murphy, William Murray, Robert Neyland, Jim Reimer, Warren Riess, Margaret Rule, Don Shomette, Roger Smith, Richard J. Steffy, William N. Still Jr., David Switzer, Richard W. Unger, Shelley Wachsmann, Gordon P. Watts Jr., Hector Williams, Robyn Woodward and Joseph Zarzynski.

The following institutions and organizations provided assistance, for which I am grateful: Association css *Alabama*, Paris; uss *Arizona* Memorial, U.S. National Park Service, Honolulu; Bateaux Below, Inc., Wilton, New York; Bermuda Maritime Museum, Mangrove Bay; British Museum, London; GRAN, Toulon, France; Independence Seaport, Philadelphia; Institute of Nautical Archaeology, Texas A & M University, College Station; Kalmar Lans Museum, Kalmar, Sweden; Lake Champlain Maritime Museum, Basin Harbor, Vermont; Mariner's Museum, Newport News, Virginia; *Mary Rose* Trust, Portsmouth, England; Museum für Antike Schiffahrt/Roemisch-Germanisches Zentralmuseum, Mainz, Germany; uss *Monitor* National Marine Sanctuary, Newport News, Virginia; National Civil War Naval Museum, Columbus, Georgia; National Museum of American History, Smithsonian Institution, Washington, D.C.; North Carolina Underwater Archaeology Unit, Kure Beach; Queensland Museum, South Brisbane; Royal Naval Museum, Portsmouth, England; Royal Navy Submarine Museum, Gosport, England; Scottish Institute of Maritime Studies, University of St. Andrews, Scotland; Ships of Discovery/Corpus Christi Museum, Texas; South Carolina Institute of Archaeology and Anthropology, Columbia; Submerged Cultural Resources Unit, U.S. National Park Service, Santa Fe, New Mexico; U.S. Naval Historical Center, Washington, D.C.; U.S. Naval Historical Museum, Washington, D.C.; Underwater Archaeological Society of British Columbia, Vancouver; Vancouver Maritime Museum, Vancouver; *Vasa* Museum, Stockholm; Vicksburg National Military Park, U.S. National Park Service, Vicksburg, Mississippi; Viking Ship Museum, Roskilde, Denmark; and the Viking Ship Museum, Oslo, Norway.

For some of the wrecks and sites mentioned in this book, I was able to dive on them or visit them in their museums, with the accompaniment, guidance or support of Fabio Amaral, George Belcher, Len Blix, John Broadwater, Arne Emil Christensen, Chris Dobbs, Andrew Elkerton, Al Giddings, Dan Lenihan, Mitch Marken, Dave

McCampbell, Bob Mealings, Larry Murphy, and members of the U.S. Navy diving community with whom I was privileged to work at Pearl Harbor and Bikini Atoll.

My family has always been supportive, both when I'm at home and when I'm in the field. Thank you, Ann, Mary, John and Beth. You've paid the price when I'm far away and joined my mother in fretting when I'm down, deep inside a wreck.

Portions of the manuscript were reviewed and invaluable criticism and advice offered by Ann Goodhart, Hector Williams, Roderick Miller, Art Cohn, Chris Amer, Shelley Wachsmann and Debbie Tardiff. Betty Marshall made the initial production of the manuscript possible. The hard-working team at Douglas & McIntyre worked their usual magic; I'd like to thank editor Maureen Nicholson and designer Gary Blakeley. Eric Leinberger produced the maps, and Michael Paris took photographs especially for this book. I'd also like to thank Carol Aitken, Isabelle Swiderski and Gayle Gibson for production assistance.

Any errors or omissions are my sole responsibility.

CHAPTER I

War on Ancient Waters

THE MEDITERRANEAN IS the birthplace of scientific archaeology under water. After more than five decades of work by archaeologists, a rich and varied understanding of the warship has emerged from both sea and soil. Archaeologists have developed knowledge about ancient ships from images painted on pottery, engraved in metal or chiselled in stone. We know more about ancient ships than we do about many other ships throughout history, because so many ancient shipwrecks have now been discovered and studied. British scholar A. J. Parker has catalogued over seven hundred Roman wrecks. Archaeologist George F. Bass, the pioneer of scientific underwater archaeology, and his associates at the Institute of Nautical Archaeology estimate that they have discovered over a hundred ancient and medieval wrecks along the Turkish coast.

But despite thousands of years of often-intense naval combat in these waters, little evidence has come from the sea. Why? Probably because ancient warships were small, light craft that were pulled out of the water when not in battle. When they fought, they did so within sight of land. After service, they were dismantled and recycled. Ancient warships that fell in battle were usually captured or disabled, drifted ashore or broke up on the surface of the sea. They were not always sent to the bottom. If destroyed, they were probably hauled onto the beach and burned, as the ancient historian Plutarch suggested more than nineteen hundred years ago. Walking the beaches near the site of the battle of Artemisium, where the Greeks clashed with the Persians in 480 B.C., Plutarch described stone memorial tablets and "a place on the beach where deep down, mingled with the thick sand, you can find a dark, ashy powder, which seems to have been produced by fire, and it is believed that the wrecks and dead bodies were burned there."

Whatever the reasons, archaeologists have extracted only tantalizing clues from the water: a handful of wrecks and a few weapons. But from the land, in combination with ancient texts, archaeologists, historians and other scholars have learned a great deal about ships of war from thousands of years ago.

FACING PAGE **Bow on, the reconstructed trireme** *Olympias* **recalls the nautical technology and naval triumphs of ancient Greece.** Trireme Trust, Paul Lipke

RIGHT **This Bronze Age Swedish rock art depicts men with boats, tools and weapons from the west coast of Sweden. It dates to c. 1100 B.C.** Vitylcke Museum, Tanum, Bohuslan, Sweden/Bridgeman Art Library

The Earliest Navy

From skin, reed and log boats, the ship slowly developed in the Mediterranean. Open-water voyages on log rafts probably occurred as humans crossed from Africa to Europe. By ten thousand years ago, people were venturing out to sea to fish, probably in hollowed logs and skin boats stretched over a wooden frame. By the early Bronze Age, some five thousand years ago, boats made of bundled reeds and wooden-planked craft had emerged.

The evolution of the ship gave rise to far-flung trade networks and to the use of the sea to extend power and control. By the second millennium B.C., the world's first navies were created by Mediterranean states. Ancient historians credited the near-mythical ruler of Crete, Minos, with the creation of the first navy. Thucydides wrote in the fifth century B.C., "[Minos] made himself master of a great part of what is now termed the Hellenic Sea. He conquered the isles of the Aegean and was the first colonizer of most of them."

Archaeologists excavating on land throughout the Mediterranean have proved the extent of Minoan trade by recovering Minoan artifacts in Egypt, the Levantine coast (now, Israel and Lebanon), the Aegean isles, Turkey, Greece and Italy, including Sicily and Sardinia. Trade goods alone do not indicate an ancient Minoan empire, but their scattered presence is evidence of Minoan naval power strong enough to protect ships carrying goods to distant lands. The excavation of the centre of Minoan power, Knossos on Crete, starting in 1900, revealed a vast palace and settlements remarkable in that they lacked protective walls. As Lionel Casson, the dean of classical maritime studies, writes, Thucydides knew what he was talking about: "The people of Crete … had been daring and active traders and the possessors of a great navy; Minoan towns needed no stone walls, for wooden ones, their ships, protected the island."

Archaeological evidence—depictions on pottery, seals and fragmentary murals from the ruins of Minoan towns and cities—indicates that these early warships were no different from merchant ships, except that instead of cargo they carried armed warriors to fight battles ashore.

Warriors fighting on the deck of a galley. This image is from a cup c. 850 to 800 B.C. found at Eleusis. Image redrawn from Casson (1991)

The First Warships and Battles Afloat

By the second millennium B.C., two types of ships began to evolve: the merchant vessel and the warship. The Mycenaeans, a scattered group of peoples on the Greek mainland, took to the sea during the height of Minoan power, and by 1500 B.C., they had conquered the Minoans. Fierce warriors, they developed the war galley, a long, oared ship suited for raiding, piracy and war. These were the ships that carried the Greeks to Troy. Homer's descriptions of the Greek warships in the *Iliad* and the *Odyssey* show them to be fast, slender and graceful craft.

They carried a single sail on a mast that could be raised to take advantage of the wind. When the wind did not blow, or in battle, the sail and mast were lowered and stowed and the men took to the oars. The smallest war galleys were about 12 metres (40 feet) long, carrying twenty oarsmen; the most common carried fifty oarsmen and may have been about 27.5 metres (90 feet) long. And yet they were only about 3 metres (10 feet) wide and with a low freeboard. Open, or as Homer termed them, "hollow ships," with a small deck forward and aft, the war galleys were probably much like a modern rowing shell.

With such sleek hulls, the Mycenaean galleys were easily beached. Casson notes that the

ABOVE Minoan ships from the frieze at Santorini, showing the gentle crescent form of the ships of this long-vanished navy and dating to c. 1600 B.C. National Archaeological Museum, Athens/Bridgeman Art Library

BELOW This Greek vase depicts Odysseus lashed to the mast of his ship as he passes the Sirens. Small and light, vessels like that of Odysseus' were the earliest Greek warships. British Museum/Bridgeman Art Library

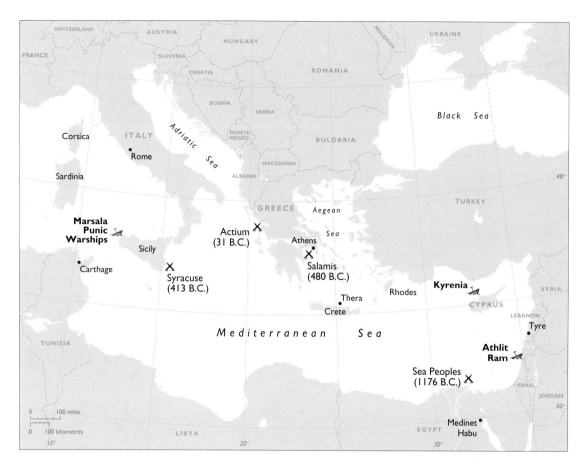

Wrecks and battles of the ancient Mediterranean.
James P. Delgado, Eric Leinberger

Odyssey describes how Odysseus made a fast getaway from the island of the Cyclops by shoving his ship off the beach with one good heave on his boat pole. But the lightness of the galleys came with a price: they were not a strong craft and working them was difficult and risky. Nonetheless, these ships were the standard Mediterranean warship beginning around 1500 B.C. Amazingly, we know nothing definitive about these ships because none has ever been discovered by archaeologists.

The power of Mycenae waned after 1250 B.C. when a major invasion of the Mediterranean by seafaring groups of Indo-Europeans occurred. Known as the "Peoples of the Sea," these seafarers destroyed Mycenaean cities and occupied the Levant. Their destructive arrival ushered in a so-called dark age and the first-recorded sea battle in history. Around 1176 B.C., Egyptian pharaoh Ramses III and his large navy met the Sea Peoples in battle, probably in the Nile Delta.

What we know about this battle comes from one remarkable source, a carved relief on the wall of Ramses' mortuary temple at Medinet Habu. Rising out of the desert, the imposing ruins tower above the sand. The wall, several storeys high with traces of bright paint and deeply carved images, is awe-inspiring. For maritime scholars, one series of scenes incised in stone is, as archaeologist Shelley Wachsmann notes, "the most important iconographic evidence" not only for the ships of the Sea Peoples, but also for "ship-based warfare before the introduction of the ram as a nautical weapon." By carefully analysing the relief, archaeologists have some sense of what the ships were like, and how the battle was fought.

Wachsmann uses the relief and an understanding of Egypt's artistic style to recreate the battle. Groups of ships, with soldiers on the decks, fought a "land battle" at sea, with the Egyptians staying out of range of the Sea Peoples' spears and shooting the invaders with archers. The relief shows Egyptian ships closing on their opponents after a volley of arrows, tossing a four-armed

ABOVE Rising from the sands of Egypt, Ramses' temple at Medinet Habu preserves the images of the pharoah's sea victory over the Sea Peoples. Bridgeman Art Library

LEFT Egyptian ships grapple with the vessels of the Sea Peoples in this view of the 1176 B.C. battle at the mouth of the Nile. Shelley Wachsmann

grapnel from the bow into the enemy's rigging and capsizing the light, shallow Sea Peoples' ships. The enemy soldiers drowned, were killed in the water or were pulled out and captured, as were their ships. The capsized ships are shown floating in the water.

The only archaeological traces of this battle might have been loose weapons scattered on the seabed. Indeed, all that we know about these ships of war comes from artistic representations, which archaeologists call iconographic evidence, and an understanding of ship construction resulting from

This seventh-century B.C. scene from the Palace of Sennacherib at Nineveh shows a Phoenician warship. These ancient mariners were accomplished traders and sea fighters. British Museum/ Bridgeman Art Library

the detailed study of Egyptian ships of the period excavated from desert sands. The most famous of these ships, the exquisitely built royal boats of the Pharaoh Cheops, were discovered in stone-lined pits next to the Great Pyramid.

As yet, no direct archaeological evidence of war at sea during the Bronze Age has been found. There are only tantalizing traces: an underwater discovery near Beit Yannai on Israel's Mediterranean coast of a late Bronze Age dagger and a Canaanite sickle sword may be evidence of an early sea battle.

Rise of the Ram

Egypt repelled the onslaught of the Sea Peoples. But it did not pursue naval control of the Mediterranean. Instead, a group of sea traders from Sidon, on the Levantine coast, expanded a commercial network of maritime trade westward, establishing colonies in North Africa at Utica and Carthage. Controlling much of the western Mediterranean and trading into the Atlantic as far north as Britain, these peoples, now known as the Phoenicians, ultimately came into conflict with a group of Greek city-states.

The Greek city-states rose out of the dark age that followed the arrival of the Sea Peoples. By 800 B.C., Corinth, Athens, Miletus, Sparta and other cities began to expand their trade, and over the next two hundred years, the Greeks established overseas colonies to the east in the Dardanelles, north to the shores of the Black Sea and west to Italy and Sicily. This expansionism brought Greece into conflict with the Persian Empire, the Phoenicians and the Etruscans, and started a series of wars on land and sea for control of the Mediterranean.

In this age, the galley—propelled by oars but also carrying an auxiliary mast and sail—was the principal fighting ship. Around 850 B.C., the Greeks added a projecting, bronze-sheathed underwater ram to the bow of their galleys. Perhaps adapted from a projecting beak at the bow of earlier warships that facilitated running the ship onto the beach, the ram changed the way ships fought at sea. Although they still grappled and men fought it out on-deck, the ram, as Lionel

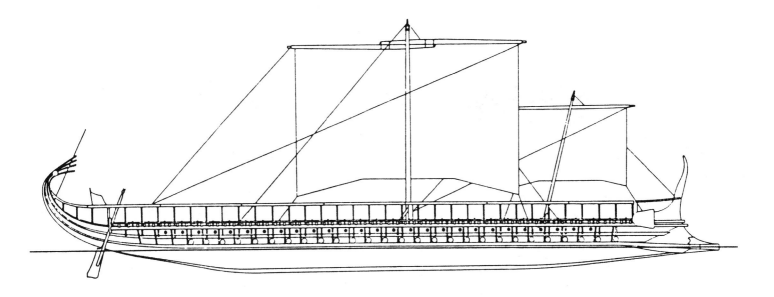

ABOVE **Profile drawing of the reconstructed trireme** *Olympias.* Trireme Trust, John Coates

BELOW **Water surges past the ram on the bow of** *Olympias* **as the ship's eyes glare forward in this graphic view of the grace and power of an ancient naval weapon.** Trireme Trust, Paul Lipke

Trireme Navies and Tactics

Ancient warships were often built quickly in times of emergency. To meet the Persians in battle at Cape Artemisium in 480 B.C., the Athenians constructed and assembled a fleet of some two hundred ships.

When not in use, the triremes were housed ashore in large, roofed ship sheds with sloping ramps that led down to the water. Archaeological study of the ruins of these sheds—particularly those from the Athenian dockyard at the Bay of Zea in Piraeus, near Athens—provided the first direct physical evidence of

the length and beam (or width) of triremes: about 36 metres (120 feet) long and 5 metres (17 feet) wide. The ships were classified according to their age as "selects," "firsts," "seconds" and so on. The oldest ships were sold, usually for breaking up, according to one ancient Greek inscription listing the scrap value of discarded bronze rams.

Triremes carried oars, masts and sails. When sailing any distance, they put in to shore at night, beaching so that the men could forage for food and set up camp. To fight, the triremes

removed their masts and sails to lighten the ship, and then they rowed out to meet the enemy. The Greek trireme carried three rows of banks of oars manned by 170 rowers, and a force of thirty marines and officers. The ships used three tactical manoeuvres: the *diekplus,* the *periplus* or the *kyklos.* The diekplus was used to break through an enemy's line of ships and ram the ships from behind. The periplus was used to encircle an enemy's ships and ram them. The kyklos was a defensive manoeuvre. The ships would form a circle, sterns touching and the bow standing out like the hubs of a wheel.

The Greeks adopted fleet tactics, with groups of ships

drilled to fight together, practising fast manoeuvres to ram and then, if needed, close in, heaving grappling irons and boarding for fierce, hand-to-hand combat on the decks. As Plutarch noted, for the Greeks in this age the key to naval victory was simple: "They learned from their own behaviour in the face of danger that men who know how to come to close quarters and are determined to give battle have nothing to fear ... They have simply to show their contempt ... engage the enemy hand to hand and fight it out to the bitter end."

Thus was set the basic form of naval warfare for the next thousand years.

This ceramic model of a galley comes from a tomb at Amathus, Cyprus, and dates to the sixth century B.C. Much of our evidence of ancient warships comes from models, engravings and scenes painted on pottery.
National Archaeological Museum, Athens/Bridgeman Art Library

Casson notes, shifted the emphasis "to the men who manned the oars." Victory went to a well-trained crew, who responded instantly and accurately to orders to drive a ram into an enemy ship.

The standard warship of the period was the fifty-oared *pentekontoros* with a ram at the bow. But a change in the design of warships resulted in a new type of vessel. Although earlier warships had been open hulled, the Greeks added a deck to protect the oarsmen and to provide a platform for the fighting men. The addition of a deck level led to a second row of oars for greater speed. These new ships are known as biremes. This development, around 775 B.C., in turn led some fifty years later to the design of a decked ship that carried three banks of oars, the Greek *trieres*, or trireme.

The trireme and the ram were the key inventions that gave the Greeks naval control of the Mediterranean for the next three centuries. The trireme, with a trained crew of citizen-volunteers (*Ben Hur* notwithstanding, the ancients did not use galley slaves), was a fast, deadly ship. The use of

the trireme dictated a change in tactics. Rather than closing and fighting with arrows, spears and boarding ladders, triremes lined up in columns and manoeuvred to ram the enemy, causing his ships to founder.

The manoeuvrability and power of the new ships was proved in battle around 540 B.C., when Greek colonists in southern France and Corsica, with a fleet of sixty triremes, defeated a larger force of a hundred Etruscan and Phoenician ships near Corsica. This victory led to history's first naval arms race. Between 540 and 525 B.C., most Mediterranean powers built large fleets of triremes.

Triremes fought the major sea battles between Greece and Persia, notably at the epic battle of Salamis in 480 B.C., when a united Greek fleet defeated the navy of Xerxes. Triremes also fought in the bitter Peloponnesian War between Athens and Sparta that followed from 431 to 404 B.C. But with dozens of battles and hundreds of ships lost, archaeologists have yet to discover a single trireme shipwreck.

Nearly a century of scholarly debate over the trireme recently ended. The arguments were often over the meaning of the facts available from the scattered evidence of artistic representations and in ancient texts. In the 1980s, collaboration between classical scholar John Morrison and naval architect John Coates resulted in the reconstruction of a trireme. Morrison and Coates built

models, then a full-scale section of a trireme to test how the three-banked oar system would work. From this, the Greek government in 1987 built the full-scale modern trireme *Olympias*.

It is an amazing sight as *Olympias* goes through the paces, rowers working in synchronized motions to move the trireme quickly, stop and turn sharply. *Olympias* looks much like ancient representations on pottery and stone, but like any reconstruction, some guesswork and deduction was necessary. The ship shows how the modern technique of "experimental archaeology" works to pull together evidence and test theories. After watching *Olympias*, most scholars agree with Morrison and Coates about the design of a trireme.

The construction of *Olympias* demonstrated that the trireme was a complex, fast (capable of 11 knots) and yet fragile craft that required a high level of skill of its crew to go into battle. The Greeks, particularly the Athenians, were skilled sea fighters with their triremes, a point that is obvious to anyone who reads ancient accounts of battles like Salamis. There, a combined Greek

LEFT This fragment of ancient sculpture, the Lenormant Relief, was one of the critical pieces of evidence used by scholars to reconstruct the trireme because it shows the position of the oars and men. Acropolis Museum, Athens, Hector Williams

BELOW Banks of oarsmen row an ancient Greek warship on this vase from the eighth century B.C. British Museum/ Bridgeman Art Library

Olympias **going through manoeuvres. The reconstructed trireme breathes life into two-dimensional images of pottery and stone.** Trireme Trust, Paul Lipke

fleet of three hundred ships defeated a Persian fleet of some eight hundred ships. Thanks to the reconstruction of *Olympias*, we now have a better understanding of how each citizen-volunteer at his oar personally contributed to a victory that saw two hundred Persian ships destroyed at a cost of only forty Greek ships.

The next phase in the development of ancient warships was the rise of the polyremes. A series of wars, fought for the control of Sicily and the seas surrounding it, pitted Carthage, the Sicilian Greek colony of Syracuse and the new power of Rome against each other. New, larger versions of the trireme, mounting greater numbers of rowers, appeared in a naval arms race that started around 400 B.C.

Quadriremes (fours) and quinqueremes (fives) were built, some ships reaching more than 60 metres (200 feet) in length. At one time, historians believed that these ships, and the "sixes," "nines" and "tens" that followed might have referred to the number of banks of oars, one bank

per level, so that a ten would be ten levels high. But such ships—towering above the water— would have been impossible to build or sail. Instead, working with a three-level system like the trireme, scholars such as Morrison and Coates have reconstructed the ships on paper with more than one man per oar, often staggering the number of men per oar on each level. A "five" would have two rows or levels of oars, three men per oar on the first level, and two men per oar on the next.

The navies of the last three centuries B.C. were a varied lot, with ships of different sizes and classes, much like later navies with their mix of battleships, cruisers and destroyers. The naval arms race of this period saw contenders for control of the sea outbuilding each other in sheer numbers of ships and in their size. Again, the key to power was seen in the number of oarsmen: tens, sixteens, twenties and forties instead of 12-, 14- or 16-inch naval guns. These were the ships used by Alexander the Great as he seized control of the Mediterranean, capturing island cities like Tyre with combined land and sea forces.

The death of Alexander in 323 B.C. started a war between his generals for control of the far-flung Macedonian empire. Antigonus, with his son Demetrius, held Greece, while Seleucus held Persia and Ptolemy dominated Egypt. Dionysus, the tyrant of Syracuse, is credited with the invention of the five; Demetrius of Greece is credited by ancient historians with the invention of the larger ships—sixes, sevens, all the way up to a sixteen. As Demetrius built larger ships with more oarsmen and larger decks carrying not just armed men, but catapults, fire pots and ballistae that fired bolts and stone shot, his ships were matched and then surpassed by those built by other rulers. Ptolemy IV, it is said, built a gigantic forty, perhaps an unwieldy marriage of two hulls into a massive catamaran.

In this age of the super-galley and varied fleets, sea battles were fierce melees as ships of different sizes closed with each other, firing missiles, bolts and darts before ramming. Armed marines, standing on decks, or in wooden turreted towers at either end of the ships, fought with long spears, arrows and swords. Grappling irons brought ships close so boarding parties could spring onto the enemy's deck.

In this period, the first direct archaeological evidence of war at sea appears in the form of iron spear points embedded in the hull of a sunken ship. The Kyrenia wreck, a Greek merchant galley, was attacked and scuttled, probably by pirates, around 306 B.C. When archaeologists from the Institute of Nautical Archaeology excavated the wreck, and the timbers were raised for preservation and reassembly, the spear points were discovered. They are the earliest direct evidence of a fight at sea.

Carefully excavated from the seabed and reconstructed, the hull of the Kyrenia ship yielded evidence of the earliest traces of a battle at sea. © Michael and Susan Katzev

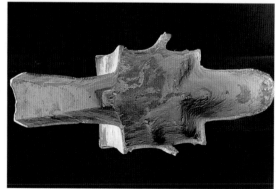

ABOVE The Athlit ram is one of the most complicated and ornate bronze castings from the ancient world—and a deadly weapon of its age.
W. A. Murray

RIGHT Now hollow, the interior of the Athlit ram was once filled with a complicated group of timbers that helped the ram pack a punch without sinking its own ship.
W. A. Murray

The Athlit Ram

Another underwater discovery provides a hint of larger warships from this period and the sophistication of the ram. Archaeologist Yehoshua Ramon, snorkelling about 200 metres (650 feet) offshore from Athlit, which lies near Haifa on Israel's northern coast, discovered the ram in November 1980. Lying in the shallows of only about 3 metres (10 feet) of water, the ram was raised for careful scientific study by archaeologists from Israel and the United States. Repeated surveys of the bay where Ramon discovered the ram yielded no additional traces of the warship that once carried the ram. It had apparently drifted close to shore after being wrecked and disintegrated, leaving only the heavy ram with remains of the warship's bow inside it.

The "Athlit ram," after cleaning and preservation, proved to be an exceptionally well preserved, cast-bronze warship ram 2.26 metres (about 7 feet) long, 0.76 metres (about 2.5 feet) wide and 465 kilograms (over 1000 pounds). This ship-killer held sixteen timbers from the bow of the lost warship inside its socket. In a meticulous, painstaking process, J. Richard Steffy of the Institute of Nautical Archaeology carefully extracted the timbers, which were form-fitted inside the ram.

Steffy's analysis of the surviving wooden structure of the ram showed a well-designed series of strakes and timbers that distributed not just the weight of the ram but the forces and stresses of the act of ramming into a heavily constructed hull bottom. Steffy believes that the "entire bottom of this ship was essentially the weapon," not just its bronze ram.

No other wooden remains of the ship at Athlit were discovered. There are only the timbers from inside the bronze ram to suggest how the original warship's hull was built. The ram timbers and wooden wales that ran along each side of the keel indicate that the ship weighed as much as one tonne per metre of length—a heavy ship indeed. This reconstruction means that not all ancient warships were lightweight.

Fast and hard-hitting was not always a good combination. Steffy points out that a motorcycle hitting a brick wall at 100 kilometres (about 60 miles) an hour will destroy itself, whereas an eighteen-wheeled truck loaded with 20 tonnes of freight will knock the wall down at 10 kilometres an hour. "Our warship was more like the eighteen wheeler than the motorcycle," Steffy says. Momentum was the key, as was remaining agile to "drive that ram home." The Athlit ram suggests that the builders of that warship discovered the right balance between the weight of the timbers and the good "punch" and the overall lightness of the vessel to enable the oarsmen to manoeuvre quickly.

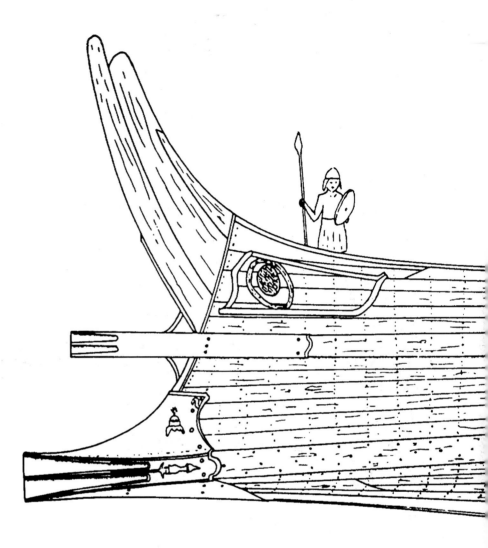

This hypothetical view of the bow of an ancient warship shows how scholars believe the Athlit ram would have fit.
W. A. Murray

Archaeological drawings document the Athlit ram. It was carefully designed to break and open the seams of an enemy ship, not bash through. J. R. Steffy

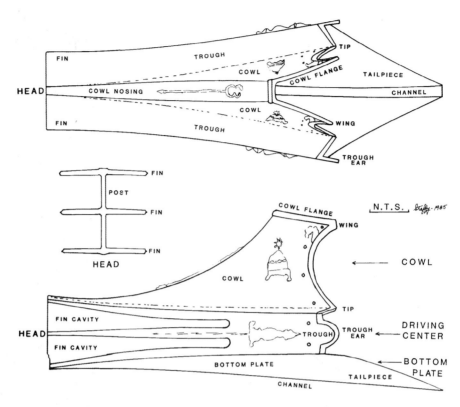

The bronze ram itself was a sophisticated weapon and very different from the bronze-sheathed ramming timber discovered at Marsala. Made of a high-grade bronze (90 per cent copper and 10 per cent tin), the ram sweeps out from the bow to a reinforced head with three "narrow fins" that spread the force of ramming into a blunt impact in a concentrated area less than a half-metre square. This impact would break planks and flood the enemy ship without smashing a hole in the side and raising the possibility of the ram getting stuck. Unlike the ram discovered at Marsala, the Athlit ram was firmly attached to its warship and could not break away without serious damage. It was not a bee-stinger, but a sophisticated, engineered "warhead" mounted on the "weapon," its ship.

How old is the Athlit ram, and what else can we say about the warship it was mounted on and how it may have been lost? Symbols cast into the bronze indicate that it dates from 204 to 164 B.C., and that the ram probably came from a Cypriot warship, probably not a trireme, but a four-banked

type known as a *tetreres*. Archaeologist William Murray, analysing the symbols and pondering how the ship came to be lost near Athlit, believes it was a smaller warship based on the Levantine coast that may have been lost in a storm or an unrecorded naval skirmish in the struggles for control of Phoenicia. The exact circumstances of the ship's loss will probably never be known, but these details are not as important as what archaeologists have already gleaned from the bronze ram plucked from the sea.

Thera Ships

Archaeologists have not discovered the wrecks of any Minoan ships. However, the well-preserved ruins of a buried Minoan city on the Greek island of Santorini in the Cyclades have provided some intriguing clues. Beginning in 1967, Greek archaeologists slowly peeled back a thick layer of volcanic ash, exposing a complex of two- and three-storey mud-brick buildings and narrow streets. The site, known as Thera, was buried in a volcanic eruption around 1628 B.C. at the height of the Minoan civilization. Archaeologists at Thera have discovered a series of plaster wall-paintings lying beneath layers of ash. Considered by scholars to be the greatest treasure at the site, they are a unique record of life from the distant past.

The Thera frieze is our most vivid record of Minoan-Cycladic ships. Long and sleek, with what archaeologist Shelley Wachsmann calls "gently curving crescentic hulls," the ships are both rowed and paddled, though some carry a single mast and sail. Only one ship has its sail set. A simple cabin at the stern, with what could be a small deck in that area, supports the helmsman and what could be a timekeeper to synchronize the rowers' strokes. The warriors in the ships carry long spears or sea pikes, which also appear in the hands of warriors ashore.

Buried for thousands of years beneath volcanic ash, the largely intact buildings of ancient Thera have yielded amazing frescoes of a vanished civilization and its ships. James P. Delgado

Romans and Barbarians Afloat

THE EXPANSION OF ROME beyond the Italian peninsula forced it to embrace the sea. Archaeologists working in the Mediterranean have excavated more Roman shipwrecks than any other vessels. However, decades of maritime and underwater archaeological work have yielded scant traces of Roman warships or sea battles.

Rome's legions are better known than its fleets, not only because of archaeology but also because scholars and the public have paid more attention to the troops and land battles. This is not surprising. Even during the heyday of Rome, its links to the sea were ambiguous, often mistrustful. The sea, with its capricious moods and risk of shipwreck and drowning, never fully appealed to the citizens of Rome. The sea was regarded as an efficient way to transport goods. Once the initial wars were fought for control of the Mediterranean and Rome's civil wars ended, the Roman navy's principal tasks were the patrol of trade routes and frontiers, and the suppression of piracy. There was no tradition of recurrent sea battles, as had so marked the Greek consciousness, nor did most Romans venture to sea for recreation or travel.

Rome's assumption of naval power resulted from its struggles with Carthage between 264 and 201 B.C. The Romans copied the captured ships of their enemies to build large fleets. By the end of the Punic Wars, Rome controlled the western Mediterranean and the Adriatic. Now the most powerful state in the region, Rome and its fleet were drawn into power struggles in the eastern Mediterranean for the next two hundred years.

The Imperial Royal Navy, A.D. 100 to 400

Following Augustus' victory at Actium in A.D. 31, the naval forces of the empire underwent two significant changes. The first was the shift from larger warships to smaller vessels. Agrippa's experience at Actium led Rome to move to a standardized force of light, small ships, the *biremis*, or *liburnian*. Just as the Romans had copied the Carthaginian warships to build a navy two hundred years earlier, they now copied the small, fast ships of the Illyrian pirates of the Adriatic. Related to the hemiolia of the Greek pirates, the liburnians were, according to illustrations, small, one- or two-level, open-decked galleys. Although larger warships remained part of the naval inventory, the liburnians became the standard Roman warship for the next four centuries.

The second naval development was the concentration of the fleets in several naval bases throughout the Mediterranean, in Britannia, Gaul and Germania, and on the Black Sea. Major bases at Ravenna and Misenum guarded Italy's eastern and western shores, and other bases occupied strategic positions that allowed the Romans to

FACING PAGE The nineteenth-century discovery of the magnificent **Oseberg ship provided modern scholars with their first detailed look at a Viking ship.** University of Oslo, Eirek Irgens Johnsen

RIGHT This fragmentary relief of two Roman warships shows rows of armoured soldiers on the deck, a reminder that the navy was a floating extension of the Roman army. National Museum, Naples, Hector Williams

This fragmentary relief of a Roman warship is believed to depict one of the ships at Actium. British Museum, Hector Williams

Souvenir of a lost cause, this Roman Denarius coin was minted between 32 and 31 B.C. by Mark Antony, who used the money to pay his troops during his war against Octavian. The coin shows a warship, complete with ram, a reminder of the final battle with Octavian at Actium when Antony and Cleopatra's fleet was defeated. Author's collection, Michael Paris

The Battle of Actium

In Western Greece, a large memorial on land overlooks the site of the Battle of Actium, the last major sea battle of antiquity. There, in 31 B.C., a Roman-Egyptian fleet of five hundred ships loyal to Antony and his consort and ally Cleopatra met Octavian's smaller fleet of four hundred ships in battle. The two armies faced each other at Actium, while their fleets clashed offshore. Antony and Cleopatra's fleet was not only greater in number but also included large ships—sixes, sevens and tens—that dwarfed those of Octavian and his able lieutenant Agrippa. Boarding and fighting was not an option, because Agrippa had roughly half the men his opponents did. To win, Agrippa had to change tactics, first by throwing fire from catapults to gain an advantage, and then by out-manoeuvring and ramming the heavier, slower Roman-Egyptian fleet.

Octavian's fleet won, as the small ships darted in and out, quickly ramming the heavier enemy ships and then retreating for another strike. Cleopatra fled the battle in her ship, followed by Antony. Their fleet, now in disarray, was left to Octavian's mercy. It was not forthcoming. Agrippa closed and used incendiary weapons to set the enemy fleet ablaze. When the flames died out, Octavian was the victor in the last major naval battle of antiquity. Pursuing Antony and Cleopatra, his conquering troops took Egypt in the aftermath of their suicides. Octavian assumed control of all of Rome and inaugurated the new Roman Empire in 27 B.C. as Caesar Augustus.

Archaeologist William Murray has searched the waters off Actium for the lost warships, but their remains are elusive. However, he has been able to learn a great deal about them by studying the memorial that Augustus built on the hillside of Mount Michalitsi, overlooking the site of the battle. The memorial's low southern wall once supported a collection of bronze warship rams from Antony and Cleopatra's fleet, which were placed there by Octavian as an offering to the gods. Murray has found evidence of twenty-three rams of different sizes, and he estimates another twelve rams once were mounted there, making a total display of thirty-five elaborate bronze weapons. For Murray, the sheer number of the rams "confirm[s] the ferocity of the final battle and support[s] the accounts that describe a great conflagration at the battle's close."

hold sway over important bodies of water and
major sea routes.

From its bases, the Imperial Roman Navy
patrolled the seas but fought no major sea battles.
The answer was simple: the Mediterranean
was considered a Roman lake known to them as
mare nostrum, or "our sea." The navy during those
centuries was an extension of the army afloat.
Armoured Roman marines, equipped with spears,
swords and arrows, formed the fighting force,
while oarsmen manoeuvred the ship into battle.
By A.D. 100, the Romans began to abandon the
heavy rams of earlier warships, emphasizing
smaller, hornlike rams similar in drawings to those
on the Marsala Punic warship wreck. As well, the
Romans had earlier added large wooden towers to

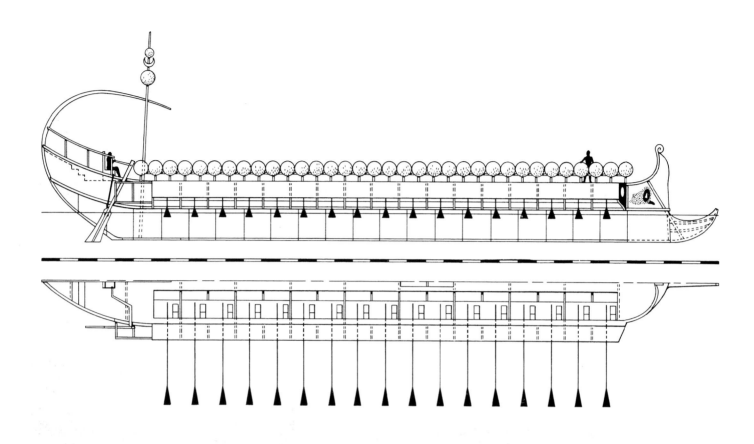

Discovered in shallow water and covered with sand, the Marsala wrecks offer a rare view of ancient warships. The flattened hull timbers, when reconstructed, revealed a long, sweeping ship with a sharp-pronged ram. Frost, from *Lilybaeum* (1981)

The Marsala Punic Warship Wrecks

Between 1970 and 1974, archaeologist Honor Frost discovered, excavated and studied the remains of two Carthaginian warships in the waters off Marsala, Sicily. The wrecks date from the First Punic War between Carthage and Rome, perhaps from the Battle of the Egadi Islands in 241 B.C.

The first wreck's hull was preserved from the stern almost to the bow. Long and sleek, the ship was 35 metres (115 feet) long, with a beam of only 4.8 metres (about 16 feet). As manageable as a modern rowing shell, the wreck was loaded with rock ballast to keep it stable. The ship carried two banks of fifteen oars, probably with two men pulling on each. With a crew of sixty-eight oarsmen,

the Marsala wreck's hull was built to cut quickly through the water.

Reconstructions of the Marsala Punic warship on paper indicate that a crew of up to thirty-four fighting men were also carried aboard. The excavation also recovered part of a human long bone. That fragment is part of the earliest documented casualty of naval combat found to date.

Carpenters' shavings were discovered mixed in with the ballast, along with leaves from a tree, caught between planks and stuck in the putty used to caulk the hull. According to Frost, these findings suggest that the ship was "built in haste and sank when new." Phoenician symbols and letters painted onto the

timbers showed how the warship was built in sections—prefabricated—and pieced together quickly. This practice demonstrates how a fleet of warships might be built as speedily as ancient writers suggested. But quickly built did not mean that the ship was poorly designed. The prefabrication of portions of the hull demonstrates a high level of sophistication in shipbuilding.

Forty metres away from the first warship wreck, Frost's divers discovered the remains of the bow from another ship. The well-preserved bow mounted a long, beaked-type ram built to gore the enemy's hull. The danger with this type of weapon was that it could stick inside the wounded

ship and sink both attacker and victim. At Marsala, however, the ram was a separate piece, joined to the hull by long iron nails. If stuck, it would break off in the damaged ship, leaving the bow of the attacking ship intact.

The builders of the two lost warships at Marsala were intelligent, experienced shipbuilders and sea warriors who could launch large numbers of ships with replaceable rams quickly and efficiently.

the decks of large warships. On these, they carried siege weapons and artillery such as catapults and bolt-throwing ballistae.

Barbarians and Warriors of the Sea

With increasing regularity after A.D. 100, rival factions fought for control of the empire. The next major Roman naval engagement after Actium was a battle in A.D. 323 when the rival Roman emperors Constantine and Licinius met in sea battle, with Constantine's two hundred liburnians emerging victorious over Licinius' 350 triremes. It was a reminder of the lesson learned at Actium: smaller ships, used effectively, could beat a larger fleet of more substantial ships.

Barbarians sacked a weakened Rome in the early fifth century. The power and authority of the Roman Empire shifted eastward to Constantine's new imperial city, Constantinople, on the shores of the Bosporus at Byzantium, now Istanbul. From there, the Byzantines, as the new Roman empire was known, controlled the flow of trade from east to west and tried to maintain control of the Mediterranean. But as Roman troops were drawn back into the heart of the empire, and as citizens on the edges of the empire were absorbed into the local cultures or were slaughtered by barbarian raids, Roman control of the fringes of the empire collapsed. The end of the fleet on the Rhine may be evident in the Mainz boat wrecks: they were

This relief from Trajan's column, Rome, from A.D. 113, depicts a liburnian, one of the small "destroyers" of the Imperial Roman Navy.
© Colin Martin

stripped of their fittings and abandoned to the mud by the early fifth century, showing perhaps that the Roman troops were gone, or that those who remained had other priorities than patrolling a river frontier.

In Northern Europe, the collapse of Roman control allowed the native seafaring peoples to start raiding each other by sea. At the same time, diverse tribes joined confederations that allowed for a greater concentration of resources and men against Rome's political, economic and military weakness. Between the third and seventh centuries, Germanic peoples pushed by ship out of the North Sea, into the English Channel and finally into the Mediterranean.

Two hundred years later, Germanic fleets had increased their activities so that the "barbarian" push against Rome was as much by sea as by wild tribes marching from the interior of Europe into Italy or pouring across Hadrian's

Wall into Britannia. The success of these ship-borne raids is particularly evidenced by the third-century construction of coastal watchtowers and fortifications by the Romans in Germania, Gaul and Britain—defensive measures against attack by sea. There are also "hoards," or coins and jewellery buried in the ground, that date from this period.

The success of the Frankish and Saxon raiders, in the range of their depredations and their ability to carry sufficient men and arms to strike and return home, shows that they had sophisticated vessels built for war. By the fifth century, and for the following two hundred years, these boats were capable not only of raiding but of conquest and migration as the Saxons poured out of Europe and into Britain. Archaeological study of ancient-boat finds in Northern Europe shows a well-developed shipbuilding tradition progressing quickly from dugout logs to planked boats of considerable size.

Archaeologists found this horde of Anglo-Saxon weapons, dating to c. A.D. 900, alongside the Nydam boats in that south Jutland peat bog between 1859 and 1863.
Landesmuseum fur vor und Frugheschichte, Kiel/Bridgeman Art Library

The Praeneste Relief, dating from the late first century B.C., and now in the Vatican Museum, shows Roman soldiers ready for combat next to a wooden tower at the bow. From Torr, *Ancient Ships* (1895)

Roman Ship Artillery

The popular image of Roman warfare at sea is huge ships with galley slaves struggling at the oars, the slaves whipped into "ramming speed" and the crashing of timbers as two galleys collide. Locked together, on fire, the decks fill with swarms of armoured men stabbing, spearing and falling screaming into the sea. That's the way *Ben Hur* showed it.

But that's not how it was. The Romans did not use galley slaves; they used soldiers who volunteered to take the oars. More soldiers stood by the board to seize an enemy ship. The objective was not to sink the other ship, but to take control of it by killing as many of the enemy crew as possible.

Cassius Dio, Vegetius, Appian and other ancient historians say that Roman naval commanders used a variety of weapons at a distant range to kill as many men as possible before boarding and fighting it out hand-to-hand. Archaeologists have excavated an amazing array of Roman weapons from land sites—stone-throwing catapults, large and small, ballistae that shot small stone balls and iron bolts, as well as the weapons for close-in fighting. But none of these weapons was discovered underwater, except for lead sling-shot excavated from a warship wreck off Capo Rasocolmo, Sicily, that may be a casualty of the 36 B.C. Battle of Naulochos.

Modern historian E. W. Marsden points out that Greek-invented torsion artillery was introduced at sea as early as 200 B.C. and "featured fairly regularly in sea-battles throughout the Hellenistic period." The Romans, following Greek practice, also carried artillery to sea, as Caesar and Appian noted, to bombard the shore, but also to fire at other ships. Marsden, working out how much weight a Roman warship could carry, estimates that a quinquireme could have carried "ten three-span arrow-firers, two comparatively small stone throwers weighing two tons apiece, expert artillery men and ammunition, and still carry forty marines."

This nineteenth-century engraving offered the first archaeological reconstruction of the form of the Nydam ship. From Englehardt, *Nydam Mosefund* (1865).

The Nydam Ships

The Nydam ships, excavated from a Danish bog known as Nydam Mose in 1859–63, illustrate the type of ship used to raid Roman and "barbarian" settlements in Europe. Dating to the fourth century A.D., the ships were deliberately sunk as an offering to the gods, along with a large number of weapons. They were probably spoils from a defeated enemy, deposited in the bog as offerings of thanks. The bog has yielded the remains of three ancient boats and a trace of a fourth. The boats were ritually destroyed, or "killed," before they were deposited. The ancient people who lived at Nydam Mose cut one boat up and with axes cut into the hulls of the others to sink them.

The most amazing of the finds, and the most famous, is a large oak warship. It is about 25 metres (over 80 feet) long and narrow, with a 3.5-metre (11.5-foot) beam. Its builders made it out of five large planks that overlap each other in a style of building known as "clinker-built." The

This copy of the Nydam ship was built in Germany in 1935 for a film. The low profile and number of rowers capture how this ancient sea raider would have performed in action. Schleswig-Holsteinisches Landesmuseum

planks were fastened together with iron rivets clenched inside the hull. Frames or ribs cut from curved branches and lashed to cleats carved into the planking strengthened the hull, making it a strong, flexible craft. Rowlocks for thirty oars were lashed to the gunwale, and a large steering oar was lashed or otherwise fastened to the starboard. There was no mast or sail.

Some scholars suggest the lack of a sail is not because the boat's builders did not know about sailing technology. As early as the first century B.C., during Julius Caesar's conquest of Gaul, his naval forces fought a large number of sailing warships of the Celtic peoples known as the Veneti, at the western end of the English Channel off the coast of Brittany. Rome's defeat of the Veneti, and the next four centuries of a Roman presence in Northern Europe, doubtless suppressed the use of the sail and led to the development of stealthier warships like the Nydam ship. The addition of a mast and sail would make the boat more visible.

Historian Owain T. P. Roberts has suggested that Northern European warships "remained as small, many-oared pulling boats until the constraints of a patrolling foreign navy were removed."

Some archaeologists see in the Nydam warship a Scandinavian shipbuilding tradition that would ultimately lead to the more famous Viking ships. But, as historian John Haywood suggests, the Nydam warship is more than a precursor of the Viking ship. It should be viewed as a fully developed ship in its own right and indicative of a specific type of warfare. Without a sail, and with a low profile, the Nydam oak warship was a good ship for a stealthy raid on neighbours. Instead of success, however, the owners of the Nydam ships died, and their vessels and weapons ended up in a bog as a spoil of war and an unintended legacy to future generations.

This illuminated manuscript image shows Saracens landing in Crete and burning Byzantine warships. The scene is from a twelfth-century Byzantine chronicle of events from 811 to 1057. Biblioteca Nacional, Madrid/Bridgeman Art Library

The Byzantine Navy

The collapse of the western Roman Empire by the late fifth century gradually allowed the rise of small kingdoms, fragmented and often isolated, that warred on one another in Northern Europe, Britain, Spain and Italy. In the east, Byzantium reigned supreme, controlling trade between Europe and the Far East. However, a new power—Islam—would soon rise to challenge that control in the seventh century. Wars between the Arabic forces of Islam and those of Byzantium raged for centuries, with each side ranging far and wide throughout the Mediterranean in battles to control land, sea lanes and trade.

Greek fire erupts from its tube at the bow of a Byzantine dromon and engulfs an enemy ship, c. A.D. 820–29. Biblioteca Nacional, Madrid

The Byzantine navy protected the sea approaches to Constantinople as well as Byzantium's overseas colonies. The warship of the Byzantine navy was the *dromon* (racer), a two-banked, oar-driven warship that also carried sail. Most probably a descendant of the liburnian, this warship represented a return to a simpler form that emphasized speed and manoeuvrability. In their push for simplicity, the naval masters of Byzantium eventually lost the secret or the desire to build the more complex triremes or quinquiremes of antiquity. But the Byzantine navy performed well in action.

Decisive military actions, supported by the navy, helped the Byzantine emperor Justinian regain control of the western Mediterranean in the sixth century. In 533, the Vandals, who had sailed across the Mediterranean to seize North Africa after the collapse of Rome, were defeated and their capital, Carthage, fell to Justinian's commander, Belisarius. This victory was followed by the conquest of Sicily in 535 and by the reconquest of Italy in 562.

Byzantium's control of the Mediterranean would not last long. Within a century, Arabs united under the Islamic banner conquered vast areas around the Mediterranean. Arab Moslems took Egypt, Persia and Northern Africa, including the Byzantine naval bases at Tyre in 638 and Alexandria in 641. Armed Arab dhows, along with captured Byzantine ships, swept into the Mediterranean, pushing across the Straits of Gibraltar to seize the Iberian Peninsula. Arab ships pushed into the Indian Ocean, encountering no resistance from small, isolated kingdoms.

Alarmed, the Byzantine navy responded with a program of construction, developing three versions of the dromon: the *ousakio*, *pamphylos* and dromon proper. The older Roman technique of ram and board remained the principal tactic, with the two-banked dromon, twenty-five oars at a bank and a hundred oars overall, crewed by two hundred men, fifty of them marines. The pamphylos carried a crew of 120 to 160, while the ousakio carried a hundred men, fifty to row on a single level and fifty on an upper deck to fight. Aiding the rowers were sails, not the older square sails of antiquity, but the more easily handled, more manoeuvrable lateen, or the fore-and-aft rig favoured by the empire's Islamic foes. We know little otherwise about Byzantine warships. The accounts of contemporary historians, and a few poor illustrations, are all that exist.

Ultimately, Islamic power gained the upper hand over Byzantium. A naval battle off Cyprus in 655 saw the defeat of the Byzantine fleet. A five-year naval siege of Constantinople followed. It ended only when the Byzantine navy employed a new weapon for the first time. "Greek fire," an intensely hot, burning liquid that could not easily be extinguished, was shot from projectile tubes mounted on the bows of dromon. Developed around 650, Greek fire was a naval technological advantage that helped keep Byzantium's capital from falling.

But the Muslims gained the upper hand else-where, taking Carthage in 698, followed by Sicily and then Crete in 827. Byzantium maintained a strong navy, repulsing another siege of Constantinople in 718, and retaking Crete in 961. New powers were also emerging to hold off the Islamic advance in the Mediterranean, sometimes allied with Byzantium, sometimes not. The Franks, led by Carolus Magnus (Charlemagne) defeated a Spanish Muslim force in the Balearic Islands, and galleys from the powerful island-state of Venice were able to control the Adriatic, warring against both Muslim and Byzantine rivals.

The Viking Ships

As Byzantine and Islamic forces struggled against each other in the Mediterranean, a new naval force arose on the North Sea. The Scandinavians, the forebears of the Danes, Swedes and Norwegians, developed open-decked, versatile warships and used them to war against neighbours and to mount extensive raids. The Scandinavians, in particular, as they went "Viking" on piratical voyages, pushed as far south as the Mediterranean. The Viking age saw the development of North Sea and Baltic craft, clinker-built ships made from planks split with axes from tall northern forests. From smaller twenty-four–oared, single-masted galleys, the Viking ship evolved into large, sixty-oared *drekkar*, or dragon ships. Whether fighting hand-to-hand or ship-to-ship, or raiding coastal settlements, the Viking ships with their dragon-headed figureheads became well-known, far-ranging and feared warships.

Viking naval warfare was more of a hit-and-miss affair, with raids against coastal settlements the more common fight than a battle between ships on the water. When a battle happened, the defend-ing ships often tied up alongside each other to form a larger fighting platform, while the attacking ships closed, until bow to bow, best warriors for-ward, with sword and axe they fought for control of the decks. Fights between ships focussed, as they did for the Romans, on killing the other crew and gaining control of the enemy vessel.

There was no single type of Viking ship or even a generic Viking warship. A diverse assort-ment of vessels, some cargo carriers, others warships, with a range of rowing craft and barges were built and used by the seafaring Scandinavians. Although the Nydam ship is the only archaeologi-cally documented pre-Viking warship, sites throughout Scandinavia, Northern Europe and Scotland provide a detailed sense of Viking ship-building and warships. Of all these sites and ships, a few stand out as exemplary. They include two "royal" ships, elaborately buried as part of a funeral rite, and two wrecks, one at Roskilde, the other at Hedeby, both in Denmark.

GOKSTADSKIBET

Bow view of the Gokstad ship.
University of Oslo, Eirek Irgens
Johnsen

ET VENIT AD PEVENE SÆ :·

The Viking Warrior of Scar

In 1991, Scottish archaeologists performed a quick emergency-rescue dig at the edge of the sea at Scar, a farm on Sanday, a northern Orkney island. High tides and surf eroding the sandy shore were exposing human bones and rusty iron rivets. They proved to be from a Viking boat burial dating from around 900. Three skeletons, those of an elderly woman, a young child and a male warrior, rested inside the boat. By the time the grave was excavated, the sea had claimed half of the boat and some of the bones and artifacts. Not much of the boat's timber had survived a thousand years of burial. Most of the wood was gone, but the positions of the rivets that once held its planks together and impressions in the sand allowed archaeologists to

reconstruct this "ghost boat" on paper to reveal a sleek 7-metre (23-foot) craft. A rich variety of grave goods buried with the boat's occupants included the man's iron sword and a bundle of iron-tipped arrows.

Although only the "ghost" of the boat survived as outlines in the sand, the bones of the dead also revealed much. Forensic analysis of human remains is a subject well known to readers of archaeological reports and murder mysteries. Bones can reveal much about how people looked, how they lived and occasionally how they died. Archaeologists are unsure how the middleaged warrior died, but his bones indicate that he had been to sea and rowed heavily as a young man.

Forensic anthropologist Daphne Home Lorimer

deduced this point from changes to some of the bones, because bone "is a plastic medium and responds to the pull and stress of active muscles." The bones of the lower body, particularly the hips, showed strong evidence of hyperextension, and the knees showed changes occasionally caused by constant squatting but also by "constant checking of the inward rotation of the knee." What caused these changes? Lorimer points out that similar changes are seen in the skeletons of drowned sailors from the 1545 wreck *Mary Rose* and result from young bones adapting to the heavy stresses caused by a ship moving on the sea. In the case of the Scar burial, the man's bones were not changed from standing on deck, but from bending and

rowing in low seats. Archaeologists are not sure if the man was a warrior, because his grave goods included both trading implements and weapons. The evidence of the bones and the presence of the weapons might suggest that as a young man, he had participated in Viking war at sea, rowing long distances to raid or fight, before settling down to a more peaceful middle age as a trader.

This scene from the Bayeux Tapestry shows the Viking-style fleet of Duke William crossing the Channel to Pevensey in 1066. Musée Tapisserie d'Bayeux/Bridgeman Art Library

Our understanding of the diversity and construction of Viking ships was dramatically increased when a cofferdam was built around the shallow-water wrecks of five ships at Skuldelev at Roskilde Fjord, Denmark, and the scuttled ships slowly emerged from the mud. Viking Ship Museum, Roskilde

The ninth-century Oseberg ship, excavated in 1904 near Oseberg, Norway, is about 22 metres (over 70 feet) long. The earliest Viking ship yet found, the Oseberg ship is an interesting comparison to the Gokstad ship, discovered under a Norwegian burial mound in 1880. The Gokstad ship was also well preserved by the wet soil. Built around 895, it is 24 metres (almost 80 feet) long and 5.2 metres (about 17 feet) wide, with a graceful curving hull made of clinker-fastened strakes. Propelled by oars or a single mast and sail, the ship has a stout oak keel, cut from a single timber. The keel and the strength of the overlapping, clinker-fastened planks made the Oseberg and Gokstad ships flexible and light, but fast on the water and light enough to beach. They also had a shallow draft. The Gokstad ship, for example, drew about a metre of water. Like the ancient Greeks, the Vikings built and used their ships more for amphibious warfare than battles at sea. The Oseberg and Gokstad finds were not run-of-the-mill warships, even though archaeologists

discovered the remains of thirty-two painted wooden shields mounted on the sides of the Gokstad ship. It was a *karve* or *karfi*, a royal Norse ship used for trade, travel or war.

Five Viking ships from around A.D. 1000, excavated in 1962 from the harbour mud at Skuldelev, Denmark, provided archaeologists with a detailed look at various types of Viking ships, including two round-hulled *knarr* or merchant ships, and two warships. None of the ships was lost in battle or storm, but they were scuttled to blockade the harbour, probably to defend it against attacking ships.

The two warships were the type used by the Danes and the Normans to conquer England. The smaller warship is a type found on the Bayeux Tapestry, which illustrates the Norman invasion across the English Channel in 1066. An "ideal amphibian in sheltered waters," the ship was reconstructed for experimental trials and "rode like a swan upon the water." It also performed well, as shown in the tapestry, ferrying troops and their

horses. The modern copy of the larger Skuldelev ship, in a 1967 experiment, loaded four horses, cruised and then landed the horses with ease.

The second ship, larger and able to carry more cavalry and horses, was another type used in 1066. It probably is the type of ship used by the Vikings to reach Constantinople in 1043 with a fleet of four hundred ships. Fleets with combined warrior-sailors and cavalry made fearsome amphibious forces whose impact could be felt strategically as well as tactically. And yet the second warship was not a giant for its age.

Large ships could be built with the clinker method in lengths greater than 37 metres (120 feet). This allowed the Vikings to build large, yet light and manoeuvrable ships. The lessons inherent in the Viking ships were not lost on the English, who under Norman rule continued to use Scandinavian shipbuilding techniques well into medieval times.

Ships built in the clinker-style of the Vikings, with square sails, remained the standard vessel type throughout Northern Europe until the Renaissance. Not surprisingly, warships of larger sizes, directly descended from the dragon ships, remained the key to naval power until larger-scale wars and new weapons combined with Mediterranean influences to challenge their effectiveness.

From the flattened, at times scarce remains, shown here on the site and as drawn by archaeologists, the ships, including this warship, were reconstructed both on paper and as models. Viking Ship Museum, Roskilde

One of the fourth-century A.D. Roman lusoriae, as found and reconstructed by archaeologists at Mainz.
Museum für Antike Schiffahrt/ Roemisch-Germanisches Zentralmuseum

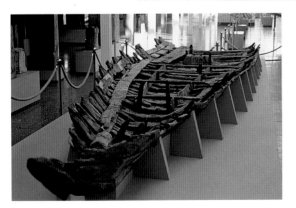

Mainz Boats

The fresh water and mud of the Rhine has preserved the remains of several Roman boats, including *lusoriae*, small light galleys that date to the fourth century A.D. and formed the naval fleets on the northern frontiers.

German archaeologists recovered the remains of five Roman boats in 1981–82, providing the first detailed look at these Roman riverine warships. Archaeologist Olaf Hockmann describes the Mainz boats as "sleek, shallow-draught, and low-sided undecked river warships with fifteen oars per side." Reconstructions of the boats show they were about 18 metres (60 feet) long, with a 3-metre (10-foot) beam, and drew only about a half-metre (18 inches) of water. Archaeologist Peter Marsden, studying the form of the boats, estimates that they cruised at speeds of about 7 knots and could reach a maximum speed of 10 knots.

Built of oak and coated with pitch on the outside, the Mainz boats show a merging of Roman Mediterranean building practices and Northern European Celtic tradition. They again demonstrate the Roman tendency to adopt a local or regional vessel into their fleets. They also show the Roman preference for standardization; the boats were assembled with the aid of temporary "moulds" or templates, which Hockmann points out "would have eased mass production by following standard plans, defined by the moulds." The reconstructions of these Roman riverine warships on the German frontier provide direct physical evidence of the appearance and form of the boats.

The Rise of the Gun

IN NORTHERN EUROPE, the Viking style of warfare, with oarsmen rowing and sailing in fast raids or with many ships in a fleet swooping onto a beach, faded away after A.D. 1000. The emergence of royal power in England, Scandinavia, France, Hungary and Poland suppressed raiding and sporadic attacks in favour of trade alliances forged by negotiation or war. To maximize their trade, the Northern European powers built larger ships, propelled by sail, not oars. These new, large ships, called cogs, required much more timber than the earlier, smaller Scandinavian cargo carriers. Strong regional rulers who held under their control a considerable number of ports and resources, were able to build a substantial navy in times of necessity. The high cost of building these new ships led to the use of the cog as a merchant trader in times of peace and a platform for fighting men in times of war.

With this shift in strategy came the reintroduction of royal ships and navies. The change in naval strategy was already under way in the late Viking period, as ninth- to eleventh-century Scandinavian campaigns were organized by the emerging kingdoms rather than by tribal leaders. These campaigns employed large fleets of hundreds of ships. The powerful naval forces represented that important shift from the Viking voyages in which several ships might join in a piratical raid to a more concentrated invasion force or seaborne extension of power. Such forces inspired similar forces to counter them. England's first "navy" was an organized royal fleet assembled by the Anglo-Saxon kings, notably Alfred of Wessex, to repulse the Vikings.

While navies arose in Northern Europe and England, the kingdoms of the Mediterranean continued a centuries-old tradition of standing navies. The typical Mediterranean warship of A.D. 1000 was still the oared fighting ship. The two-banked dromon of the Byzantine Empire, and the oared galleys of the various Islamic powers, battled back and forth the Mediterranean, supported and countered by the oared galleys of the powerful Italian city-states emerging from the shadow of Byzantine domination.

The rise of new kingdoms altered the balance of power in the region while Byzantium's power waned. Venice, Genoa, Pisa, Spanish Aragon, France and the Kingdom of the Two Sicilies vied for power in the Mediterranean between 1253 and 1381. Venice finally won the upper hand. The key to its success was a large navy, with impressive fleets of two-banked, three-masted "great galleys." Unlike the descendants of the Vikings, these Mediterranean powers returned to the multilevel oar-powered warship. In the south, rowing and ramming, the time-honoured tradition of naval warfare in the Mediterranean for nearly three thousand years, remained the principal tactic. By 1380, following a decisive defeat of Genoa's navy, Venice controlled the western Mediterranean with its own fleet of eighty great galleys.

However, the rise of another power threatened Venice and the rest of Christian Europe. Where the scattered Islamic caliphates had been unable to break the power of Byzantium or conquer the new kingdoms on the Mediterranean's northern shores, a consolidated power was pushing out of the east. The Ottoman Turks took to the sea to establish their dominance in the region. They built a fleet at Gallipoli and met Venice in a sea battle in 1416. Venice's navy defeated the Ottomans. Undeterred, the Ottoman ruler, Mehmet the Conqueror, built a new fleet. With it and his army, he besieged and took Constantinople in 1453. The Ottoman navy moved on to conquer the Aegean and the Black Sea. Venice was able to hold off the Ottoman advance into the rest of its territory, then weakened, losing three naval battles to the Ottomans off Greece in 1499. The age of Venice was passing. New naval powers such as England, France, Portugal and Spain were on the rise in the west. Some of these powers, particularly the united Iberian powers and the "Holy Roman Empire" of Germanic and Balkan states, would stand against the Ottomans in the early sixteenth century.

FACING PAGE **This fifteenth-century manuscript shows Swiss soldiers in a small, cannon-armed ship.** Private collection/Bridgeman Art Library

Men pour from galleys onto the shore during the capture of Constantinople. From the painting by Jacopo Robusti (Tintoretto), Palazzo Ducale, Venice/Bridgeman Art Library

Ottoman galleys pursue a Christian ship from Peljesac (Croatia) in this sixteenth-century scene. Private collection, Michael Paris

Hulks, Cogs and Crusaders

A different type of warship was employed by the new European powers. The northern and western Europeans built hulks and cogs. These clinker-built ships grew out of both the Scandinavian ships and the Germanic-designed, flat-bottomed coastal trading vessels of the Hanseatic League. Much of what we know about them comes from literary references, and from images such as the official city and port seals of Northern Europe in the thirteenth and fourteenth centuries. Although no "war cogs" have been discovered by archaeologists, one essentially complete merchant cog was excavated near Bremen, Germany, and other cog wrecks and parts of cogs have emerged from underwater sites and river mud to reveal how these round, clinker-built ships were constructed.

They were not the longships of war developed by several cultures over the past millennia. They were instead stout platforms with flat bottoms that kept them stable and made them capable of carrying great weight. In times of war, massive timber structures could be erected on them, making seagoing fortresses. These structures, sometimes only at the stern, other times at bow and stern, were known as stern castles and forecastles.

Occasionally, a castle was added to the top of the mast. Experience gained in the Crusades showed how these larger ships, with greater height, allowed men to carry the day by towering over the row galleys, which rested lower in the water. They also prevailed in fierce sea battles by overpowering another ship with sheer numbers, or by delivering death from a great height with archers, heavy stones or Greek fire.

The ships fought by approaching with the wind, turning and heading for the midships area at right angles to try to ram the other ship amidships. The men in the castles would sweep the enemy's decks with arrows and missiles before coming alongside. Men in the mast tops hurled heavy stones or pointed iron bars called gadds onto the decks of the enemy vessels. Only then did the troops attempt to board and fight it out. The defending ship would manoeuvre to place its stern to the enemy, so that the heavily fortified castle was the focus of the attackers. This type of sea battle from the Crusades influenced the conduct of war at sea when the Crusaders returned home. It also influenced the ships, as the larger ships allowed builders to add more masts and introduce the lateen rig, gunpowder, Greek fire and other fire

Model of a cog, showing its
distinctive, towering hull with
fore and stern castles. This
feature made the cog a more
formidable warship than the
earlier Viking-style ships.
Model by A. Martinovic Izanin,
Private collection, Michael Paris

weapons, and finally guns. But from 1000 to about 1400, warships closed in, archers and crossbow men rained death from the skies, and then ships grappled as men swarmed onto each other's decks to fight it out with sword, javelin, battle-axe or pike.

The earliest castles on ships were temporary structures. This approach worked when rulers and naval powers equipped their merchant fleets for war on an as-needed basis. But as the demand for a standing fleet grew, the castles were built into the ship to become a permanent part of its structure. This step was important in the evolution of the fighting ship, particularly galleons with their high, armed stern castles. But these new ships were not descended from cogs. The Northern Europeans replaced their flat-bottomed cogs with hulks. Archaeologists have yet to discover the wreck of a hulk, and so we have little knowledge about this type of ship. What we do know is that the hulk's rounded bottom made it stronger and better equipped to ride the waves, whereas its blunt bow and stern created more room for carrying cargo, armament or fighting men.

The Introduction of the Gun

Chinese alchemists discovered the magic mixture of sulphur, saltpetre and carbon around A.D. 300, but the transition from laboratory accident to tool of war took many centuries. A Chinese military encyclopedia of the eleventh century known as the *Wu Ching Tsung Tao* (Collection of the Most Important Military Techniques) describes gunpowder bombs wrapped in paper, much like a giant firecracker. In 1221, the Chinese were packing their powder into hollow iron bombs they called *chien-t'ien-lei*, or "heaven-shaking devices." They used catapults to throw the bombs. Sixty years later, invading Mongol troops in Japan carried these bombs with them across the Tsushima Strait, and an illustration on a Japanese scroll shows one of these bombs exploding in mid-air, much to the consternation of a nearby samurai and his horse.

The heaven-shaking devices and the *huo-ch'iang*, a pole-mounted "fire lance" (imagine a large Roman candle at the end of a long stick, thrust into an enemy ship's sides, sails, or into the face of an enemy boarding party), were all used aboard Chinese naval ships in battle. By 1259, another invention, a bronze tube called the *t'u huo ch'iang*, is mentioned in the official history of the Sung Dynasty. An early cannon, it fired small projectiles from its mouth for a distance of about 140 metres (450 feet). The Chinese also developed gunpowder rockets and missiles in the late thirteenth century, firing them in large numbers as fleets closed for action. Some of the projectiles were hooked with barbed ends to catch on sails and set them on fire. A 1272 account of a Sung naval battle with the Mongols notes that every ship in the Sung fleet was "equipped with fire-lances, trebuchets [catapults] and bombs, burning charcoal, large axes and heavy crossbows."

The Chinese also used chemical weapons, including ceramic containers filled with gunpowder and other ingredients to create toxic smoke. These weapons were still in use in the mid-nineteenth century when Britain and China clashed during the Opium Wars. British sailors called them "stink-pots," describing how the war junks would come alongside while men at the mastheads threw the pots on the enemy's deck, "and woe betide any unlucky boat that received one of these missiles, for the crew would certainly have to jump overboard or be stifled." Another invention, dating to the mid-thirteenth century, was an underwater mine, the *shui ti lung wang phao* (submarine dragon king). Made of cast iron and wood, these mines were encased in an ox's bladder to keep the water

---

The Bremen Cog

In October 1962, workers dredging the banks of the River Weser, near Bremen, uncovered the remains of a wooden ship. This fortuitous German discovery yielded the best-preserved example of a cog yet found. The Bremen cog, excavated in 1965, chemically treated and carefully reconstructed at the Deutsches Schiffahrtsmuseum, provides a detailed, three-dimensional look at a cog—the typical Northern European cargo carrier and warship of medieval times. Analysis of the timbers showed the cog was built around 1378.

Until the discovery of the Bremen cog, details of how cogs were built and their appearance were unknown. The 23-metre-long (75-foot-long), 7.6-metre-wide (25-foot-wide) cog has a flat bottom, a sharp turn at the bilges and rounded sides made up of overlapped, edge-sided planking. The bow and stern rise from the keel at sharp angles, with a rudder, only recently introduced to Europe, fixed to the sternpost. A single mast carried a square sail. The stern castle at the aft end of the ship, trapezoidal in shape, overhung the sides of the deck. Study of the Bremen cog allowed archaeologists to identify other wrecks, not as well preserved, as cogs, adding to the body of knowledge about these long-lost types of ships.

The Deutsches Schiffahrtsmuseum has built a sailing replica of the Bremen cog. Its angled sides, towering over the water, gave men on the deck an advantage over attackers in smaller ships or boats who had to climb up the sides while defenders on the deck fired down into them. The size of the cog made it capable of carrying a large cargo or a number of fighting men. It was a worthy successor to the Viking ship and the next major step in the evolution of what would become the gun-carrying wooden warship of the sixteenth century.

Emperor Kang Shi's tour of Kiang-Han in 1699, after Chaio Ping Chen (1661–1722): the emperor's troops disembark from their ships (ink and watercolour on silk-backed paper). British Library/Bridgeman Art Library

out. A long fuse, usually a stick of incense, floated above the mine in a waterproof container and could be trimmed to explode at a set time. All of this ingenuity was exercised well before Europe even thought of such weapons, and nearly half a millennium before the first western warship was sunk by a submerged mine in 1862.

The invention of gunpowder and the gun made their way from China to Europe by the early fourteenth century. Europeans probably carried the first guns aboard ships early in the century, but it was not until the Hundred Years' War between England and France (1338–1453) that cannon were first used aboard ships in an otherwise traditional boarding action off Sluys in 1340. The guns proved ineffective in the battle. In time, cannon dominated battles at sea, but that day was yet to come.

Chinese Sea Power

The introduction of the cannon came just as the Chinese reached the apex of their naval power in the fourteenth and fifteenth centuries. During these centuries, the Chinese built the world's most incredible ships and a navy unrivalled elsewhere on the globe. It grew out of the eagerness of the Mongol rulers of the Yuan Dynasty to continue to expand China's overseas trade.

Annam, Champa and Java, despite their successful defeat of the Mongol fleets and armies, wanted to continue to tap into China's lucrative trade market. So the rulers of these kingdoms accepted nominal Mongol sovereignty and sent "tribute" to continue their trade relationship with China. The reverses of the Mongol navy notwithstanding, China's merchant fleet continued to expand and trade far and wide, taking

A Chinese war junk of the nineteenth century. Its form remained relatively unchanged from the sixteenth century through the early twentieth century. Vancouver Maritime Museum, Michael Paris

control of the spice trade and ranging into the Indian Ocean. But while overseas trade to Southeast Asia grew, China's coastal trade declined. The Japanese, eager to avenge the Mongol invasions of 1274 and 1281, ravaged the coast with pirate raids. The Mongols responded by pulling much of China's internal trade off the coastal routes and back into the interior, and by building fleets of patrol boats to police the canals and rivers.

The buildup of the internal waterways and an inland navy was a sign of growing weakness in the Yuan Dynasty. The Mongol rulers of China and their dynasty were overturned, beginning in 1351, by rebellions that spread through the country. The struggle ended when one rebel leader, Chu Yuang-Chan, defeated both his rival rebel leaders and the remaining Mongol forces to found the Ming

Dynasty nearly two decades later. Chu came to power gradually, amassing both territory and control of the Yuan navy on the lower Yangtze. By 1359, the war for control of China centred on the Yangtze and a struggle between the states of Han and Ming. Ming controlled the lower Yangtze, but the middle part of the river remained under Han control. The matter was decided in battle, on Lake Po-yang, on the Middle Yangtze, in 1363. The Han ruler, Ch'en-liang, built a fleet of large, three-decked warships, armoured with iron plates, armed with heavy cannon and manned by crews as large as two thousand to three thousand. Chu met the fleet with a mixed force. Some of the Ming ships were large, but most were smaller vessels and no match for the giant Han warships.

Chu's ships were pushed back across the lake by the Han fleet, and several of the Ming vessels ran

The samurai meet the Mongols on the beach in this nineteenth-century Japanese print. Torao Mozai

The Battles of Kublai Khan

Under Kublai Khan, conquering Mongols by 1279 ruled all of China. The Khan sought to enlarge trade by using the navy as a tool for Mongol expansion, conquering distant lands otherwise isolated from the Mongols by sea. Japan was his first target. The relatively narrow straits of Tsushima, spanning some 177 kilometres (110 miles) between Korea and Japan's Kyushu coast, would be the highway of war.

The Mongol fleet embarked twenty-three thousand Mongol, Chinese and Korean soldiers and seven thousand sailors in October 1274 and attacked Japan. The battle proved unequal in both numbers and tactics. By October 20, the Japanese had retreated from the beach at Hakata Bay (near modern Fukuoka), falling back 16 kilometres (10 miles) to an ancient abandoned fortress at Mizuki. That evening, however, a storm struck the coast with such violence that the Mongol fleet was mauled by the waves, and some

three hundred ships and 13,500 men were lost.

Battered and depleted, the surviving Mongols retreated, arriving home more than a month later on November 27, leaving the Japanese to cheer their salvation at the hands of what they termed the *kamikaze*, or "divine wind."

Kublai Khan did not forget Japan. After his demands for surrender in June 1279 were rejected—with his envoys executed on the beach at Hakata—he ordered Koryo to build a new fleet of nine hundred ships. In China, he assembled the Chiang-nan Division, a fleet of nearly thirty-five hundred ships, most of them captured Sung warships, and an invasion force of a hundred thousand Chinese warriors. The Koryo Eastern Route Division carried thirty thousand Mongol and ten thousand Korean warriors and seventeen thousand sailors. It set sail on May 3, 1281, retaking Iki Island on June 10.

The Chiang-nan Division sailed in June and met with

the Eastern Route Division at Hirado. The combined fleet struck the garrison on the small island of Takashima in Imari Bay, 50 kilometres (30 miles) south of Hakata, and then poured ashore. A two-week battle ensued. The crews of the Mongol ships chained their vessels together and constructed a planked walkway to build a massive floating fortress in preparation for the inevitable waterborne assault by the small defence craft of the Japanese.

The principal fight, however, was ashore, where losses on both sides mounted as the invasion dragged on. The stalemate was finally broken when the Mongol fleet was mauled by another sudden storm on the evening of July 30. Driving rain, high winds and storm-driven waves smashed into the Mongol fleet. Nearly four thousand ships sank as the fleet tried to disengage from one another and flee the bay through the narrow harbour entrance. Most did not make it, and nearly a hundred

thousand men drowned.

Kublai Khan abandoned his dreams of a Japanese conquest in 1286 when he abruptly cancelled preparations for a third invasion.

Some seven hundred years later, Kublai Khan's fleet was rediscovered. For years, Japanese trawlers in the waters off Imari Bay had dredged up artifacts from the lost Mongol fleet. Then, in 1980, Torao Mozai, a professor of engineering at Toyko University, used a sonoprobe—a sound-wave device that geologists use to discover rocks buried in ocean sediment—to survey the seabed off Takashima Island. In Imari Bay, Mozai's team pinpointed the wrecks of as many as seventy ships in 25 metres (about 80 feet) of water. His preliminary reconstruction of the Mongol fleet suggests a complex naval force of 1170 large war junks. Each ship was about 73 metres (240 feet) long, carried about sixty crew and towed a landing craft known as a *batoru* that could transport about twenty men. Mozai also

found smaller warships, including three hundred Korean two-masted fighting ships. By far the most numerous vessels were supply ships.

Many ships are believed to lie in deeper water; Tsushima Strait drops to a depth of about 90 metres (300 feet), and in its waters, fishermen have dragged up intact pots that indicate the presence of other shipwrecks. These artifacts attest to the diversity of the invading force, its weapons and provisions. Mozai's discoveries made international headlines and sparked the creation of a Mongol museum on Takashima Island. The project and the museum's opening also inspired a number of fishermen to donate their own discoveries.

aground on the shallows, including Chu's flagship. In desperation, the Ming ruler fell back on the ancient tactic of fire ships. As the Han fleet massed to renew their attack, Chu sent some fishing boats, manned by a few volunteers, and packed with reed and gunpowder, into their midst. The Han fleet, caught by the ruse, began to burn as cannon and powder magazines exploded. According to contemporary accounts, "several hundred" ships were destroyed and sixty thousand Han troops and sailors died. But some of the Han ships remained afloat and ready to fight. Chu and the Ming fleet finally won by harassing the Han fleet as it split up to avoid more fire ships and tried to retreat back up the Yangtze. The smaller Ming ships cut off the huge Han warships and whittled them down in a battle marked by cannon blasts, flames, grappling and boarding. When it ended, Ch'en was dead, the survivors on the last Han ships surrendered, and Chu was master of much of the Yangtze.

Using the victory at Lake Po-Yang as a springboard, Chu pushed into northern China, seizing the remaining states and pushing out the Mongols. Incorporating the remaining Han ships into his fleet, Chu swept into the South China Sea and conquered the coastal ports. Ming completed the seizure of control in China from 1363 to 1382. Amazingly, the country emerged from these wars both prosperous and powerful. The new Ming rulers did not forsake naval power, and under Chu's thirty-year reign, as well as those of his successors, the emperors Hui-Ti and Yung-lo, a large navy was built to control the interior and the coast and to range far overseas. By the 1420s, China's navy was the largest in the world, with 400 large war junks stationed at Nanking; 1350 warships, river and canal patrol boats stationed elsewhere; 3000 merchant vessels that could be converted into fighting ships if needed; 400 huge grain transports; and 250 "treasure ships," overseas warships that brought back riches from far-flung missions of trade and diplomacy.

Under the command of Admiral Zheng Ho, a fleet of these huge junks—some over 60 metres

(200 feet) long—armed with cannon, rockets and guns, carried Chinese naval power and trade throughout Southeast Asia and into the Indian Ocean, pushing back pirates and reopening trade with India, Arab East Africa and the Ottoman Empire between 1405 and 1433. Archaeologists and historians argue over the size of Zheng Ho's ships. Some insist that the ships could have been as long as 135 metres (almost 450 feet) and as wide as 55 metres (180 feet).

The argument rages on, aided or confused by the discovery of a gigantic rudder post believed to be from one of the warships. Excavated from the mud in a backwater of the one of the Ming naval shipyards at Nanking, the rudder post is 12 metres (about 40 feet) long and a half-metre (about 18 inches) in diameter. Naval architects estimate that the rudder attached to the post was nearly half its length in height and breadth. That means that thirty men could comfortably lie down on it. The ship to which such a rudder belonged would, following the rules of thumb for Chinese ship construction, be at least 120 metres (400 feet) long. But one rudder post does not represent a fleet, archaeologists are quick to point out. It is still an intriguing hint at a navy of gigantic ships that outweighed, outgunned and outclassed anything afloat in a European navy of the time.

European powers, just then adapting cannon to warships and starting the progression towards large warships of their own, never came into contact with the "treasure ships." After 1433, a new emperor, fearing the perils of foreign contact, withdrew the overseas and coastal navy and scrapped it as China again confined most of its trade and traffic to rivers and canals. Chinese merchant junks on the high seas and coast were left to the mercy of Indonesian, Vietnamese and Japanese pirates. And the seas were open to the Europeans, primarily the Portuguese, Spanish and Dutch, who by the early sixteenth century were regularly arriving. They seized control of the overseas trade in spices, silks and other commodities with ships that could not have withstood the Ming navy at

The magnificent warships of China's internal waters included multi-storeyed vessels that could only manoeuvre on the protected rivers and lakes. This A.D. 1044 image of a *Wu-ya hsient*, or five-ensign battleship, from c. A.D. 636, shows a form that survived for centuries. From the *Wu Ching Tsung Tao*, after Needham

The Sung Navy, 1100–1299

While Mediterranean kingdoms and empires rose and fell, ancient cultures at the other end of the world were also taking to the sea. One of those cultures, the Chinese, created a naval force unrivalled by any other in the world of its time.

The fall of the Tang Dynasty in 906 had divided China into warring entities. But by 960, the victors of the struggle established the Sung Dynasty, which united the country and dominated it for the next three hundred years. The Sung built up the inland water-transportation links with new canals, locks and a haul-way for moving cargo-laden craft up the Yangtze against the current. China experienced a boom

in shipbuilding, in which shipbuilders learned from innovations brought into China by Arab, Singhalese and Persian traders. The result was a merchant fleet that grew larger in number and size of ships from the eighth to the twelfth century.

The Sung used this fleet of ocean-going junks and sampans to encourage overseas trade, expanding routes that linked China with Indochina, Malaya, Korea and Japan, and introducing porcelain to a growing market. This peaceful expansion of trade into distant waters encouraged the development of a naval force, but the major factor in the rise of the Sung navy was the arrival of invaders.

Two enemies, the Ruzhen Jin and the Mongols, warred against the northern border of the empire. The Ruzhen Jin occupied northern China after 1125, weakening the Sung, who retreated south to a new capital at Hangzhou. The Sung then turned even more to the sea. They responded to the threat at their borders—and on the coasts—with an energetic campaign of warship construction and the creation of China's first permanent navy. As Chang I wrote in 1131, "China must now regard the Sea and River as her Great Wall and substitute warships for watchtowers."

By 1170, a traveller on the Yangtze described naval

manoeuvres by a fleet of some seven hundred vessels, "about 100 feet long, with castles, towers, flags flying and drums beating." This fleet, drilling and training, was needed to keep both the Ruzhen Jin and the Mongols at bay. The Chinese also introduced new weapons such as gunpowder, catapults and incendiary devices to naval combat.

With eleven naval squadrons, a substantial navy of three thousand men and control of the Yangtze, the Sung were able to thwart a Ruzhen Jin naval invasion in 1160. The two fleets met in battle off the Shandong Peninsula, where the three hundred ships of the Sung fleet apparently used rockets

or gunpowder-filled fragmentation bombs to set their enemies on fire. The Sung gained control of the Yellow Sea with this victory.

By 1232, the Sung navy stood at twenty squadrons and fifty-two thousand men. Joseph Needham sums up the Sung contribution to China's naval history: "The navy of the Southern Sung held off the Chin Tartars and then the Mongols for nearly two centuries, gaining complete control of the East China Sea. Its successor, the navy of the Yuan, was to control the South China Sea also—and that of the Ming the Indian Ocean itself."

the height of Chinese naval power decades earlier. One of the greatest archaeological prizes that remains to be discovered in the ocean is the wreck of one or more of Zheng Ho's "treasure ships." Had they remained on the seas, the history of the world might have been very different.

The Rise of the Gun in Europe

Archaeologists have discovered and studied a number of shipwrecks from the period 1400–1650. These wrecks, and their guns and equipment, provide the first detailed look at lost warships and life and combat aboard them. Historians, working from literary sources and illustrations, date the wide-scale introduction of guns on European ships to after 1400. Although ship crews used guns to fight before 1400, the practice was not widespread. Archaeologist Ian Friel, looking at the evidence, finds that long bows and crossbows were the most effective shipboard weapons—for killing the other crew—with "guns coming a very poor third, at least before the late fifteenth century." As the use of cannon aboard ships increased, so did the problems with the guns.

The earliest guns on ships were small, swivel-mounted cannon mounted on the rails, out in the open. Firing small balls, or scrap iron known as *langrage*, these weapons were used to kill men, not ships. A shotgun-like blast of langrage was a cheap and effective way to cut down fighters on another ship's deck. The larger guns, made of iron staves (much like a barrel) and held together by metal bands, were mounted on the main, or weather deck, or in the castles. The earliest guns at sea rested on wooden platforms, not wheeled carriages. Unwieldy and hard to manoeuvre, these cannon were not powerful enough to breach another ship's hull.

Three warship wrecks from between 1416 and 1545 not only include early guns. They demonstrate how the first purpose-built warships were adapted to the gun. The first wreck is a "great ship," presumably *Grace Dieu*, a massive ship built for King Henry V of England as part of a naval buildup in response to French raids on the English coast. *Grace Dieu* is a departure from the tradition of the war cog and the rowed galley of the Mediterranean. It is a direct ancestor of the wooden ship of the line, the standard warship of the world's naval powers until the nineteenth century.

The wreck of *Grace Dieu* rests in the thick mud on the banks of the River Hamble in England. Antiquarians rediscovered the wreck in the nineteenth century, but it was not until 1933 that researchers were able to identify the wreck. Since then, archaeologists working during spring low tides and underwater have partially excavated the wreck and learned more. Historical records show that *Grace Dieu* was a large ship, built to tower over cogs and hulks with a huge forecastle that allowed the ship's archers and other fighting men to overlook and overpower their opponents. It also carried four cannon. Built in 1417, the ship never saw action. A brief 1420 voyage ended in mutiny, and the ship was laid up in the River Hamble. She remained there until a fire burned her to the waterline in 1439. Today, only the very bottom of the hull survives about a metre above the keel.

Archaeologists studying the wreck mapped the long, broad hull and discovered that, although now 40 by 12 metres (130 by 40 feet), *Grace Dieu* was originally some 38.1 metres (125 feet) long at the keel and 54.9 metres (180 feet) long on the deck. The hull was 15.24 metres (50 feet) wide at its maximum beam—making *Grace Dieu* the largest European warship when built. *Grace Dieu*'s builders constructed the ship using the Scandinavian method of clinker construction with overlapping planks. But this centuries-old method was reaching the limits of its utility with *Grace Dieu*. To construct the ship so large, the builders used three layers of planks, effectively giving *Grace Dieu* a triple skin. Closely spaced frames attached to them by thick wooden treenails reinforced the planks of the hull.

ABOVE Archaeologists excavating the interior of *Lomellina* discovered some of the earliest guns recovered from a European wreck. This view shows the banded form of the iron gun and its carriage as excavated. CNRA-IRAA BSO, K. Hurteau

BOTTOM Site plan of the round-hulled *Lomellina*. GRAN

The warships of this period, large, clinker-built craft, were the ultimate expression of Viking and Anglo-Saxon shipbuilding technology: built plank by plank, "skin first" and then reinforced with a skeleton of frames or ribs. The introduction of the gun had no effect on their construction. But by 1500, major changes were afoot. Although earlier guns were mounted on the superstructure or on open weather decks, by 1501 an innovation, guns below the deck, resulted in major change. To cut gun ports through a hull, a new type of ship construction was needed, one that did not rely on the planks of the hull for strength, but instead used an internal skeleton or frame.

Another benefit of this "frame-first" construction was that the hull, without clinker-style planks overlapping each other for strength, now provided a simple, reinforced surface that could be pierced for gun ports and other portholes. The earliest wreck to show a gun port is a Genoese ship. *Lomellina* foundered off Villefranche-sur-mer, France, on September 15, 1516. The ship was under repair when it sank; archaeologists discovered sawdust and chips of wood between the frames and a worker's plane lying nearby. Resting on its port side, the ship had heeled over as it sank. Not a large ship, measuring some 46.5 metres (153 feet) long with a breadth of 14 metres (46 feet), *Lomellina* was carvel planked and according to archaeologist Max Guérout was a *navi*, a cross between the Mediterranean row galley and the Northern European "round ships."

This sleeker, well-armed type in time became the basis of the new fighting ship, the galleon. *Lomellina* was a hybrid in more than her hull. The wreck site included fifteen guns, some of which may have been for combat ashore because the wreck site included huge wheels for gun carriages. Other guns were intended for the ship, as their carriages and the gun ports show. But guns alone were still not seen as the key to naval victory. Among the finds from the wreck of *Lomellina* were crossbow parts and four different types of hand grenades. Guns were just part of the equation as fighting ships came into conflict.

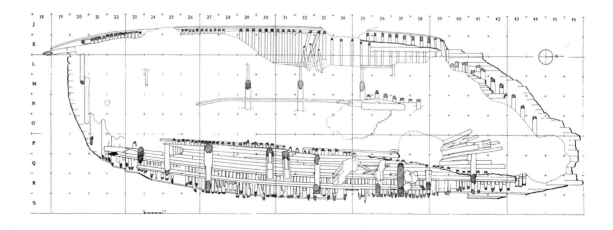

The Wreck of *Mary Rose*

The earliest warship wreck to yield a tremendous amount of information to archaeologists and historians is the well-preserved *Mary Rose*. The ship, with a crew of six to seven hundred men, sank suddenly on the morning of July 19, 1545, off Portsmouth, England. Manoeuvring into battle with an invading French fleet, *Mary Rose* was top-heavy and heeled over as the crew set sail and ran out the guns. Water poured in open gun ports, which lay dangerously close to the sea. The ship capsized on her starboard side, quickly filled and sank as men fought to get away. As guns, ballast, equipment and men crashed through broken compartments and into a broken jumble inside the ship, *Mary Rose* settled on to the bottom. Fewer than forty of the crew escaped to nearby boats.

Archaeologists slowly excavated the wreck from 1971 to 1982 and recovered more than nineteen thousand artifacts. The excavation revealed

This modern painting of *Mary Rose* is based on an archaeological study of the wreck. *Mary Rose* Trust

This isometric view of the surviving portion of *Mary Rose*'s hull gives a clear sense of the massive structure of the Tudor warship. *Mary Rose Trust*

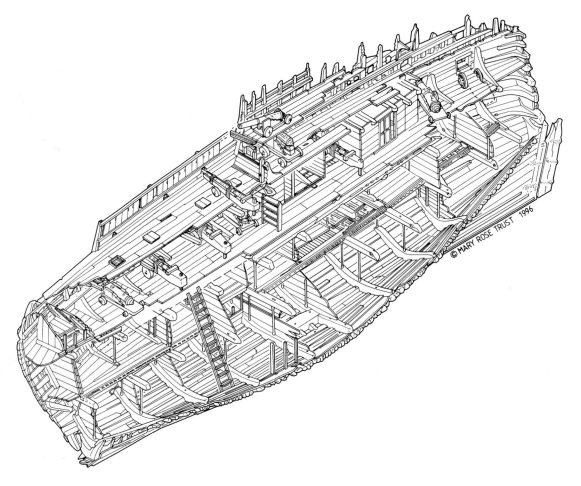

that *Mary Rose* lay on her starboard side, with more than half of the ship, four deck levels in all, intact with guns, equipment and personal belongings jumbled in the hold, decks and cabins exactly where they had fallen when the ship sank. Archaeologists raised the intact hull in 1982 and continue to study it while preservation work is done on the water-saturated timbers.

The remains of the ship have allowed archaeologists to make a detailed reconstruction of *Mary Rose*. The ship was a carrack, a huge and modern (for its day) purpose-built warship. Its builders equipped her to fight as much with her guns as with other weapons. Among the weapons found inside the ship were swords, daggers, pikes, bills and incendiary darts used to set an enemy ship on fire. But the most common weapons discovered were bows and arrows. Accounts of medieval battles talk about the power of the English longbow

and how lines of archers would fill the skies with deadly volleys of arrows. Some bows were capable of piercing armour. Even more amazing is that until the discovery of *Mary Rose*, not one medieval bow or arrow had survived.

Thanks to the wreck of *Mary Rose*, we have detailed knowledge of the weapons and the men who used them in battle on land and sea. Excavators found 137 complete and 3 broken English longbows, 2497 complete arrows and 1471 broken arrow tips. Some of the bows and arrows were still stowed inside boxes, and groups of the arrows were bundled together, twenty-four to each bundle. A leather disk, with twenty-four holes, kept the bundles together but prevented the arrows from crushing each other's feathering. Archaeologist Margaret Rule suggests they were an ammunition clip.

Skeletons lay buried inside the sunken ship.

One of the men's bones rested on the deck, along with the remains of his leather jerkin, or undershirt. A leather belt or thong with a spacer full of arrows loosely circled his spine, showing he was an archer. Another body, with only the bones left, was also discovered to be an archer. His bones showed that the man had worked with the bow for many years.

Other skeletons lay tangled beneath a mass of rope that covered the open deck. The rope, woven into a diamond-shaped mesh, formed antiboarding netting to keep the enemy off the decks when *Mary Rose* grappled with another ship. But the netting also trapped the crew when *Mary Rose* sank. It was strung atop a planked wall of panels that armoured the deck. Called "blindage," these planks were movable. The crew could pull them out to provide a protected port for an archer or gunner to fire at a nearby ship's crew. The blindage, the netting and the hand weapons all point to a reliance on fighting at close quarters. Although *Mary Rose* and her contemporary warships represented the ascendancy of the gun, it was a time when the guns were meant for the other ship's crew, not its hull.

Mary Rose has a long gun deck and gun ports, and iron and bronze cannon, some still mounted to their wooden gun carriages, lie inside the wreck. The types and ages of the guns are mixed. Some of them were practically antiques. Archaeologist Margaret Rule, who supervised the excavation of the ship, feels that the mix of guns represents a hasty arming in a time of national emergency. Anthropologist Richard Gould argues that gun manufacture and guns themselves were rapidly changing at this time. The mix of types could reflect tactical indecision as to which types worked best. Three "hailshots" are primitive, rail-mounted shotguns that fired cubes of cast-iron shot into groups of enemy soldiers or marines. The hailshot is a weapon that predates the cannon and was used in Asia and Europe beginning in the fourteenth century. The presence of the hailshots may suggest a deliberate decision to include

LEFT Diver hovers over the wheel from a seagoing gun carriage on the *Mary Rose* site. *Mary Rose* Trust

BELOW *Mary Rose*'s mix of antique and more modern guns included this reinforced iron bombardeta and a cast bronze gun. *Mary Rose* Trust

The thick timbers of the gun deck supported the rows of guns and the weight of many fighting men. The mass of the ship was poorly centred, though, and *Mary Rose* capsized, taking most of her crew. Still undergoing preservation through chemical spraying, the ship and its artifacts are a rare legacy of Tudor times and early war at sea. *Mary Rose* Trust

antipersonnel weapons in the time-honoured tradition of killing the enemy crew and not just focussing on damaging the other ship.

Mary Rose carried many deadly antipersonnel weapons, even for use with the large "modern" guns. Archaeologists discovered wooden cases, some made with staves like small barrels, others with a hollowed-out cylinder split into two halves. These artifacts are canister shot, much like giant shotgun shells. Each was packed with different materials—including sharp pieces of flint—that would scatter when the gunners fired the shot at an enemy ship.

The weapons aboard *Mary Rose* clearly indicate that her officers envisioned a typical sea fight, with the ship as a floating castle pitting men against men. But they also took advantage of adaptations to the ship to fit newer, heavy guns more suited to damaging enemy ships than picking off their crews. The invention of the gun port and the development of the gun deck, shown so strongly in the wreck of *Mary Rose*, was the essential step in turning the warship into a destroyer of other ships, not just a platform on which men fought at sea.

The hull of *Mary Rose* gives archaeologists a rare opportunity to see how these early gun ports and decks were fitted into a carrack hull. The ship's hull has notched frames, or ribs, that were originally cut for clinker planking. But this type of planking does not allow shipwrights to cut many holes for gun ports. The strength of a clinker-built hull is found

in the joining of the overlapped planks. At the same time Henry VIII's shipwrights were building *Mary Rose* in 1509–11, they were also converting *Sovereign* from a clinker to a carvel-planked hull. Why spend time and effort to remodel one ship while building another with the out-of-style method? It may be that the ship was a throwback. Although records of the time list her with many guns, *Mary Rose* probably carried them on the open weather deck and in the superstructure.

Henry VIII had *Mary Rose* rebuilt in 1536. At this time, the ship may have been re-planked with a carvel hull, and the continuous gun deck and ports added. The strategic position of England had changed with Henry's divorce of his wife, Catherine of Aragon, and his excommunication by the Pope. The Catholic powers of Europe, particularly France and Spain, were considerable foes, and these international tensions may have led Henry to rebuild ships like *Mary Rose*. The gun deck is supported and braced with internal frames and riders. The evidence of these timbers—some are poorly fitted—suggests to Margaret Rule that they were quickly added in response to a deteriorating political and military situation. Analysis of the wreck discovered that dry rot inside the ship's older timbers was neglected in the rebuild. The reconstruction of *Mary Rose* to enable her to take heavier guns appears to have been driven by emergency.

One of the greatest risks, of course, was that a hull strong enough to take more guns was not necessarily safer. *Mary Rose* sailed into battle on July 19, 1545, carrying some ninety-one cannon. The higher the guns were placed on a ship with high fore and stern castles, the more unstable and easily capsized the ship. The surviving superstructure of the *Mary Rose* shows evidence of lighter planking inside to make it less top-heavy, and the gun decks and ports are placed lower in the hull to help provide balance. Unfortunately, this effort to diminish the risk of capsizing did not work, and within moments of moving into position for battle, *Mary Rose* heeled over and sank.

The Rise of the Sailing Warship

Although *Mary Rose* and other carracks of the sixteenth century represent the rise of the large, heavily armed warship, two types of fighting ships, the caravel and the galleon, quickly replaced them. These ships were responsible for spreading European control over a broad area of the globe, particularly the empires of Spain and Portugal. The caravel was developed on the Iberian Peninsula, probably from coastal fishing boats that increasingly ventured offshore. Starting around 1440, Portugal used caravels as the principal ships of exploration and commercial expansion. Pushing down the coast of Africa, around the Cape of Good Hope and into the Indian Ocean, and thence into Asian waters, the Portuguese used their caravels and larger galleons to win tremendous trade advantages. They did so literally at the end of a gun, seizing control of principal trade routes, defeating Ottoman, Indian and Southeast Asian naval forces.

Spain, Portugal's neighbour and rival, also used the caravel and the galleon to push west across the Atlantic and into the Americas. The caravel in American waters was the first naval assertion of Spanish power in the New World. We know surprisingly little about these ships. The remains of three probable caravel wrecks in the Caribbean, a few documents, artistic representations and informed speculation are all the evidence we currently have.

One of the wreck sites, at Molasses Reef in the Turks and Caicos Islands, dates to the early sixteenth century. Very little of the wooden hull had survived in the shallow, 6-metre-deep (20-foot-deep) water of the site. But iron guns and composite lead and iron shot provided a detailed look at ship's armament. The guns included breech-loading bombardetas and breech chambers. The fact that more of the chambers were found than guns suggested to archaeologist Joe Simmons that they were kept loaded with powder so that a rapid rate of fire could be maintained. Smaller, swivel-mounted guns known as versos, along with the bombardetas, indicate that the guns of the Molasses Reef wreck were intended to kill men, not seriously damage ships. The other weapons excavated from the wreck, including crossbows, swords, shoulder arms and grenades, are consistent with this speculation.

Similar guns and more extensive hull remains from another site, at Highborn Cay in the Bahamas, give us some clues about these small, but sturdy ships. The caravel hull was used for both warships and armed merchantmen, and the

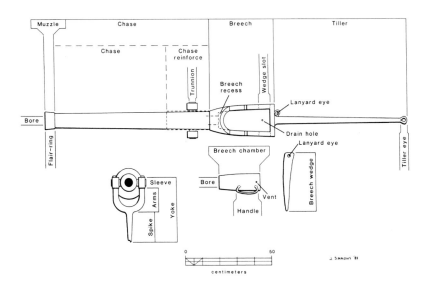

Drawing of a swivel-mounted verso from the Molasses Reef wreck—a weapon to kill men, not ships. Ships of Discovery

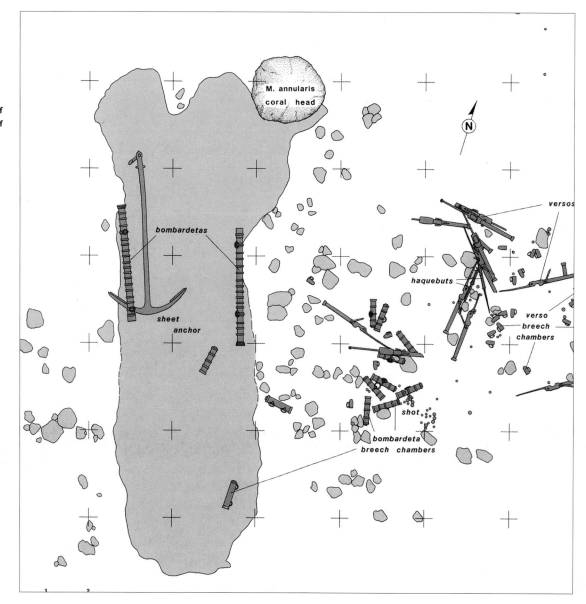

Site plan of the Molasses Reef wreck showing the position of the ship's many guns. Ships of Discovery

ships served as powerful tools for sixteenth-century imperial expansion. Ironically, the caravels sailing into the Indian Ocean, arriving within decades of China's withdrawal from the seas, could have been met by larger, better-armed Ming warships and easily defeated. Instead, Portugal and Spain built larger, better-armed ships—galleons—to meet any foes. Galleons supplanted caravels and fought in a series of actions that pitted Spain and Portugal against each other, as well as against the new naval powers in the Netherlands and England.

As these sail-powered warships came into ascendancy, the heyday of oar-powered warships was passing. The switch to larger hulls, capable of carrying many guns, gradually made the row galleys that dominated the Mediterranean

The Battle of Lepanto, 1571.
Painting by Juan Luna y Novicio,
Palacio de Señado, Madrid/
Bridgeman Art Library

obsolete. Larger, many-gunned, oar-powered
ships called galleasses represent an attempt to
merge the new technology of the gun into the
millennia-old row galley, but the age of the galley was passing. The last major battle under oars
came in the Mediterranean, off the coast of
Greece at Lepanto on October 7, 1571. A fleet
of 225 Ottoman Turkish galleys met an allied
European fleet of 210 galleys. The victorious
Europeans were able to repulse the last major
Islamic thrust against the west in a decisive naval
action. Ramming and boarding were the principal tactics, though cannon were also used, but
they did little to influence the outcome. Within
two decades, a decisive naval engagement would
demonstrate that the age of the gun and ships
large enough to carry many guns was at hand.

The Spanish Armada

Another significant European naval campaign of the sixteenth century was the running sea battle between England and Spain. Lasting from July 31 to August 8, 1588, the series of engagements between the English and Spanish ships fleets culminated in what historian Geoffrey Parker and archaeologist Colin Martin describe as "the longest and fiercest artillery action which had ever taken place at sea." The mauling of the Spanish Armada was more a result of storms than gunfire. But the storms that wrecked many of the Spanish ships left a rich archaeological record on the sea floor. Over the last four decades, archaeologists studying the wrecks of

eight ships from the Spanish Armada have added much to our understanding of the ships, the weapons and the naval combat of the time, as well as providing a new appreciation of why the Armada failed to successfully engage the English fleet and invade England's shores.

The intended invasion of England was the result of decades of tension between the Catholic church and Protestant England in the aftermath of Henry VIII's divorce from Catherine of Aragon and his subsequent renunciation of Catholicism. Spain's control of the overseas trade, Philip II's conquest of Portugal and Spanish involvement in plots to replace Henry's daughter Elizabeth with a

Long thought to be the Spanish Armada, this scene is now believed to be the Battle of Cadiz in 1596. Nonetheless, it captures the type of ships and action seen in the Channel in 1588. Painting by Hendrick Cornelisz Vroom, Private collection/Bridgeman Art Library

Catholic monarch angered the English court. In turn, England's support for the rebellious Netherlands in their fight against Spanish rule, and the increasingly outrageous attacks on Spanish ships and New World ports by English freebooters, enraged Philip. An undeclared war between the two nations, one a mighty global empire, the other a beleaguered island kingdom, culminated in Philip's orders for a large fleet to seize control of England's shores. A Spanish army, aided by European mercenaries, would then cross an English Channel swept free of English ships, march on London and depose Elizabeth.

Initial Spanish plans called for a fleet of five

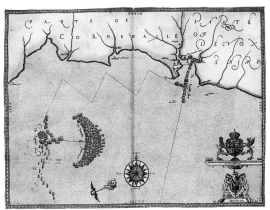

This 1588 map by Augustine Ryther shows the route and the crescent-shaped mass of the Spanish Armada as it moved into the English Channel. Soon, the tactics of the English, weather and the sea would scatter the fleet. Private collection/Bridgeman Art Library

A wheel from a siege gun's carriage, discovered on the seabed by archaeologists excavating the wreck of *La Trinidad Valencera*.
© Colin Martin

hundred ships and thirty thousand troops. When the "invincible armada" finally sailed, only 130 ships and twenty thousand troops were available. The Spanish fleet included Mediterranean row galleys; hybrid "galleasses" that carried guns, sails and oars; galleons from the New World treasure fleets, and huge merchantmen from Portugal, Italy, Dalmatia and Northern Europe that the Spaniards had converted into fighting ships. Some of the fleet were transports, loaded with artillery, siege trains, fortifications and weapons for the invading troops.

The Spanish Armada entered the English Channel on July 31. The English fleet, 170 ships strong, included seventy merchantmen converted to warships. Over several days, the two fleets closed and fought a series of actions that demonstrated a new approach to war at sea. The English ships sailed in a line, keeping just within firing range of the Armada, and they unleashed a barrage. Spanish naval tactics called for their ships to grapple with the enemy, use their guns to sweep the other's decks and then board and take the enemy with overwhelming force.

The well-armed, well-trained troops on the Spanish ships never got a chance in the Armada's encounters with the English. In a few hours, the furious rate of English fire peppered the galleon *San Juan* with over three hundred rounds. The Spanish response was not as intense; one Spanish officer estimated they had fired 750 rounds against two thousand English shots.

The battles continued over the next week as the Armada, massed together into a large formation, lumbered up the Channel. The English picked off a few stragglers that separated from the Armada's massed bulk. Their success was not in destroying the Armada as a fighting force but in preventing it from landing. When the Armada reached Calais for provisions and to rendezvous with the invasion force on August 6, it was still intact and formidable. The pursuing English disrupted the anchored Armada in a bold attack with blazing fire ships. Panic instead of flames swept the Spanish fleet, and many ships cut their anchors free and fled to sea, where the English rejoined the battle.

The Armada began its slow return home, circumnavigating the British Isles. Of the 130 ships that sailed against England, only sixty returned to Spain. Very few were lost in battle. The majority foundered on the shores of England, Scotland and Ireland, or on the open seas, lashed by storms the English believed were heaven-sent.

Wrecks of the Spanish Armada. James P. Delgado, Eric Leinberger

Atlantic Ocean

Route of the Armada

El Gran Grifón

SCOTLAND

San Juan de Sicilia

North Sea

Trinidad Valencera

Girona

IRELAND

Santa María de la Rosa

ENGLAND

Calais

Plymouth

FRANCE

0   40 miles

0   40 kilometres

A modern navy gun crew experiments—and fights—with the difficult task of loading and firing a reconstructed ship's gun carriage from *La Trinidad Valencera*. Too long for the decks and unwieldy, the carriages slowed the rate of Spanish fire and were one of the reasons for the defeat of the Armada.
© Colin Martin

Wrecks of the Armada

Divers, treasure hunters and archaeologists have discovered a number of Armada wrecks on the shores and waters of Scotland and Ireland, and careful archaeological work has revealed the identity as well as detail about four of these ships. One wreck, *San Juan de Sicilia*, was systematically plundered for treasure. Evidence was scattered and removed. However, the dean of Armada shipwreck research, Colin Martin, working with the evidence from four excavated wrecks—the transport *La Trinidad Valencera*, the armed merchantman *Santa María de la Rosa*, the galleass *Girona* and the armed merchantman *El Gran Grifón*—has rewritten the story of the Armada.

Historians have suggested that the Armada's failure resulted from its huge ships being outmanoeuvred by smaller, more agile English ships, from firing all of their heavy shot early in the battle or from having too many short-range guns. Martin, working with historian Geoffrey Parker and others, and combining the evidence from the wrecks with

meticulous research in English, Spanish and other archives, has determined that these suggestions are incorrect. The problem lay in Spain's failure to adapt to the technological revolution sweeping Europe. The explanation is not just in the English tactic of line-on attack and bombardment without boarding. It lies in the disparate rate of fire between the two fleets. The Spanish ships, with twenty-five hundred pieces of artillery, were a match for the English. And the Armada sailed into action with its guns loaded, ready for action. A cannon recovered from the wreck of *El Gran Grifón* demonstrates the Spanish practice of always keeping a gun loaded, so that a volley of shots would precede a ramming and boarding.

But the Spanish fleet was not ready to repeatedly load and fire. The principal problem, Martin found, was lack of standardization. Coming from various parts of the empire and Europe, manufactured by different foundries, the "Spanish" guns and shot simply did not match. In the heat of a battle, the men of the Armada had to search

ABOVE Resurrecting an ancient and fearsome weapon, a team experiments with a "bomba," or fire lance reconstructed from examples excavated from *La Trinidad Valencera*. These weapons, first invented by the Chinese, were part of the Armada's arsenal. © Colin Martin

LEFT A small bronze gun rises from the wreck of *La Trinidad Valencera*. © Colin Martin

A contrast in arms. The ornate casting of Philip II's escutcheon on a bronze siege gun from *La Trinidad Valencera* shows a different level of craftsmanship than the off-centre bore of a gun from the wreck of *El Gran Grifón*.
© Colin Martin

among their shot, measuring each cannon ball to see if it would fit into their guns. In the wreck of *La Trinidad Valencera*, archaeologists discovered a wooden "gunner's rule" used to calibrate shot. This vital tool was "useless," Martin notes, because "the graduations are so inaccurate and inconsistent" on one side, whereas on the other, "a fundamental arithmetical misconception has rendered these graduations entirely spurious." Some guns, such as one raised from the wreck of *El Gran Grifón*, were hastily cast to meet the needs of the Armada. The bore of the gun was off-centre, making it worthless.

Archaeological excavation of *La Trinidad Valencera* also recovered huge gun carriages. These 6-metre-long (20-foot-long) wooden carriages mounted two wheels at the front and swept back to rest on the deck. The carriages sat on a gun deck only 12 metres (40 feet) wide. They were unwieldy. After firing, each gun was pulled back, swabbed and reloaded by its muzzle. In a telling display of experimental archaeology, Martin supervised a test in which a crew loaded, fired, cleaned and reloaded a gun on this type of carriage. Then the crew did the same with an English gun on its shorter, four-wheeled carriage. Examples from the wreck of *Mary Rose* show that the English were mounting their guns on these small, stout, more manoeuvrable carriages in the sixteenth century. Not surprisingly, the modern gunners completed their job with the four-wheeled carriage in half the time.

The excavation of the Armada wrecks yielded significant information about the armament of the soldiers who sailed aboard, including the earliest surviving examples of fire pots and pole-mounted *bombas* that spewed flames and projectiles—the same types of weapons used by the Chinese a continent away in their sea battles. In the aftermath of the Armada, naval warfare shifted to a global perspective, with new types of ships and tactics that would dominate sea fights for more than two centuries.

Nineteenth-century engraving of a Venetian galley. From Shippen, *Naval Battles Ancient and Modern*

The Lake Garda Galley

The galley was the instrument of the sea power of the Italian city-states. Introduced around the end of the ninth century, it was a medieval adoption of the time-honoured Mediterranean tradition of rowed warships. This ship remained a staple of Mediterranean naval warfare for nearly six centuries. The Battle of Lepanto, in 1571, is generally considered the end of galley warfare. Although illustrations of medieval galleys exist, and documents discuss their dimensions and number of oars, little was known about the construction of these craft until the discovery of a Venetian galley in Lake Garda in Northern Italy.

Divers working under the direction of archaeologist Enrico Scandurra discovered the wreck in 27 metres (about 90 feet) of water, buried in mud. Built around 1438, the galley was part of a Venetian fleet transported overland to fortify Lake Garda during a war with the Duchy of Milan in 1439. Venice won the war and retired the fleet to the eastern end of the lake. In 1509, war again threatened Venice as the League of Cambrai attacked the island republic. Venetian commander Zaccaria Loredani prepared the remaining galleys on Lake Garda for combat. Outnumbered, with only one large and two small galleys, Loredani scuttled his fleet in the lake in June 1509, loading them with stones and setting them on fire.

Scandurra's divers located the wreck of one galley and excavated it between 1962 and 1965 to reveal the well-preserved bottom of the hull beneath the layer of stones used to sink it. Approximately 40 metres (130 feet) in length, wide and shallow, the galley was a stable rowing and fighting platform. Scandurra reconstructed this typical Venetian galley as a broad platform supporting a wooden outrigger, on which the oars rested. A large platform forward, known as the *rembata*, supported the fighting troops and the galley's weapons, be they stone-firing mangonels or cannon. Since Scandurra's work in the 1960s, archaeologist Marco D'Agostino has continued the study of the Lake Garda galley.

CHAPTER 4

Wooden Walls

THE BEGINNING OF the seventeenth century until the mid-nineteenth century was the heyday of the wooden warship. Nations waged war on the seas for empires and occasionally survival. During these years, Spain and Portugal lost control of the seas to the growing power of the Dutch, the French and the English. The Dutch waged an eighty-year war for independence from the Spanish empire. This struggle left the Dutch with a formidable navy and far-flung interests in trade and empire that included incursions into the Far East.

Neither England nor France was able to counter the growing influence of the Netherlands, and the three powers struggled until the triumph of British sea power in the early eighteenth century. Anglo-Dutch wars between 1652 and 1654, and 1664 and 1667, were marked by intense sea battles. Those wars ended with no clear victor and a new rival to contend with. France's King Louis XIV built a large navy to challenge the Dutch and the English as well as the Austrians and Spanish. French naval victories over Spain in the western Mediterranean and the naval buildup made France the major sea power, a position the French held until the Dutch and English formed an alliance under English naval leadership. A battle off Beachy Head, England, in 1690 ended in French victory, but France did not press its gains, giving the alliance time to prepare another fleet.

In 1692, when the French navy met the alliance in battle, the result was disastrous for France, with defeat at the battles of Barfleur and La Hougue. England's experiences in the war with France led the government to create a large, permanent navy. By 1697, when the war ended, the English navy had 323 ships, and England was the world's greatest naval power. New threats, particularly from a resurgent France under Napoleon, challenged England's mastery of the seas, but the "wooden walls" kept the nation safe and allowed the British to create an overseas empire.

The hallmark of this age was the expansion of Europe's wars to a global stage. After centuries of conflict within the confines of the Mediterranean, large-scale naval warfare expanded into northern seas by the sixteenth century, then spread with the development of overseas empires throughout the world. The sea fights of Portugal, Spain, the Netherlands, France and England sent ships and fleets into combat far from home, leaving sunken warships in African, Indian, Asian and American waters. At the same time, Russia, Sweden and Denmark fought for control of the Baltic.

The rise of the gun in the late sixteenth century, and widespread adoption of weapons designed to smash and sink other ships, led the various sea powers to build larger ships capable of mounting increasing numbers of cannon. The typical heavy warship of the early seventeenth century, the galleon, developed into two types of ships: the "ship of the line" and the frigate. But it was not just an age of hulking, towering ships bristling with cannon. Smaller warships, carrying fewer guns, join the wrecks of the large ships to provide a rich archaeological record of the age of the wooden walls.

Archaeologists studying warship wrecks from this period have also examined an extensive collection of artifacts. These finds not only document fighting at sea and the use of weapons. They also provide a detailed look at life aboard. The man-of-war, from 1600 to 1850, carried crews the size of small towns and villages. Archaeology reveals much about how these men worked, ate, slept, sought recreation and fought.

FACING PAGE *Vasa*'s wooden walls, gun ports open to expose the snarling lions' heads. The huge galleon was as much a psychological weapon as a platform for cannon. *Vasa* Museum, Hans Hammerskiold

RIGHT The personal effects of a *Vasa* seaman, recovered from the wreck. *Vasa* Museum, G. Bauer

Vasa floats again in Stockholm harbour. Swedish salvage divers patched the ship on the bottom to make her watertight. Vasa Museum

The Wreck of Vasa

One of the world's great archaeological treasures is the completely intact Swedish galleon Vasa. Built for King Gustaf II Adolf of Sweden, the great galleon was part of a naval expansion designed to prevent the Habsburg Empire from extending its control into the Baltic. Gustaf II Adolf wanted to expand Sweden's power over the Baltic, and he built up a navy to control the region. One of those ships was Vasa.

On August 10, 1628, Vasa cleared the naval dockyard in Stockholm and crossed the harbour on her maiden voyage. As a crowd of some ten thousand watched from the shore, Vasa fired two salutes with her guns, and she set sail. Strong gusts of wind made the huge ship careen sharply, and as the officers shouted orders for the men to take their stations and loosen the sails, the ship heeled

again. Water poured in through open gun ports and flooded the lower decks. The ship continued her roll, then went under on her port side. Sails still set, flags flying, Vasa sank. Out of a crew of 133, little more than half survived.

According to Swedish records, an English salvor managed to get the wreck off her side and upright within days of the sinking. Attempts to raise the wreck were not successful, but between 1663 and 1665, divers working from a diving bell managed to pull up many of the ship's guns. After a brief salvage project in 1683 that raised one cannon, the wreck of Vasa was abandoned for more than three hundred years.

In 1956, persistent efforts by researcher Anders Franzen rediscovered the wreck resting in 32 metres (105 feet) of water in Stockholm harbour. Hard-hat divers sent down to find the ship

reported walking up to a solid wall of wood. The dark waters of the Baltic are not as salty as other oceans, and the marine organisms that eat submerged wood elsewhere in the world are absent. Other than the damage from early salvage attempts, centuries of anchors hitting the submerged hulk and the rusting away of iron fastenings, *Vasa* was preserved. The discovery prompted the Swedish government to devote the time and money to raise the ship from the depths.

Between 1958 and 1961, divers prepared the wreck for raising. Working with high-pressure hoses, they cut into the clay beneath the hull, passing slings underneath her. The slings were then used to slowly move *Vasa* into shallower water. Finally, the hull was raised out of the ocean in April 1961 and moved into a special dry dock for treatment and restoration. Spraying the hull with preservatives until 1977, the Swedes rebuilt missing portions of the decks and stern castle, and reattached sections of the ship and her ornate, carved decorations. The reconstructed ship now rests in a specially built museum that opened in 1990.

Vasa was large and exceptionally well decorated for her time. She was a special *royalskeppet* or royal ship. She embodies the new role of the warship as a symbol of regal power and national pride, as well as the changes in ship design that fully adopted the gun as the principal weapon of war at sea. Galleons like *Vasa* were the next step in warship development after huge carracks like *Mary Rose*. Sleeker, without a heavy forecastle and with a more compact stern castle, galleons were built with cannon in mind as their principal armament; they were the first purpose-built, all-gun warships.

Workers clearing the mud from the decks of *Vasa* faced a daunting task of shifting heavy guns and ballast along with tons of mud. They were rewarded with fresh glimpses of the past, from crushed skeletons of *Vasa*'s crew to ornate carvings with traces of original paint. *Vasa* Museum

By the time of *Vasa*, the galleon was a ship in transition. Galleons were growing larger to accommodate more guns below the decks. *Vasa* has two gun decks mounting an impressive number of cannon. She held sixty-four guns in all, forty-eight of which were large 24-pounders. These guns were potential ship-killers. To counter the threat of the enemy's guns doing just that to *Vasa*, she was built with thick timber sides and heavy framing to help the hull absorb the hits. An impressive amount of timber and money went into *Vasa*'s 69-metre (226-foot) length, 11.7-metre (38-foot) width and 1210 tons.

Vasa was designed to carry 145 crew and three hundred soldiers. Although the guns were the primary armament, fighting men on the ship discouraged boarders who might try to close and take the ship in hand-to-hand fighting. *Vasa*'s masts, when recovered, included a fighting top, a large platform from which men armed with muskets could shoot at the enemy's decks or at boarders on their own deck. *Vasa*'s ammunition for the cannon also included bar-shot and pike-shot. These balls and spikes, mounted on sliding bars, spread to whip through the air and cut through rigging to drop masts or plow through the unprotected flesh of the enemy's crew.

ABOVE Reconstructed and once again ornate and beautiful, *Vasa*'s quarter deck was the battle station for her officers. *Vasa* Museum, Hans Hammerskiold

RIGHT Gilded and painted carvings covered *Vasa* with a host of nationalistic, mythological and religious symbols. *Vasa* Museum, Hans Hammerskiold

One of the most striking conclusions reached by the archaeologists and other scientists who removed more than fourteen thousand artifacts from the wreck was the disparity between the ship's majestic, imposing appearance and life aboard the ship as experienced by her crew. *Vasa* is covered with hundreds of carvings, in their time brightly painted and gilded, with symbols depicting the power of the Swedish crown, images of life and death, religious icons and mockery of their enemies. Carvings show two Polish noblemen, enemies of Sweden, humbled and crawling on the floor under a bench. The figurehead, a huge, snarling lion and the roaring lions' heads on the gun port lids were all part of a deliberate attempt at floating propaganda to impress all who saw *Vasa*.

Although most of *Vasa*'s guns were salvaged shortly after her sinking, the empty carriages on the gun deck give a sense of the heavily armed ship's ability to fight. Unfortunately, the ship and her crew never had the chance to do so. *Vasa* Museum

LEFT Inboard profile view of *Vasa* as reconstructed by **Gunnar Olofsson.** *Vasa* Museum

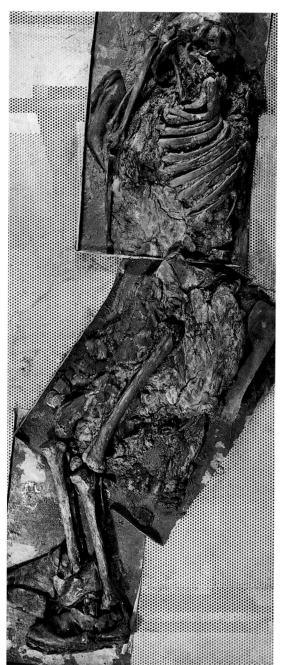

When *Vasa* heeled over, her guns and their heavy oak carriages (top right) broke loose and rolled across the decks, crushing men. This broken, flattened skeleton was the result of one of those "loose cannon." Deaths caused in this way gave rise to that now commonly used term.
Vasa Museum

Lars-Ake Kvarning, former director of the *Vasa* Museum, notes how the archaeological finds, when cleaned and analysed, turned "a rare mixture of apparently worthless bits of wood" into "imaginative carvings," whereas other finds showed what life aboard was like "behind this showpiece façade." Life, Kvarning points out, was revealed by the finds inside the ship to be "plain and hard." The sailors and soldiers did not have uniforms, and they had to wear whatever they themselves brought aboard. Archaeologists, unpacking well-preserved sea chests belonging to the sailors, found no "extra clothing for cold nights on deck and no wet-weather clothing." The men, who sailed with their families, lived on the decks. Hammocks for sleeping were unknown. The food, eaten on wooden plates with wooden spoons, was boiled salted beef and pork, as well as salt herring. Fishing gear found inside the hull indicates that the crew caught fresh fish to augment their diet. The remains of twenty-five people discovered in or around the wreck showed the traces of hard work and previous injuries, including healed fractures of arms and legs that had been broken by "severe blows."

The wreck of *Vasa* points out that the transition to many-gunned warships came at a price. Like *Mary Rose*, *Vasa* was top-heavy and prone to capsize. Surviving Swedish archives describe a lengthy investigation that came to no definite conclusion as to why *Vasa* sank. What seems clear from looking at the ship today is that she was built top-heavy, without enough room for ballast in her hold. The gun carriages, often still on their four wheels, were discovered lashed in place. *Vasa* sank because she was built in a time of national emergency, built larger than other ships and quickly rushed into service with a critical design flaw that sent her to the bottom before she even cleared the harbour.

ABOVE **Diver examines one of *Kronan*'s bronze guns on the seabed.** Kalmar Lans Museum

LEFT ***Kronan* explodes in the height of battle.** Kalmar Lans Museum

The Wreck of *Kronan*

The incredible preservation of wooden wrecks in the Baltic, first seen with the wreck of *Vasa*, was demonstrated again by the 1980 discovery of the wreck of *Kronan*. This warship, built in Stockholm between 1665 and 1672, was a huge, three-decked 60-metre-long (197-foot-long), 2140-ton warship. Armed with 126 guns, *Kronan* was a heavily armed and lavishly decorated instrument of Swedish naval power.

Sweden's quest for domination of the Baltic, beginning in the late sixteenth century and lasting into the early eighteenth century, led to conflicts in that enclosed sea. By 1660, though, Sweden's power in the Baltic was at its peak, with an empire that controlled most of the coast and the sea itself. But Sweden's empire was contested by other European nations, notably Russia and Denmark. In 1675, Denmark and her ally, the Netherlands, declared war on Sweden. *Kronan*, the flagship of a Swedish fleet sent against a Danish-Dutch fleet, engaged the enemy off the southwest coast of Sweden on June 1, 1676.

While turning to fight, *Kronan* capsized in a squall. Only forty-two of some five hundred crew members survived.

Archaeological excavation of *Kronan*, which lies in 26 metres (85 feet) of water, under the direction of Lars Einarsson of the Kalmar County Museum, has documented the preserved remains of about two-thirds of the port side of the ship and recovered more than twenty-three thousand artifacts. The wreck site has been described by the archaeologists as "a fantastic sight that is at the same time frightening," as they swim over large, scattered timbers, bronze cannon, ornate decorations and wooden sculptures from the ship, pewter plates, clay pipes and skeletons. Like *Vasa*, the wreck of *Kronan* is a remarkable archaeological legacy from the heyday of Swedish naval power.

From Galleon to Ship of the Line

The battle for domination of the seas was more a
naval arms race than a succession of wars. The
naval arms race of the seventeenth and eighteenth
centuries was characterized by competition not
only to build large numbers of ships, but also to
build bigger, heavier ships to carry more guns.
These large ships were a reflection of prestige for
the monarchies that commissioned them. As well,
the development of the "great ships," as the English
called them, changed the way battles were fought.

The only way to place larger numbers of guns
(and heavier guns, too) on a ship was to build gun
decks to mount them, side by side. Two-decked
ships like *Vasa* and three-decked ships of the same
period, like the famous English warship *Sovereign of
the Seas*, had only one effective way to fight. They
sailed alongside the enemy and fired all the guns on
whatever beam, or side, faced the other ship. These
"broadsides" ultimately led to ships fighting in rows
or lines, sailing alongside each other to discharge as
much shot as possible into each other. The naval
powers built their ships heavy to carry as many heavy
guns as they could and to absorb punishment from
the enemy's guns while keeping afloat. These huge
wooden fortresses, the "ships of the line," became
the standard warship of the eighteenth century.

Several wrecks from the late seventeenth and
early eighteenth centuries provide a detailed look at
warships in this time of naval expansion. These
large fleets reintroduced the concept of standardization. The problems of standardization of guns and
shot, one of the elements that helped defeat the
Spanish Armada, were resolved in the seventeenth
century. Wrecks of warships, beginning in this
period, include guns captured from an enemy
adopted for use on a rival's ships. The hulls of the
ships, too, show the beginnings of standardization
in construction, the development of "classes" of
ships as more than one vessel was built to a single
plan and the transition of ideas and techniques as
the naval innovations of one power were copied by
another—just as Rome had done with Carthage
two thousand years earlier.

The Duart Wreck

A chance discovery by a diver in the waters off
Duart Point, at Mull, Scotland, has provided
archaeologists with a detailed look at a small warship lost in 1653. Under the leadership of archaeologist Colin Martin, excavation of the wreck is
slowly yielding her secrets. The Duart wreck is
probably the pinnace *Swan*, a small warship built in
1641. If *Vasa* was a seventeenth-century battleship,
then *Swan* was a destroyer. Light and fast, *Swan*
represented a class of warship built to defend the

English Channel. In the early seventeenth century, North African, Turkish, French and Dutch pirates and privateers regularly raided English shipping and settlements in the Channel with small, fast pinnaces that outmanoeuvred the English navy's galleons.

The "nimble dwarfs" of the pirates inspired the English to copy them. During the reign of Charles I, the navy launched English-built pinnaces. These ships were not as successful as the pirates' ships, largely because English shipwrights insisted on bulking the pinnaces to make their hulls stronger than the lightly built enemy ships. In 1637, an Irish noble, Thomas Wentworth, bought a Dutch pinnace for the protection of the Irish coast. In 1641, Charles I ordered a copy of Wentworth's "extraordinarily good sailer." The new ship, *Swan*, entered service in July of that year, patrolling Irish waters and Scotland's west coast.

Swan was soon swept up in England's Civil War and in 1645 was "captured" by Parliamentary forces

The age of Cromwell was a time of war on land and sea — a struggle that caught up the tiny warship *Swan*. This scene by Willem Van de Velde the Younger captures the style of the fighting ships of the time. The broken wreck of *Swan* now allows us to fill in the details. Private collection/ Bridgeman Art Library

Diver examines a small gun carriage on the wreck site of *Swan.* © Colin Martin

when her unpaid crew, at anchor off Dublin, were approached by a Parliamentary ship whose captain offered to pay their wages. By 1649, when Parliament proclaimed the English Commonwealth under Oliver Cromwell, *Swan* had spent much of her eight-year career fighting her own countrymen. The pinnace's end came during another campaign in home waters, this time in the Sound of Mull on Scotland's west coast.

Following the execution of Charles I in 1649, Cromwell moved to crush royalist sympathizers in Ireland and Scotland. The dead king's heir, Charles II, landed in Scotland in 1650 to fight for his crown, but in September 1651 was defeated by Cromwell's forces. Charles escaped to the continent, but his supporters fought on. A 1653 rebellion in Scotland, supported by the Macleans of Duart, inspired Cromwell to send a naval force and troops to subjugate the region and capture

the Macleans' castle at Duart Point. The Commonwealth's six-ship, thousand-man force landed at Duart Point to find that the Macleans had retreated. The success of the expedition came to an abrupt end on September 22, when a fierce storm swept through the Sound of Mull. "Wee lost a small Man of Warre called the Swan," a correspondent wrote Cromwell. Two other ships were lost, all of them "in sight of our Men att land, where they saw their friends drowning, and heard them crying for helpe, but could not save them."

The wreck of *Swan* was not seen again for more than three hundred years. In 1979, naval diving instructor John Dadd discovered the wreck, but he kept his find quiet for twelve years. In 1991, Dadd finally reported his discovery to authorities, who visited it and agreed that it was significant. Other divers, from the Dumfries and Galloway Branch of the Scottish Sub-Aqua Club, also found the wreck

A general plan of the wreck of *Swan*. Detailed mapping of the scattered wreckage allows archaeologists to reconstruct the ship and how it was built, sailed and wrecked.
© Colin Martin

0
5

metres

Part of a human pelvis
revealed during excavation
of the wreck of *Swan*.
© Colin Martin

in 1992. The Archaeological Diving Unit, acting on both discoveries, reported that the wreck was being exposed by erosion of bottom sediments. Iron cannon, wood—including carved decorations—and human bones were in danger of being swept away. Colin Martin began excavating the wreck in 1993 to preserve it from the ravages of the sea.

Swan lies jumbled and collapsed into herself, with the retreating sediments exposing exceptionally well preserved organic materials such as fabric, rope, leather, bone and wood. In the remains of the cabin of Edward Tarleton, *Swan*'s captain, archaeologists have retrieved panelling, "an elaborate door, more suited to an elegant drawing-room than to the interior of a small warship," the ship's binnacle, one compass and the disarticulated remains of a human skeleton—or skeletons. Two of the discoveries, as Martin explains, hint at the richness of the site. Two masses of rusted concretion, when x-rayed, revealed an "almost intact pocket watch, its brass

shell miraculously preserved within an outer shell of corrosion," and a steel rapier with an ornate handle. When conservators cleaned the rapier, corrosion had claimed the steel, but the concretion had preserved the shape, outline and details of the blade, guard and tang. The conservators were able to extract and save the hilt, an elaborate creation of tightly wound silver and gold wire.

Although excavation has not yet exposed major portions of the ship's hull, a series of beautifully carved decorations have come to life. They include a helmeted warrior's head, a winged cherub, a scroll and a portion of a heraldic badge with three ostrich feathers, a coronet and the words *Ich Dien*. The carvings are amazing on two counts, according to Colin Martin. They are the remnants of the ornate stern decorations of *Swan* and date to her construction as a royal ship. The badge is that of the Heir Apparent of England—a hated item that Cromwell's men would have, or should have, removed from the ship once it came into Commonwealth hands. The fact that the carvings remained aboard *Swan* eight years after her capture by the Commonwealth is a reminder that ships, like men, can and often do change sides.

Dartmouth

The archaeological study of a small English warship—an early frigate—of the late seventeenth century offers a look at the origins of standardization. It is also a reminder that more warships were lost to age and accident than combat. *Dartmouth* was a fifth-rate ship of the line. It was so designated because in the progression of a naval fighting force, the more guns a ship carried, the higher its rate. A first-rate carried a hundred guns, whereas a fifth-rate like *Dartmouth* carried thirty-two guns. Built at Portsmouth in 1655, *Dartmouth* was 24.4 metres (80 feet) long, with a beam of 7.62 metres (25 feet), and carried up to 135 men. The thirty-two guns were a mixture of 9-, 6- and 3-pounder iron cannon. Colin Martin

describes *Dartmouth* as "an early member of a small, lightweight class of warship … which were designed for patrol and reconnaissance work."

After a long career at sea, *Dartmouth* was not retired. Rather, the Royal Navy "refitted" the ship with extensive repairs in 1678. On October 9, 1690, *Dartmouth*, then an aged, decrepit ship, wrecked on the coast of Scotland in a gale when its worn-out anchor cable parted. Driven onto the rocks, the ship sank with most of her crew. Only six men survived.

Divers rediscovered the wreck in 1973, and two seasons of excavation recovered the scattered remains, including the intact hull structure as well as guns and other artifacts. Colin Martin found evidence of standardization in the placement of the frames or ribs of the hull. The shipwrights who built *Dartmouth* placed each frame exactly one foot apart. One surviving lodging knee, used to support the main deck, showed that it fit exactly within a 5-foot module and that the deck was laid out and built in a modular

One of the decorative carvings from the wreck of *Swan*. These symbols of royalty were carefully stowed away in the ship. © Colin Martin

A lodging knee in situ on the wreck of *Dartmouth*. From the broken, disarticulated timbers of the wreck, archaeologists have gained a clear image of the worn-out warship and her destruction.
© Colin Martin

fashion, much like a modern home. The need for nations to build large fleets of similar ships led to the standardization of types of ships and ship construction. Martin's analysis also showed that the keel, or backbone, of the ship was built of three large pieces of timber, each scarfed or fitted together with a complex joint. Each section of keel was 29.5 feet (9 metres) long, or just about as long as a mature English elm could grow to provide a timber 13 inches (0.33 metres) square.

Archaeological study of the surviving hull of *Dartmouth* showed that the ship had been pushed beyond her limited life, even with a major rebuilding. The keel had been cut out and replaced, and the thick frames or floors of the hull were clamped down with a thick timber. But outer-hull planks showed that some of the wooden treenails used to fasten the planks to the frames had been placed nearly atop older treenails, probably to tighten up loose fastenings. And the hull was, at the time of the wreck, worm-eaten and leaking,

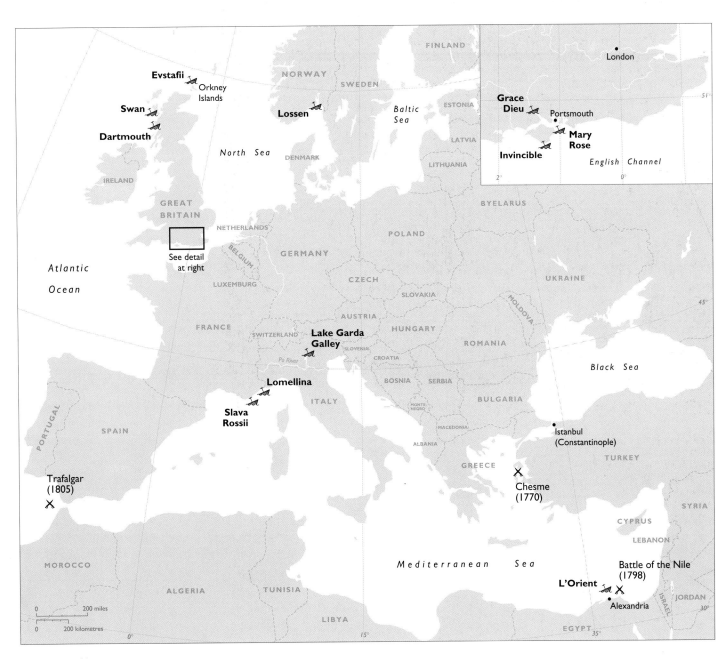

European warship
wrecks, 1500s to 1700s.
James P. Delgado, Eric Leinberger

The Wrecks of La Hougue

England's revenge against the French for Beachy Head came with naval victories in 1692 off the coast of Normandy at Saint-Vaast–La Hougue and Cap Barfleur. Since 1990, a French archaeological team led by Michel L'Hour of the Department of Underwater Archaeological Research has studied the remains of five first-rate French warships defeated and burned to the waterline by the English. Lying in four to eight metres of water, the wrecks were subjected to centuries of salvage but nonetheless have yielded important information about their construction—including one wreck, believed to be first-rate *Ambitieux*, which is covered with a resinous coating along the waterline, illuminating a practice that the records of the period indicated was done to speed up slow, poor sailers. More than 350 artifacts were excavated and are now in the collections of the Maritime Museum on Tatihou, the small island next to Saint-Vaast–La Hougue.

with the rigging worn, confirming Captain Edward Pottinger's complaint to the Admiralty, just a few weeks before the ship was lost, of these defects. Pottinger's list of the ship's defects included the anchor cable "so extremely worn as not to be trusted." Indeed not, as the loss of the ship and the remains of *Dartmouth* show a navy grappling with the need for growth both by building standard ships and by pushing them and the men who crewed them beyond their limits.

Lossen

Norwegian archaeologists discovered the wreck of the Norwegian frigate *Lossen* in 1963 near Hvaler at the entrance to Oslo Fjord. Built in 1684, *Lossen* entered service in 1686. In 1717, the 24-gun frigate was protecting convoys running from Norway to Denmark during the "Great Nordic War" with Sweden. The war was then in its seventeenth year. *Lossen*, caught in a storm on December 23, ran north for the protection of Oslo Fjord, only to be driven onto the rocks at the entrance. Of the 109 aboard, only fifty-four survived.

The wreck, lying in about 10 metres (30 feet) of water, was buried in soft mud that preserved the lower hull of the 28.7-metre-long (94-foot-long) frigate. Inside the hull were thousands of well-preserved artifacts that included all twenty-four cannon—eighteen 6-pounders and six 3-pounders—as well as shot, grapeshot and barbell-headed bar-shot. The galley equipment, including a large copper cooking pot recycled from an older, just retired Norwegian warship, joined cutlery and eating utensils to give a sense of how the crew ate. Barrels of salted pork and sheep, as well as fish, were cooked in the pots and served on round wooden trays. Small barrels of butter and liquor, as well as numerous wine and other liquor bottles, showed that alcohol was no stranger to the ships, for the officers or the men.

Although clothing had disintegrated, the excavation produced 925 buttons, most of them different, which suggested to the archaeologists that the crew of *Lossen* did not wear uniforms, but like the crew of *Vasa*, nearly a century earlier, wore their own clothes. The crew of *Vasa* slept on the deck or wherever they could find a spot, whereas *Lossen*'s crew slept on hammocks. Brooms and brushes showed that the Norwegian navy was concerned about hygiene, as did combs with double rows of closely set teeth used to comb out lice. An interesting find was evidence of how the crew spent their time when not working the ship or fighting. Like countless generations of sailors, they smoked pipes, took snuff and carved wood. Twenty-four half-finished wooden spoons, carved wooden boxes and a small, "elaborately carved child's rattle" were discovered in *Lossen*, all evidence of the activities of a crew seeking relaxation, or an extra way to make money in the midst of the rough and tumble world of a warship.

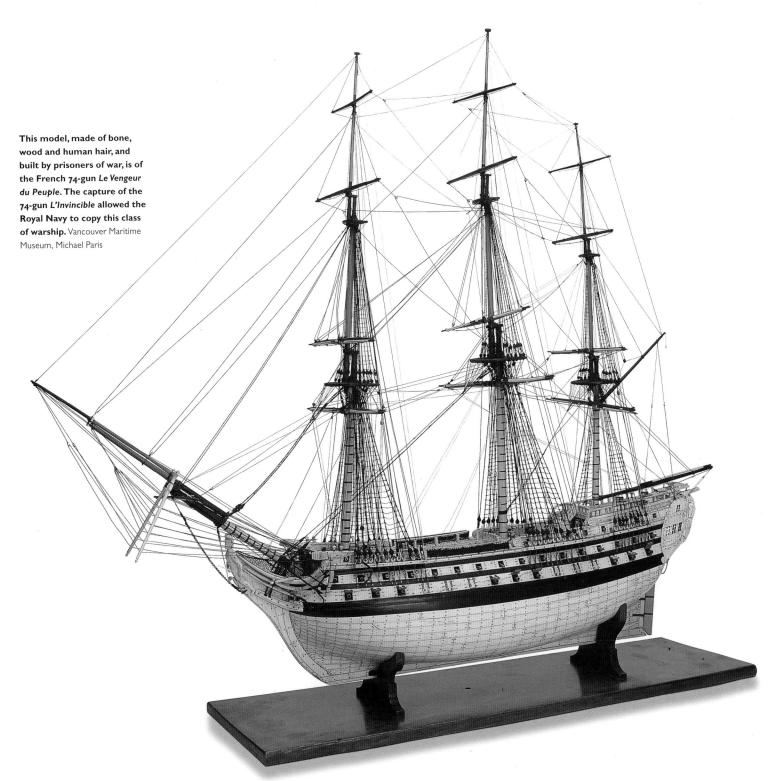

This model, made of bone, wood and human hair, and built by prisoners of war, is of the French 74-gun *Le Vengeur du Peuple*. The capture of the 74-gun *L'Invincible* allowed the Royal Navy to copy this class of warship. Vancouver Maritime Museum, Michael Paris

The Wreck of *Invincible*

The wreck of an eighteenth-century French ship of the line, captured by the English and incorporated into the Royal Navy, speaks not only of standardization, but also of how navies of the time, notably the English, copied each other's ships. *L'Invincible*, built at Rochefort and launched in 1744, was part of France's naval buildup. She also embodied a new design perfected by the French for large, seaworthy,

74-gun ships. *L'Invincible* proved her mettle in battle in 1745, when, alone, she fought off three English warships. But on May 14, 1747, *L'Invincible* met her match when confronted by a fleet of fourteen English ships at the First Battle of Cape Finisterre off the Spanish coast. Captured and towed back to Portsmouth, *L'Invincible* excited the interest of English naval officers, including Admiral Lord Anson, her captor, who proclaimed the

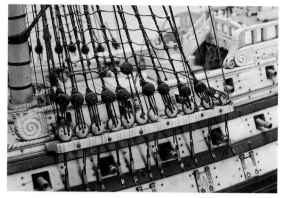

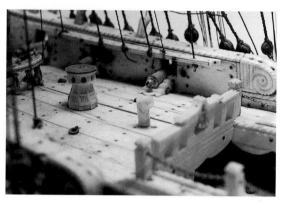

Details of *Le Vengeur du Peuple* provide an artistic view of a "74." Excavation of Invincible has yielded the details of the ship and life aboard. Vancouver Maritime Museum, Michael Paris

French 74 "a prodigious fine ship, and vastly large."

Although the Admiralty did not immediately pursue Anson's plans to copy *L'Invincible*, and two ships laid down to copy the French warship were cancelled due to lack of funds (and the end of the war with France), the ship was copied in time. In 1757, the Royal Navy laid down two new 74s on *L'Invincible*'s lines, and thus began the long line of English 74s—the "backbone" of the Royal Navy— that lasted for nearly a century. The original, incorporated into the Royal Navy as HMS *Invincible* in early 1748, remained in service for ten years. At the end of her career, *Invincible* was used against France in the Seven Years' War to raid and seize French possessions in the North America. After one season in Canadian waters, the ship was ready to sail with a large squadron when she ran aground on a sandbank off Portsmouth on February 19, 1758. Despite the efforts of the crew, *Invincible* was holed by her own anchor and sank. After some salvage, the Royal Navy abandoned the

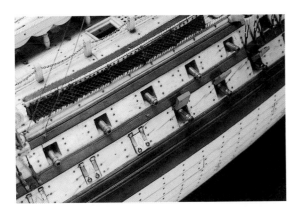

ship to the sea.

The wreck of *Invincible* remained undisturbed until fisherman Arthur Mack snagged it with his nets in 1979. Excavation began in 1980 and continued in 1991 as a volunteer effort undertaken with great difficulty, sustained by the personal energy of Arthur Mack and archaeologist John Bingeman. *Invincible*'s wreck is a veritable time capsule of ship and ordnance stores as remarkably well preserved as those of two centuries earlier excavated from the nearby wreck of *Mary Rose*. The artifacts include mid-eighteenth-century rigging blocks, lines, bosun's tools and stores, navigational instruments and the mess kits of the crew. The mess kits included square wooden platters that the crew ate from. (These platters were the origin of the term "a square meal.")

Although the guns themselves were salvaged after *Invincible*'s loss, a number of fragile, expendable items listed in records or known only from illustrations were well preserved by the mud of the Solent. They include fifty intact powder barrels, and tampions used to plug the ends of cannon to keep moisture out. The tampions, spooled together in groups of six, suggested to Bingeman that they were constantly replaced, and that the ship's guns were kept loaded with the tampion in place. The first shot of the gun would have cleared the tampion, which would be replaced after battle.

The excavation also yielded structural information about *Invincible*. One of the features of interest to the English was the use of iron fittings such as braces and knees to help support the heavy weight of the gun decks. This feature was adopted in many warships in the late eighteenth century, helping "stretch the limits" of wood to build stronger vessels, and to satisfy the requirements of the Royal Navy as it built up into the world's largest naval force, overwhelming the ability of England's forests to provide the necessary timber.

Excavation of *Invincible*'s lower gun deck revealed many of the iron knees and an interesting feature: a nut at the lower extremity that apparently was used to tighten the knee, which could—and would—work loose in heavy seas or from the vibration of gunfire. French shipwrights appear to have been taking advantage of the new material—iron—in a way not possible with the thick, heavily pinned wooden knees of the past. *Invincible* was not only a harbinger of change for the Royal Navy as the progenitor of a new class of 74s; she anticipated the changes wrought by the increasing use of iron.

L'Orient

A casualty of naval war—and a victim of Nelson's—is the French 120-gun ship of the line *L'Orient*. Flagship of a fleet sent by Napoleon to invade and occupy Egypt in 1798, *L'Orient* was one of thirteen ships anchored at Aboukir Bay on August 1, 1798, when Nelson caught it unprepared and at anchor. Nelson had searched the Mediterranean for the French fleet before finally cornering it in the small bay at the mouth of the Nile.

The "Battle of the Nile" ended in disaster for France. Nelson's eleven ships sank four of the French warships and captured the other nine in an evening action. The destruction of *L'Orient* shocked both sides into a temporary ceasefire that gradually ended as ships started firing again at each other.

French archaeologist and explorer Jacques Dumas discovered the wrecks of *L'Orient* and the 40-gun frigate *Artemise* in 1983. In 1996, Franck Goddio, who also located the wreck of the frigate *Serieuse*, continued Dumas's work. Goddio's divers recovered artifacts from the wrecks, and photographed a number of others, including French carronades and the largest naval guns used in the battle, iron 36-pounders. The copper-sheathed remains of *L'Orient*'s 11-metre-long (36-foot-long) rudder hints at its massive size.

The Founding of St. Petersburg, a bas relief by Bartolomeo Carlo Rastrelli (1675–1744) and Andrei Konstantinovich Nartov (1693–1756), 1723 (bronze). Hermitage, St. Petersburg, Russia/Bridgeman Art Library

The Rise of Russian Sea Power

The eighteenth-century struggle for naval supremacy occupied regional as well as global concerns. The end of the seventeenth and the first decades of the eighteenth century were times of war as the Dutch, French and English sparred. But they were also times in which the Baltic states of Sweden, Denmark, Poland and Russia fought for control of the northern seas. Russia, beginning with Peter the Great, established a navy, learning by copying foreign warships and hiring experienced constructors and officers. Peter's ambitions in the Black Sea and the Baltic, and Russia's desire to thwart the designs of the other Baltic states and the Ottoman Turks, brought decades of war to both seas. By 1721, Russia was the dominant sea power in the Baltic, but it maintained an uneasy stalemate with the Ottomans. Another Russian-Ottoman war in the 1730s ended with an Ottoman victory, aided by Britain, which sought to maintain a balance of power in Europe by discouraging a more powerful Russia.

The European wars of the mid-eighteenth century shifted the balance of power, particularly as Britain, France and their allies slugged it out in the Seven Years' War of 1755–63. The Russian ruler, Catherine the Great, pulled Russia out of the war after she ascended the throne in 1762. The respite

This painting of a Turkish warship on fire, done in 1868 by Constantin Bolanachi, recalls the rise of Russian sea power.
Leeds Museums and Galleries (City Art Gallery)/Bridgeman Art Library

SLAVA ROSSII

TOPOGRAPHIE

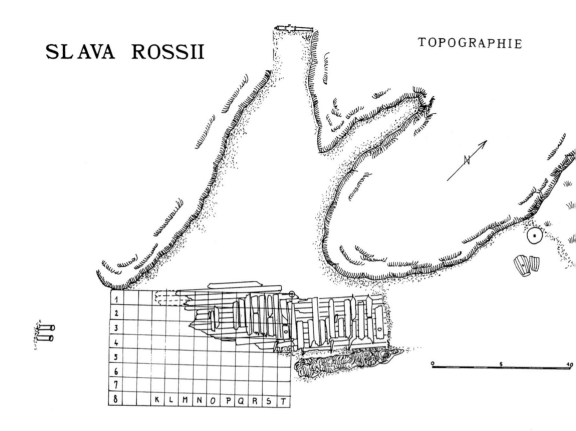

allowed Britain's continental ally, Prussia, fighting Russia and Sweden, to be more of a counter to France and helped end the war. Britain rewarded Russia by supporting Catherine's ambitions in the Black Sea and Mediterranean.

Catherine built up a larger navy, pulled some of her heaviest warships out of the Baltic for duty in the Mediterranean and hired British naval officers to command some of her ships as she determined to end Ottoman naval power in the region. The Russo-Turkish War of 1768–74 commenced in earnest in 1770, when the new Russian Mediterranean fleet arrived from the Baltic. The Russian fleet of only twelve ships met the Ottomans off the Aegean island of Chios, close to the Turkish mainland at Chesme, on July 5, 1770. The Turkish fleet—twenty-one ships of the line and a number of row galleys—were pushed back into Chesme's harbour when the Russians launched a fierce attack. A follow-up attack at dawn on July 7 ended in Russian victory as their ships destroyed

The bronze icons excavated from the wreck of *Slava Rossii* are testimony to the importance of religion for the officers and crew. GRAN

the Ottoman fleet. The war continued for four years, with Russia emerging as a major new naval power in the Baltic and Mediterranean.

Two Russian warship wrecks from this period recall the war and Russia's rapid rise to naval power. The first, the pink (naval transport) *Evstafii*, wrecked off the Shetland Islands on September 17, 1780. Built at Archangel in 1773, *Evstafii* was a 39.6-metre-long (130-foot-long), 38-gun ship. Sailing south from Archangel to Kronstadt, Russia's Baltic naval fortress, *Evstafii* struck the rock Griff Skerry in a gale and sank with 189 officers, crew and passengers. Only five of the crew survived the wreck. Wreck hunter Robert Stenuit discovered the wreck of *Evstafii* in 1972. Stenuit's divers found metal artifacts, including guns, shot, pieces of muskets and pistols, sword hilts, belt buckles, hardware, and 220 Russian and Dutch gold, silver and copper coins. One of the more interesting finds was a corroded silver medal, struck to commemorate the Russian victory at Chesme.

The other Russian naval wreck of the period is the 66-gun warship *Slava Rossii*, also lost in 1780. Part of a Russian naval visit to the Mediterranean to underscore a new treaty of armed neutrality, *Slava Rossii* sailed from Kronstadt with five other ships, visiting Copenhagen, Texel, Dover and Lisbon before heading into the Mediterranean to reach Livorno, Italy. Bad weather caused Captain Ivan Abrasimovich Baskakov to lose his position. Separated from the rest of the flotilla, *Slava Rossii* struck the rocks off Levant Island, a French possession off the Provençal coast, and sank in 40 metres (about 130 feet) of water with a loss of eleven lives. A fisherman, Louis Viale, snagged the wreck with his nets in 1957. Pioneering French archaeologist Philippe Tailliez raised ten cannon from the site that year, but scientific excavation of *Slava Rossii* did not start until 1980.

Under the direction of archaeologist Max Guérout, divers surveyed and excavated the wreck in a project that continues more than twenty years later. They found additional guns, including three bronze cohorns (8-pound mortars) for use by the ship's infantry ashore, shot (including hollow shells, grapeshot, chain shot and round shot), equipment, small arms and apparel and equipment for both the crew and the Russian naval infantry aboard *Slava Rossii*. A portion of the hull survived, and it helps demonstrate a continuity of form and construction for Russia's 66-gun warships. The first Russian "sixty-six" was built in 1731 by Scotsman Joseph Nay, hired and brought to Russia by Peter the Great several years earlier. The Russians learned not only to draw from the experience of other nations, but also to adhere to what was viewed as a successful design for many years. *Slava Rossii* when launched in 1774 was one of the last of a line of fifty-one 66-gun ships built for the Russian Imperial Navy between 1731 and 1779.

Guérout notes that the excavation recovered shipboard equipment and fittings which "if not always spectacular, certainly gave insights into the way the very young Russian navy absorbed the knowledge brought in from abroad…there are no significant differences … between the wreck of *Slava Rossii* and other naval wrecks of the period," except one. The French archaeological team discovered sixty-three copper-alloy religious icons in the wreck. Like so many other artifacts from lost warships, the icons are also a powerful reminder of how humanity faces the realities and risks of war.

The Heyday of the Wooden Walls

Throughout the eighteenth and nineteenth centuries, the world's most powerful navy—and nation—was that of Great Britain. The united kingdoms of England and Scotland (joined by the Act of Union in 1707) expanded into a global empire. Although Britain's control of the seas was never absolute and was constantly challenged, the Royal Navy remained the world's dominant navy, expanding British trade into North America, the Caribbean, Pacific, Indian Ocean and the Far East. These years were also a period of overseas scientific study and exploration, using the resources of the Royal Navy to map the Pacific, the southern continent of Australia, and the Arctic and Antarctic regions. The major challenges of this incredible expansion overseas were the colonial wars for the Americas and the drawn-out conflict with France and its allies from 1783 to 1814. The wars of the period were global, as Britain fought in American waters, the Mediterranean, Caribbean and the Baltic.

Other naval powers fought extended wars during these years, including renewed conflict between Russia, Sweden and Ottoman Turkey. Catherine the Great's navy fought from 1788 to 1790 for greater control of the Baltic and Black Sea. But the principal struggle between Britain and France began in 1792. A series of engagements, skirmishes and battles involved hundreds of ships and horrendous loss of life. But the wooden walls had grown so big and formidable that few ships were sunk as a result of action. Heavy-calibre guns smashed through the thick hulls, blasting splinters and pulverized wood through the enclosed gun decks to leave a gory wake of destruction. Grapeshot and chain shot swept across open decks and into the masts, slashing rigging, sails, yards and occasionally cutting through the masts and dropping them into the water. In a heavy battle, huge ships of the line would lie crippled, unable to manoeuvre or to fight, thousands of the crews dead or dying. But unless a ship's magazines were hit, setting off a fire and explosion, these massive wooden fortresses, with their thick hulls, did not sink.

The eighteenth century was an age of new tactics as well as a return to older forms of fighting. Like war on land, where troops lined up, facing each other to kneel, stand and fire as they marched towards the enemy's line, ships also fought in lines. Opposing lines of ships sailed alongside each other, firing broadsides of shot. But these fights were often a mutual slaughter and a standoff. Some commanders, like Britain's Horatio Nelson, were inspired to abandon the strict discipline of the line-on attack and try bold "melee" attacks, sailing into an enemy's line to break it up and ships closing for one-on-one duels.

The toll of war at sea in this age was better measured by mangled bodies and amputated limbs dropped over the sides of the ships after a battle than by sunken vessels. But ships did go down, sunk in accidents or by storms. Divers, fishermen and archaeologists have discovered several warships from this period, and these submerged time capsules join a small group of surviving ships still afloat—notably Nelson's *Victory*—to provide insights into the world of the ships of the line in the climactic age of wooden warships.

HMS *Victory* and USS *Constitution*

Two of the world's most famous warships are survivors from the age of the wooden walls. Unlike *Vasa*, neither ship is an archaeological discovery. Instead, they were preserved, occasionally rebuilt and ultimately maintained as naval memorials, shrines and museums. HMS *Victory*, a 100-gun first-rate ship of the line, was built at Chatham, England, between 1759 and 1778. *Victory* served as Nelson's flagship at the Battle of Trafalgar on October 21, 1805. Nelson, striding on the quarterdeck, was mortally wounded by a French sharpshooter. He died below just as news of

his victory was brought to him. *Victory* returned to England with Nelson's body. Ironically, Nelson was buried in a coffin made from the shattered mast of *L'Orient*, the French flagship lost in Nelson's earlier victory at the Battle of the Nile.

Retired from sea service in 1835, *Victory* remained afloat at Portsmouth, England, as a permanently moored flagship. In 1922, the ship was brought ashore and preserved in a dry dock. Restorations and continual rebuilding have left little of the original ship intact, but the quality of work and attention to detail gives visitors to the Royal Naval Museum in

Portsmouth an excellent sense of the ship and life and fighting aboard her.

USS *Constitution*, also known as "Old Ironsides," was built as a 55-gun frigate for the U.S. Navy. Launched in 1797, this most famous of American warships gained fame during the War of 1812 when she defeated the British frigates *Guerriere*, *Java* and *Cyane*. She earned her nickname of "Old Ironsides" when some of the British shot was observed bouncing off her hull. Like *Victory*, *Constitution* was retired from sea duty after a long career, but unlike the British warship, she has remained afloat.

Maintained as a commissioned warship of the U.S. Navy, *Constitution* toured the United States in the 1930s before a major restoration, and she was again extensively rebuilt in the 1990s. Displayed at Boston's Charlestown Navy Yard, *Constitution* is one of its best-known attractions.

TOP The simply decorated transom of USS *Constitution*.
James P. Delgado

RIGHT The ornately decorated bow of HMS *Victory*.
James P. Delgado

Wars for America

THE STRUGGLES BETWEEN various European powers for empire played out in the Baltic, the Mediterranean, the English Channel and the Americas. The New World and its waters were contested, not only with the native peoples who lived there, but also between European nations seeking trade and empire. The Dutch and English challenged Spain and Portugal's sixteenth-century domination of the New World, particularly in the Caribbean. Voyages of privateering and outright piracy gave way to colonial wars in the seventeenth and eighteenth centuries. The result of these wars was an eclectic grouping of Caribbean colonies for Spain, Britain, France and Holland, ensuring that whenever global conflict arose between these nations, war would follow in the Caribbean.

Conflicts in Europe extended to North America, where by the eighteenth century the principal colonial powers contending with each other were Britain, France and Spain. Russia extended its ambitions to the New World in the North Pacific by the mid-eighteenth century, but the czar's possessions were a concern only for Spain, which belatedly extended its own colonies up the Pacific coast in the late eighteenth century in response to Russia. The principal contest in the Americas centred on conflict between Britain and France. The battleground was the coast of New England, Nova Scotia and Newfoundland, as well as the reaches of the St. Lawrence and the waterways that ran between Quebec and New England such as Lake Champlain.

The Lost Wreck of *Elizabeth and Mary*

England's struggle with France left a rich underwater archaeological legacy in Canada and the northeastern United States. The earliest wreck associated with one of America's colonial wars is the ship at L'Anse aux Bouleaux on the north shore of the Gulf of St. Lawrence. A local diver, Marc Tremblay, discovered the wreck in December 1994 as he was pulling in the mooring lines for his boat. The wreck, lying just in front of Tremblay's

FACING PAGE Diver examines a musket on the wreck of *Elizabeth and Mary*. The decorations show it was a privately owned, personally modified weapon belonging to a militiaman. Parks Canada, Peter Waddell

RIGHT Parks Canada diver on wreck examining the hull timbers of *Elizabeth and Mary*. Exposed in shallow waters by winter storms, the wreck was a difficult challenge to excavate and document. Parks Canada, Peter Waddell

ABOVE Archaeologists preparing to document the exposed remains of *Elizabeth and Mary.* Parks Canada, Marc-André Bernier

BOTTOM One of the critical pieces of evidence in the identification of the wreck as *Elizabeth and Mary* was this pewter porringer marked with the initials of Increase and Susan Mosely. Centre de Conservation du Québec, Michèle Elie

cottage, was in less than two metres (6.5 feet) of water and had probably been exposed by winter storms that stripped away sand to reveal timbers and artifacts in an area measuring 10 by 4 metres (33 by 13 feet). Tremblay reported his discovery to Parks Canada and worked with Parks Canada archaeologist Marc-André Bernier. Over the next three years, the team completely excavated the wreck and identified it as the merchant bark *Elizabeth and Mary*, lost in 1690 while retreating from a failed siege of Quebec.

In 1689, as war raged in Europe between France and England, British colonists in New England were alarmed to learn of French plans to invade from Canada and seize New York. The French plans called for a naval push down Lake Champlain and the Hudson River. The plan was formulated, notes archaeologist and historian Kevin J. Crisman, by government officials in Paris, "who had no appreciation of the difficulties of logistics and warfare in the wilderness." Instead of following the plan, the governor of New France instigated a guerrilla war, with attacks by French troops and their Indian allies against outposts, farms and towns on the frontier. The war that followed was known in America as King William's War. The British colonists raised troops and prepared to strike back with two invasions, one by way of Lake Champlain, the other by sea and down the St. Lawrence to strike at Quebec, the heart of New France.

The Champlain invasion stalled for lack of boats to travel up the lake, but the St. Lawrence

expedition, commanded by Sir William Phips of Massachusetts, sailed from Boston in August 1689 with thirty-four ships and twenty-two hundred militiamen. Phips's fleet, many of them merchant ships impressed into wartime service, anchored off Quebec City on October 16 and demanded the French surrender. The French governor general, the count of Frontenac, replied he would answer Phips "par la bouche de mes canons" (from the mouths of my cannon). Phips bombarded the city and landed troops, but Quebec held fast, and in early November Phips retreated with the onset of winter. Four of his ships did not make it home, wrecking along the way. Although the fates and locations of the lost ships were generally known, *Elizabeth and Mary* was lost without a trace with a company of militiamen from Dorchester, Massachusetts. Marc Tremblay's discovery solved a three-hundred-year-old mystery.

Although not a warship, *Elizabeth and Mary* was in use as a ship of war. The impressment of this merchant ship for naval use reflects just how much Phips's campaign against New France was on a distant frontier, with a fleet of only six warships and more than two dozen hastily impressed merchant ships filled with citizen-soldier volunteers. The majority of artifacts excavated from the wreck are the arms of the militiamen. They include muskets, pistols, bandoliers for powder and shot, cartridge boxes, the remains of a cartridge pouch with twelve preserved paper and powder cartridges, shot, belt axes and swords. Many of these items were personally owned, with

some of them decorated with the initials of their owners.

Other artifacts recovered from the wreck also speak evocatively of the militiamen: the remains of their clothing and shoes, and personal items like combs and clay pipes, as well as fish and mammal bones from the provisions that they ate. One of the most poignant personal artifacts was a small pewter porringer. The handle's decoration included three letters: "M, S and I." The initials are those of Increase and Sarah Mosley of Dorchester, and the porringer, carried with Increase as he sailed with Phips's expedition, is a personal link to him. Increase Mosley died with his fellow militiamen when *Elizabeth and Mary* wrecked. Sarah waited patiently for news of him for thirteen years, remarrying finally in 1703 when it was clear he would not be coming home. The wreck of *Elizabeth and Mary* is more than a look at the human face of war. It is a reminder of how the sea swallows men and ships.

Bateaux Below and the Land Tortoise

The French and Indian War of 1755–60 left a number of wrecks in American and Canadian waters. Many of them are located in Lake Champlain and Lake George, which lie near each other on the New York–Vermont-Quebec border. Lake Champlain in particular was one of North America's most strategic waterways, its 185-kilometre (115-mile) length and nearby waters, like the Hudson and Richelieu Rivers, connecting New France with New England. Running from New York and Vermont into Quebec, the north-south axis of the lake made it a natural waterway for trade or invasion. During the French and Indian War, both sides used Champlain's waters to ferry thousands of troops. Battles to control Lake Champlain's land-locked waters resulted in naval arms races. Once the war was over, many of the ships and boats not lost in combat were laid up in the backwaters of the lake—as well as nearby Lake George—only to slip beneath the surface and be rediscovered by archaeologists centuries later.

Reconstruction of a bateau from the French and Indian Wars in Lake George. Bateaux Below, Inc., Mark Peckham

**Bateaux exposed on the
beach of Lake Champlain.**
Lake Champlain Maritime Museum

Fortification of Lake Champlain's shores to control the waterway proved ineffective in times of war, as troops overwhelmed defences to take the forts. Both France and Britain used lake-built ships and boats to ferry troops and supplies and attack each other on Champlain's waters. The French schooner *Le Vigilente*, launched in 1742, was the first warship to patrol Lake Champlain, but others would soon follow.

Both sides used bateaux—sturdy, flat-bottomed craft averaging 10 metres (39 feet) in length—to conduct the first campaigns on the lake. Easy to build, bateaux carried troops and arms as readily as the heavy cargoes they transported down rivers and across the lakes during peacetime. Carpenters built hundreds of them during the French and Indian War. To store the boats in winter, the British sank them at the southern end of Lake George, where they would be safe beneath the water and ice until the spring and the resumption of the war. Dozens of bateaux were never recovered, perhaps because they were sunk too deeply. British military records report that hundreds of bateaux were intentionally sunk in 1758 to preserve them in the cold lake waters. Local divers rediscovered the bateaux in the 1960s, and portions of several were raised. Work on the bateaux continues to this day by a dedicated volunteer group of avocational archaeologists known as Bateaux Below, Inc. Led by Joseph Zarzynski, the Bateaux Below divers have mapped concentrations of bateaux on the lake bed as well as the construction details of these once-common but until recently undocumented craft.

A far more significant discovery made by Bateaux Below, however, came in 1990 when the divers encountered a multisided wooden wreck in nearly 33 metres (108 feet) of water near the sunken clusters of bateaux. The oldest intact warship wreck in North America, it is also the only known example of a *radeau*—a floating, self-propelled gun platform. Shipwright Samuel Cobb of Maine built two radeau on Lake George in 1758 to assist a planned British assault on Fort

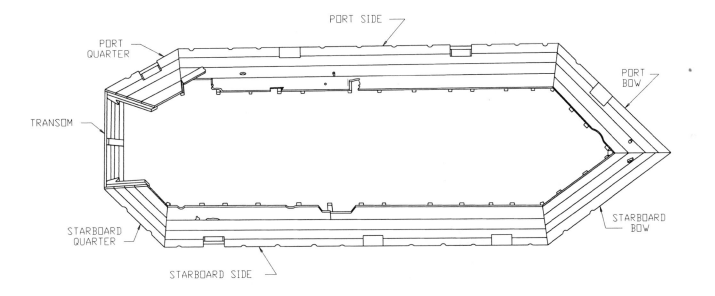

PORT SIDE

PORT QUARTER

PORT BOW

TRANSOM

STARBOARD BOW

STARBOARD QUARTER

STARBOARD SIDE

Ticonderoga. Launched in October, the radeau were apparently scuttled for the winter along with the bateaux fleet. If dozens of bateaux were sunk too deeply, so too was one of the radeau, a vessel named *Land Tortoise*. Never mentioned again by the British, it was this stocky gun ship that the divers encountered in 1990.

Other than a sketch in a journal kept by a Connecticut militia colonel and a brief note of *Land Tortoise*'s dimensions, no documentation of this unique colonial warship has surfaced. But the intact, well-preserved wreck, still solid after two and half centuries in Lake George's cold, fresh water, has yielded her secrets. Seven-sided with a pointed bow and more blunted stern, *Land Tortoise* is essentially a flat-bottomed barge with sloping sides forming a floating casemate for seven cannon. The dimensions of the actual craft, recorded underwater, are a close match to the historical description at 15.8 metres (52 feet) by 5.5 metres (18 feet).

Large curved wooden frames and stanchions support the wooden walls, and although the construction is crude, it is solidly held together with hand-forged iron nails and wooden treenails. But if the crudeness of the construction indicates haste, the layout of the radeau reflects the skill of the shipwright and the military engineers who helped design it. The gun ports are asymmetrical: three on the starboard side and four on the port. This design staggered the cannon and allowed the crew to work their guns without interfering with each other— and to keep the guns from hitting each other when they recoiled while firing. Two view ports on the upper slope of the bow, on each side, allow an observer to steer the ship or observe the action without exposing himself to enemy fire.

Although the divers discovered the steps for two masts in the lower hull, sailing *Land Tortoise* would be impractical. The Bateaux Below crew documented the holes for twenty-six oars, or sweeps. Protected by the sides from gunfire, the crew of the radeau could slowly manoeuvre the clumsy craft into position. The discovery and documentation of *Land Tortoise* has not only provided a rare look at a unique colonial warship. The work of Bateaux Below is another example of the often-overlooked, yet significant contributions of volunteer archaeologists, historians and divers to archaeology.

Plan view of the radeau *Land Tortoise*. This National Historical Landmark is a rare and unique warship and legacy of the French and Indian War. Bateaux Below, Inc.

Shown rising from the lake and in her gallery at the museum, the intact little warship is one of the United States' oldest. Lake Champlain Maritime Museum/NMAH

RIGHT Now preserved inside the National Museum of American History at the Smithsonian Institution, *Philadelphia* is one of the oldest American warships on display. NMAH/Smithsonian Institution.

The American Revolution on Lake Champlain

The ultimate British triumph in North America in 1760 was followed within decades by the American Revolution. French warships returned to American waters to fight the Royal Navy. At the same time, the new nation of the United States took to the sea to fight for its independence and for the right to trade on the high seas.

When Britain's American colonies rose up in revolt in 1775, the power of the Royal Navy was seemingly absolute. Britannia ruled the waves, and control of the seas and a blockade of the American coast ensured the isolation of the rebellious colonists and the confinement of the war to skirmishes and battles on the land. France aided the colonial cause, and battles on the sea in favour of American independence were therefore between the French and the British. As a weak, new power, the United States could not hope to build a fleet capable of joining the conflict as an equal. But the United States did take its war to sea, outfitting armed merchant ships as privateers to prey on British merchant shipping. It also hastily built fleets of small warships for fights on the inland waters, particularly Lake Champlain, once again a strategic waterway.

American forces seized the lake in 1775 and used it as a highway to invade British-held Canada. The promise of British retaliation led American forces, under the command of General Benedict Arnold, to prepare for a naval assault by building a fleet of vessels to keep Champlain in American hands. Arnold's fleet included a new design, a flat-bottomed gunboat. In the summer of 1776, shipwrights assembled eight gondolas and other craft. Although under the command of the Continental Army of the United States, the Lake Champlain squadron of sixteen vessels was the first American navy.

The two naval forces met for the first time at the Battle of Valcour Island on October 11, 1776. Arnold's small squadron went into battle with soldiers joining the ship's crews because there were not enough sailors. The British, with a larger force of twenty-nine vessels, sank two of Arnold's fleet, the schooner *Royal Savage* and the gunboat *Philadelphia*. Arnold was able to withdraw from the action, but on October 13 the British caught up with him and destroyed most of his remaining ships. Only four of the American ships escaped. By November 2, 1776, the British fleet withdrew to the northern end of the lake for the winter, giving the Americans time to build up their forces. The delay caused by the Lake Champlain campaign of 1776 kept the British from linking their troops in Canada with troops in New England. In October 1777, the Continental Army defeated unreinforced British troops at Saratoga, New York. The American victory was a deciding factor in France's decision to support the United States' bid for independence, and for France's navy to take to the seas in support of the Americans.

In 1935, diver and salvage engineer Colonel Lorenzo F. Hagglund of New York rediscovered the wreck of Arnold's gunboat *Philadelphia* in 17 metres (56 feet) of water off Valcour Island. The cold, fresh waters of Lake Champlain had

Battle of Valcour Island. Lake Champlain Maritime Museum

preserved the completely intact ship. Hagglund, working with professional salvage diver William Lilja, raised *Philadelphia*. The colonel toured Lake Champlain with the wreck on a barge, charging tourists to visit the oldest American warship. Hagglund made arrangements that after his death the Smithsonian Institution would acquire *Philadelphia*. This bequest occurred in 1961.

Archaeologists and historians have carefully studied *Philadelphia* and drawn detailed plans. Originally built without plans by shipwrights who followed Arnold's basic instructions, the gunboats were based on flat-bottomed cargo-carrying boats from New England known as "gondolas." The construction of *Philadelphia* used heavier, stronger timbers to support the weight of a 12-pounder cannon at the bow, two 9-pounder guns amidships and eight small swivel guns mounted on the gunwales. The wreck demonstrates the resourcefulness as well as some of the desperation of the

RIGHT **A remotely operated vehicle explores the intact wreck of** *Spitfire* **at the bottom of Lake Champlain.** Lake Champlain Maritime Museum

BELOW **The bow gun on the wreck of** *Spitfire.* Lake Champlain Maritime Museum/Benthos, Inc.

BOTTOM **The junction of** *Spitfire*'s **lower mast and topmast; the mast assembly towers more than 15 metres (50 feet) over the wreck's deck.** Lake Champlain Maritime Museum/Benthos, Inc.

American cause. Cannon were in short supply, and so the 12-pounder at the bow was discovered to be a Swedish-manufactured gun about one hundred years older than the ship. Paint was in short supply, and *Philadelphia*'s builders coated the gunboat with tar instead.

A single mast carried two square sails, but to manoeuvre the gunboat in action, the crew used fourteen sweeps, or oars. In battle, the gunboats had to come in close to the enemy, and hand-to-hand fighting, not heavy gun action, defined the American tactics. The swivel guns were antipersonnel weapons, and when Hagglund raised the wreck, he found Army muskets, with bayonets, balls and buckshot, ready for use by the soldier crew. Sitting on deck, the crew were "protected" only by bundles of saplings and twigs known as fascines. The fascines and wooden hull were little protection, and before *Philadelphia* could close to fight, a British 24-pounder cannon ball sank her. Hagglund discovered the fatal cannon ball still lodged in the broken timbers of *Philadelphia*'s bow.

In 1997, archaeologists from the Lake Champlain Maritime Museum, as part of a comprehensive underwater survey of the lake, discovered the remains of another gunboat, *Spitfire*, near the bottom of the 122-metre-deep (400-foot-deep) lake. Nearly identical to *Philadelphia*, *Spitfire* is another incredible legacy from the beginnings of America's navy and a desperate fight to control a strategic waterway. The sunken ships also recall a tactical defeat for the Americans that bought time for a more strategic victory on the distant battlefield at Saratoga.

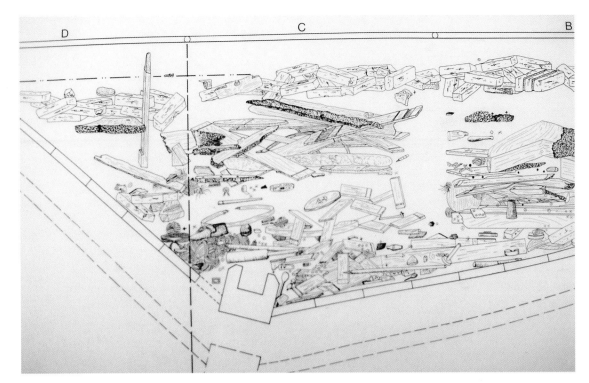

This archaeological drawing by Cynthia Orr shows the layers of debris inside *Defence*. When excavated, the debris spoke volumes about the ship, life aboard and her fiery demise. David Switzer

Defence

Another sunken warship recalls a more disastrous defeat, when the United States lost thirty ships during the Penobscot Expedition on the coast of Maine. The destruction of that fleet was one of the greatest naval disasters in American history. The Penobscot Expedition's thirty-seven to forty-one ships sailed from Boston in 1779 with some two thousand troops to drive out a British force that had come from Halifax to occupy the Maine coast and control the Penobscot River. The force that sailed from Boston was the largest American naval expedition of the Revolution. It faced a smaller British force, protected only by three warships. But six large British warships, easily outgunning the smaller American transports and gunboats, were on their way.

The Penobscot Expedition landed and dug in. Had the troops pressed their advantage they could have won. Instead, they waited for the British reinforcements to arrive and retreated in the face of the enemy's superior strength. Blockaded in Penobscot Bay by the British ships, the American fleet could not retreat down the coast. Running up the Penobscot River, the fleet was pursued by the British. Trapped, the American commanders decided to scuttle their ships to keep them out of British hands. Most of the ships, on fire, sank before the British could capture them. The small

brig *Defence*, one of the last left afloat and uncaptured, was chased into Stockton Harbor. The crew set *Defence* on fire and rowed to shore. As the British closed in, *Defence* blew up and sank.

Since 1779, periodic dredging of the Penobscot has yielded cannon and fragments of the lost fleet. In 1972, a detailed survey of the area by students and faculty from the Maine Maritime Academy revealed the remains of *Defence* in 8 metres (26 feet) of water. Excavation of the wreck began in 1975 under the auspices of the Institute of Nautical Archaeology, the Maine Maritime Academy and the Maine State Museum. Five years of excavation seasons, under the direction of archaeologist David Switzer, revealed a well-preserved wreck and artifacts beneath the mud of the Penobscot.

The crew of *Defence* set the fire to scuttle the ship at the stern, where the ship's powder magazine was located. Before the flames swept through the ship, the magazine exploded, sinking *Defence*. The blast damage was enough to tear out the sternpost and several frames, as well as crack the keelson, but *Defence* had not been blown apart. The results, when the ship's interior was carefully excavated, were a detailed look at the ship's fittings, furnishings and equipment, most of them lying in proximity to where they had been used aboard. The finds included the gear and tools of

These small wooden artifacts were wooden mess tags, used by sailors to mark their share of meat as it was cooked in the communal pot. Phil Voss (right) and Maine State Museum (far right)

the bosun, the ship's carpenter, the gunner and the sailors in the crew. The highly regimented life of the "wooden walls" of the large ships of the line was duplicated, in a smaller scale, as shown by the recovery of the crew's mess kits near the galley.

To organize and feed a large number of people quickly, warships separated the men into "messes" of eight men. Like the larger ships of the time, *Defence* was also organized into messes. The discovery of sixteen carved wooden tags at first mystified the archaeologists until they realized these tags were "markers" placed with cuts of salted meat. Sailors ate salted pork or beef packed in barrels—a number were discovered, bones still inside them, as work progressed on *Defence*. One member of each mess would approach the pork or beef barrel as the cook doled out a portion, receive the "whack" for his mess mates and mark it with the wooden tag engraved with their mess number. The mess then retrieved their boiled meat, with the tag, at mealtime. Spoons, mess kits, pewter plates and ceramic mugs, some of them marked with the initials of the crew, were also excavated. The initials on the items marked them as personal property, not ship's issue. The days of a navy issuing mess gear or bedding were still far off, and a sailor was responsible for his own "kit," whether on a man-of-war or a merchantman.

This "Revolutionary War time capsule" also included shoes, belt buckles and clothes. None of the crew wore naval uniforms. That practice had not yet come into use, but a small button, marked USA, came from a soldier's uniform. The button may be a clue that soldiers were used to fill out the crews of the Penobscot fleet, or that a sailor was wearing a discarded or otherwise acquired army uniform item. The button may have also

been a souvenir kept by one of the sailors. A range of ordnance, including grape and canister shot, round shot and the gunner's equipment was recovered, but the ship's sixteen 6-pounder cannon were not. Probing the mud outside the hull revealed that some of the guns were buried there after falling off the wreck, but the archaeologists did not excavate outside the hull for fear of collapsing *Defence*'s hull once the mud cradling it was removed.

But the excavation of *Defence* did completely clear the interior of the hull. The relatively small, 30.5-metre-long (100-foot-long) *Defence* was crowded with equipment, guns and a hundred-man crew that ate and slept in a 6.1-by-7.6-metre (20-by-25-foot) amidships section. And yet this crowded, small warship was able to work effectively, leading historian John Sands to reflect that she was in all "a remarkably complex machine." *Defence* was also not a slow, crudely built ship. The remains of the hull showed that *Defence* was built quickly, with a few shortcuts, such as a roughly shaped crutch hacked from the trunk of a large oak and placed at the bow with two of its lopped-off branches still attached to the trunk to reinforce the ship's stem. But the shortcuts could not disguise the sharp lines of the hull, with a V-shaped form and a sharp bow. Too small and outgunned by larger British ships, *Defence* was a precursor to the later "clipper"-formed merchant ship and warships built in the United States in the nineteenth century. Built to outrun a larger, heavier ship, *Defence* was better suited to attack the unprotected merchant ships of an enemy. Trapped with no place to run, and up against a superior force, all *Defence*'s crew could do was send their ship to the bottom, denying its fast hull and arms to the British.

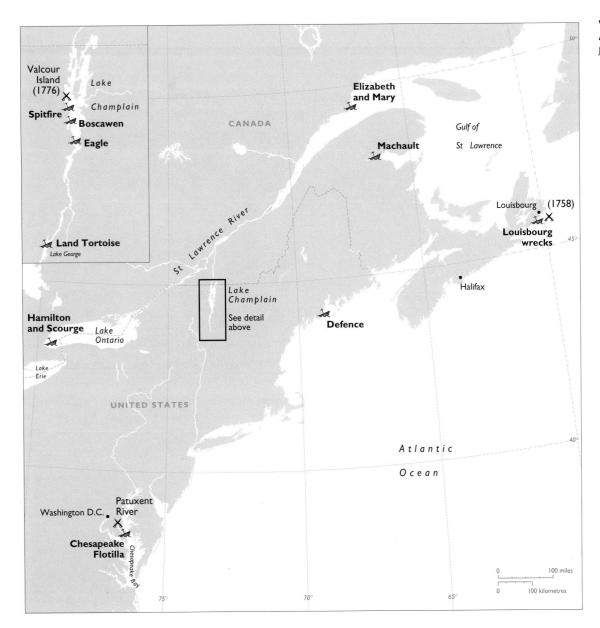

Wrecks and battles of North America, 1690 to 1814.
James P. Delgado, Eric Leinberger

Valcour
Island
(1776) ✕

Lake

Champlain

Spitfire

Boscawen

Eagle

Land Tortoise

Lake George

CANADA

St Lawrence River

**Elizabeth
and Mary**

Gulf of

St Lawrence

Machault

Louisbourg ✕ (1758)

**Louisbourg
wrecks**

45°

Halifax

*Lake
Champlain*

See detail
above

Defence

**Hamilton
and Scourge**

*Lake
Ontario*

*Lake
Erie*

UNITED STATES

Atlantic

Ocean

40°

Washington D.C.

**Patuxent
River**

✕

**Chesapeake
Flotilla**

Chesapeake Bay

75°

70°

65°

0   100 miles

0   100 kilometres

The might of British sea power, while tested by the United States and others in the early nineteenth century, remained paramount. Painting of unidentified battle scene attributed to Poale, Vancouver Maritime Museum, Mary and William Everett Family Collection

The War of 1812

The wrecks of *Defence* and *Philadelphia* are the only American warships of the Revolutionary War excavated by archaeologists. They stand in contrast to the numerous British warship wrecks of the period found elsewhere. A small, inferior force, the U.S. Navy was an auxiliary of the Continental Army, and at best American privateers on the high seas could hope to raid British merchant shipping while the major sea battles were fought on behalf of the United States by a vengeful French navy.

At the conclusion of the Revolutionary War, the few ships—gunboats and schooners—of the United States' navy were sold and their sailors sent home. But American ships were appearing on every sea, trading with other countries. The United States was a weak nation without a navy to protect it, and American ships were seized and their crews forced to become members of the crews of British warships, or slaves of Barbary "pirates" in the Mediterranean. Almost begrudgingly, Congress voted to build a new navy in 1794. Unable to afford the costs of the 100-gun ships of

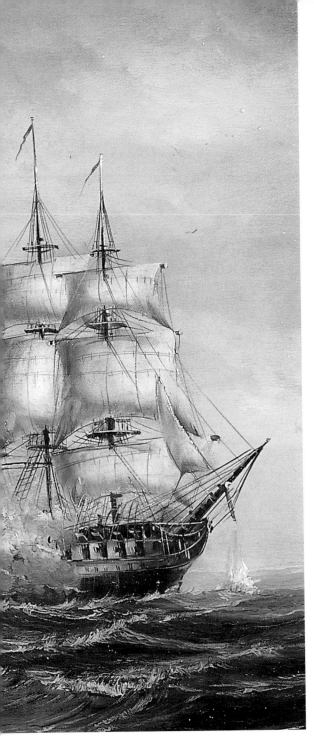

As in the French and Indian War, and the Revolutionary War, Lake Champlain and the Great Lakes were a strategic theatre of a war that left a number of warship wrecks on their lake beds. Some of the most significant underwater archaeology in North America has taken place on the lakes. But other work, particularly on the reaches of Chesapeake Bay, provides a detailed look at the unprepared navy, a victim of political whims, that nonetheless struggled against the odds against a superior navy and managed to play a role in the United States' retention of its independence.

The War of 1812 commenced in June 1812, and in the next few months, the frigates of the United States navy met and defeated British warships in single-ship actions—some of them, like the defeat of HMS *Guerriere* and HMS *Java* by USS *Constitution*, were important symbolic victories with little strategic value. The first significant naval contest came in 1813, on the waters of Lake Erie. Lieutenant Oliver Hazard Perry took command of a squadron in early 1813, and in short order, the hard work of men under the direction of New York shipwrights Adam and Noah Brown had assembled and built a fleet of warships, including the 20-gun brigs *Lawrence* and *Niagara*.

The British and American fleets met in battle at the southern end of the lake on September 10, 1813. The fleets, more or less equally matched, fought a fierce battle with heavy casualties. Perry was forced to leave the badly damaged *Lawrence* for *Niagara*, breaking the British line with her and finally winning the battle. The entire British squadron was taken, and Perry sent a famous dispatch to his superiors: "We have met the enemy and they are ours." Lake Erie was now under American control, but adjacent Lake Ontario remained contested as both sides built ships and skirmished without any climactic battle. But the actions did result in the sinking of two ships that today are the best-preserved wrecks of the War of 1812.

the line, they opted for a number of smaller 44-gun frigates, including the famous "Old Ironsides," USS *Constitution*. These ships were to play a major role in the establishment of fledgling American sea power over the next few decades, first in a struggle with Revolutionary France and again with Britain in the War of 1812.

To many, the most famous naval battles of the War of 1812 were those engagements on the open sea, particularly the exploits of "Old Ironsides." But most battles during the two-year conflict were fought close to shore, particularly on the lakes.

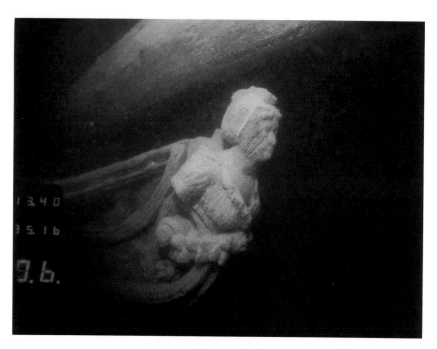

TOP The cold, fresh water of Lake Ontario has nearly perfectly preserved *Hamilton* and *Scourge*. This image of *Hamilton*'s figurehead recalls the brig's earlier career as the merchant schooner *Diana*.
Photo by Emory Kristof, © *Hamilton-Scourge* Foundation/City of Hamilton

BOTTOM Line drawing of *Hamilton* reconstructs her appearance and rig at the time of her loss in 1813.
Drawing by Ian Morgan, © *Hamilton-Scourge* Foundation/ City of Hamilton

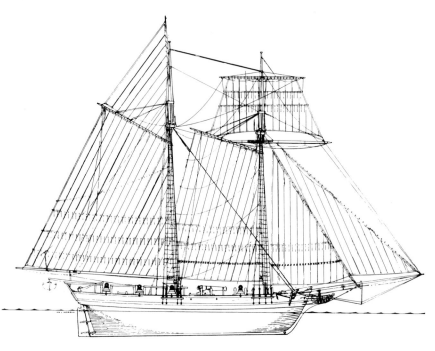

Hamilton and Scourge

The inland naval battles of the War of 1812 were marked by an arms race in which both sides tried to put as much firepower as possible on the water. This naval arms race included building warships as well as refitting merchant vessels for war. Not all of these converted "warships" were particularly effective, as the loss of two topsail schooners on Lake Ontario in 1813 demonstrated. At the outbreak of war, the British naval presence on the lake was larger than that of United States. The 16-gun brig uss *Oneida* was the only American warship, countered by Britain's 22-gun ship *Royal George* and as many as five smaller warships. After a thwarted British attack on the base at Sackets Harbor, New York, the American commander, Captain Isaac Chauncey, assembled a larger fleet of merchant schooners, and in November 1812, he launched a 20-gun ship, *Madison*. By 1813, Chauncey had added two more warships, the 24-gun *General Pike* and the 16-gun schooner *Sylph*, as well as a fast dispatch schooner. The British met the challenge by building two 24-gun ships.

Archaeologist Kevin Crisman, the pre-eminent authority on the shipwrecks of the War of 1812, points out that the two sides exchanged long-range cannon fire and skirmished without much result, both "reluctant to risk a full-scale battle unless victory was absolutely assured." Chauncey was worried about the performance of his squadron, for although he had twice as many ships as his British counterpart, "the unequal sailing qualities" of the custom-built warships stood in sharp contrast to the armed schooners. It was a "very clumsy squadron under sail." It was also a risk for some of the ships to sail at all. The schooners *Hamilton* and *Scourge*, one an American-built vessel, the other a seized British trader, had been armed by Chauncey to build up his forces in 1812. *Hamilton* was 22 metres (72 feet) long, with a beam of 6.7 metres (22 feet), whereas *Scourge* was smaller at 18 by 6 metres (60 by 20 feet). Two-masted topsail schooners, each ship was fitted with cannon, *Hamilton* with ten and *Scourge*

The remains of one of *Scourge*'s dead sailors lie on the bottom near the wreck. Photo by Emory Kristof, © *Hamilton-Scourge* Foundation/ City of Hamilton

with eight guns. The additional weight of the guns made each ship dangerously unstable.

Ned Myers, a crewman aboard *Scourge*, reported, "This craft was unfit for her duty, but time pressed, and no better offered. The bulwarks had been raised on her, and she mounted eight sixes [guns], in regular broadside." As well, Myers complained, the "accommodations were bad enough, and she was so tender that we could do little or nothing with her in a blow. It was often prognosticated that she would prove our coffin." Myers's prediction came true on August 8, 1813. The two squadrons had skirmished on August 7, and each stood off for the evening. A storm came up and the top-heavy schooners capsized, sinking within minutes.

Myers made it into the water, while other men, trapped on or in the sinking *Scourge*, struggled to get free. He watched an officer try to wriggle out of a stern window, and then the ship and the man were gone. Myers saved himself by finding the ship's boat adrift, and he went on to rescue several shipmates. But *Hamilton* and *Scourge* had gone down with most of their crews.

In 1973, the intact wrecks were found 400 metres (about 1300 feet) apart in 91 metres (300 feet) of water. A survey led by a

RIGHT **The muzzle of an 18-pounder carronade is visible on *Hamilton*'s deck near a deadeye from the ship's standard rigging.** Photo by Emory Kristof, © *Hamilton-Scourge* Foundation/ City of Hamilton

BOTTOM RIGHT **One of *Scourge*'s 4-pounder guns on the deck.** Photo by Emory Kristof, © *Hamilton-Scourge* Foundation/City of Hamilton

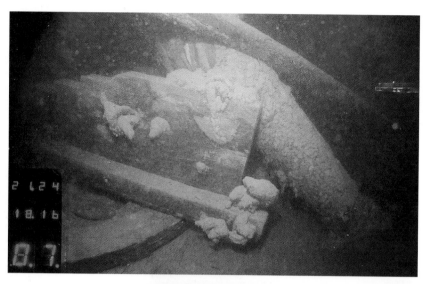

TOP The 12-pounder swivel gun, on its carriage, dominates the centre of *Hamilton*'s deck. Photo by Emory Kristof, © *Hamilton-Scourge* Foundation/ City of Hamilton

BOTTOM Boarding axes line the bulwark of *Scourge,* ready for axing when the ship came alongside an enemy's vessel. Photo by Emory Kristof, © *Hamilton-Scourge* Foundation/ City of Hamilton

St. Catherine's Ontario, dentist, Dr. Daniel Nelson, and sponsored by the Royal Ontario Museum, located targets that year believed to be the ships. In 1975, a sonar survey revealed the ghostlike image of the intact *Hamilton* on the lake bed. Since then, surveys of the wrecks by Jacques Cousteau in 1980, the National Geographic Society, with archaeologists Kenneth Cassavoy and Kevin Crisman, in 1982, and a 1990 detailed mapping of both ships by a team led by Dr. Robert Ballard and Dr. Anna Marguerite McCann have captured incredible photographs and produced detailed site maps of *Hamilton* and *Scourge* as they lie in the darkness.

The significance of the two wrecks lies entirely in their level of preservation. The 12-pounder carronades and the single long 24- or 32-pounder on *Hamilton* and the 6- and 4-pounder guns on *Scourge* remain on their carriages, on the decks. Lying nearby are powder ladles, rammers and other equipment, with cutlasses and boarding pikes. The open hatches, the masts rising towards the distant surface, the unbroken glass in the stern windows and *Hamilton*'s ship's boat, still at the stern where it was suspended from davits, make the wrecks a unique time capsule. It is as if the crew were standing ready to fight, though the upended guns and scattered equipment are clear evidence of each ship's roll into her grave. Archaeologists have spotted the remains of at least five of the crew, with one skeleton, bones tangled in rigging that dragged him down with the ship, lying alongside *Scourge*'s port side. The bodies are harsh evidence of the necessities of war compelling the U.S. Navy to put out to fight an enemy—and the elements—with ill-suited ships.

The wrecks of *Hamilton* and *Scourge* belong to the City of Hamilton, which is actively planning to conduct further work on them and determine a course of action, ranging from raising the ships to on-site interpretation of the "ghost ships" in their underwater museum. Unforgettable, each wreck is a rare glimpse into the past, an archaeological treasure and a grim reminder of the costs of war.

The Chesapeake Flotilla

Hamilton and *Scourge* were unsuitable warships, and yet they were better equipped than the U.S. Navy's largest group of fighting vessels: hundreds of gunboats. The result of an ill-advised naval policy of the Jefferson administration, the small, shallow-draft gunboats were constructed to patrol and defend the coastal waterways of the United States. Jefferson had placed an embargo on all foreign trade and virtually isolated the United States by sea. The government reasoned that without an overseas merchant trade, a large seagoing navy was not required—only sufficient numbers of gunboats to keep watch at the coast for smugglers and hostile visitors.

At the outbreak of the War of 1812, the U.S. Navy was no match for the Royal Navy as a result of the government's emphasis on gunboats. The victories of uss *Constitution* and her sister ships were important morale boosters, but they did nothing to stop the Royal Navy from blockading the American coast and landing an invading army. Swept aside by the superior forces of the Royal Navy, the gunboats were unable to prevent the British from attacking coastal settlements, towns and ports—and ultimately, from sailing up the Potomac to capture and burn the capital at Washington, D.C.

In early 1813, the Royal Navy blockaded the entrances to Chesapeake Bay and the ports and settlements in the "Tidewater" on the shores of Delaware, Maryland and Virginia. The British actively raided the region with impunity, inspiring a Revolutionary War veteran and hero, Joshua Barney, to petition the U.S. Navy to place him in command of a defensive force of gunboats and hastily built armed barges. By spring 1814, Barney's "flotilla" was not yet ready, but increasing British pressure led him to attack the principal Royal Navy stronghold at Tangier Island on Chesapeake Bay. Joining forces with a gunboat squadron from Norfolk, Virginia, Barney's armed barges, along with his flagship, the sloop *Scorpion*, a row galley and a number of merchantmen, attacked the British on May 31, 1814.

Discovered on the Outer Banks near Nags Head, North Carolina, in 1939, this wreck was first thought to be an ancient vessel, perhaps even a Viking ship, Instead, National Park Service archaeologist Thor Borreson's careful research showed it to be Jeffersonian Gunboat No. 146, lost during the War of 1812, and nearly identical to the gunboats later discovered on the Patuxent. National Park Service

The British outgunned Barney's flotilla, and after a brisk fight, as reinforcements arrived to crush the Americans, Barney withdrew his ships from the bay and into the Patuxent River. They would never leave. The Royal Navy blockaded the river, pushing Barney's flotilla farther up into a shallow tributary, St. Leonard's Creek. Six separate British attacks tried to destroy Barney's forces, but failed. Finally, the cornered Barney struck back. Coming out of the creek and into the river in the darkness of June 26, 1814, just before sunrise, Barney's ships badly damaged two British frigates before retreating again. In the retreat, two gunboats and several merchantmen were scuttled to avoid capture.

The end for Barney's flotilla came in August 1814 as the British pushed up the Patuxent to capture Washington, D.C. Pulling back up the river as the British advanced, Barney was trapped by shallow water by the third week of August. Unable to continue up river, and not wanting his fleet to fall into British hands, On August 22, he ordered the barges, gunboats, schooners and the sloop set on fire and scuttled. Sixteen vessels slipped beneath the muddy waters of the Patuxent. Barney's men joined the land forces opposing the British advance. Two days later, on August 24, they were defeated at the Battle of Bladensburg, leaving Washington open. As the government fled, the triumphant forces of Admiral Sir George Cockburn put Washington to the torch. The burning of the capital did not bring surrender or the end of the war, as other important cities remained uncaptured.

In 1978, archaeologist and historian Donald Grady Shomette, with the assistance of the Calvert Marine Museum of Solomons, Maryland, and with federal funding, began a survey of the Patuxent to locate Barney's flotilla. Years of dredging and wreck removal by the U.S. Army Corps of Engineers to clear the river as a navigable waterway had left few traces. But in 1980, Shomette's persistence paid off with the discovery and partial excavation of a nearly intact wreck in the mud of the upper Patuxent. Shomette's excavation of a portion of the wreck revealed charred and scattered timbers at the bow—traces of the scuttling fire and blast that sank many of Barney's flotilla. The blast damage was confined to a small area, with a thick plank bulkhead keeping the blast and fire out of the hold. As divers slowly vacuumed up the thick mud from inside a cofferdam and groped in the dark water, they discovered the surgical tools and medicines lost by the ship's doctor, Thomas Hamilton. Other finds included a cup with the name of the ship's cook, Caesar Wentworth, clothing and shoes, carpenter's tools, weapons, a box of munitions and the oars and benches the crew sat on while rowing the ship into action.

Shomette located two buried wrecks in the mud of St. Leonard's Creek in 1996 that he believed were gunboats Numbers 137 and 138. Limited excavation of the wrecks began in 1997 and continued through 1999 with a diverse group of participants including Maryland State archaeologists, volunteers from the Maritime Archaeological and Historical Society, all under the direction of Shomette and archaeologist Lawrence Babits of East Carolina University. The excavation of the 16-by-4.3-metre (52.5-by-14-foot) vessels revealed that these small craft were nearly identical, heavily built to carry the weight of cannon, but unwieldy and slow. The wrecks of the Chesapeake flotilla are more than a reminder of a desperate action to stop the British naval advance. They are tangible evidence of a misguided naval policy that allowed the British to carry the war past the coast and into the towns and settlements—and finally to the capital—of the United States.

Eagle

While the naval war went poorly for the United States on the mid-Atlantic coast, the U.S. Navy was able to seize control of the Great Lakes and Lake Champlain. Oliver Hazard Perry's victory at the Battle of Lake Erie on September 10, 1813, is perhaps the most famous American naval engagement on inland waters, but the more significant battle in terms of ending the war was the Battle of Lake Champlain on September 11, 1814. Lake Champlain, again a strategic highway for an invasion out of Canada and into the United States, was the setting for a naval arms race that mirrored those on the Great Lakes.

The outbreak of the War of 1812 found Lake Champlain practically undefended, though the U.S. Navy did maintain a negligible presence on the lake with two half-sunk, laid-up gunboats. The navy sent Lieutenant Thomas MacDonough to Lake Champlain in October 1812, and for the next few months, MacDonough purchased and armed six merchant schooners that gave him control of the lake—for a while. In 1813, two of MacDonough's ships, *Growler* and *Eagle*, sailed into a British trap after entering the Richelieu River in pursuit of three gunboats. Well inside Canadian waters, the two vessels were surrounded by troops on the banks and started to retreat. Harassed by the gunboats, the two American ships ran low on ammunition and finally surrendered. The British repaired the damaged *Growler* and *Eagle*, and with their gunboats and a small flotilla of bateaux, they descended onto Lake Champlain to wreak havoc, burning buildings and military equipment at Plattsburgh, New York, as well as capturing several American merchant vessels.

MacDonough added two armed merchant sloops and two gunboats to his squadron and managed to keep the British at bay for the rest of 1813. But during the winter of 1813–14, he learned that the British were busy building a squadron of their own at Isle aux Noix, on the Richelieu River. To counter the British threat, MacDonough needed to add more vessels to his own squadron.

Reconstruction of *Eagle*.
Kevin Crisman

MacDonough had shipwrights built six 25-metre-long (82-foot-long), 4.5-metre-wide (15-foot-wide) row galleys with carronades at each end— and, in response to news that the British were building a warship, he also ordered a 24-gun sloop of war. Under the supervision of master shipwright Noah Brown, workers built and launched MacDonough's new vessels within sixty days.

They also purchased a steamboat, still on the stocks in her shipyard, and completed her as the armed schooner *Ticonderoga*. This naval force was able to keep the British at their end of the lake, but by early summer, MacDonough learned that his enemies were rushing to complete even more vessels to gain naval supremacy. The anxious lieutenant pushed his superiors for funds to build one more vessel, and with approval from President James Madison in hand, he signed a contract for the additional vessel with Noah and Adam Brown in early July. Adam Brown rushed men and supplies to Vergennes, Vermont, and built the new vessel in nineteen days, launching the 39-metre-long (128-foot-long) brig *Eagle* on August 11.

Eagle joined MacDonough's squadron with just enough time for two weeks of manoeuvres and training. The crew, also hastily assembled, included soldiers, convicts from an army chain gang and army musicians. On September 11, 1814, the long-awaited British invasion swept down the lake and along its shores as ships and troops moved south. MacDonough, thanks to *Eagle*'s quick launch, was able to match the British, gun for gun. Meeting at Plattsburgh Bay, scene of the earlier successful British raid, the two fleets clashed for a bloody two and a half hours. MacDonough and his ships won the battle, losing fifty-two men in the action whereas the British lost at least fifty-four. Shot and splinters horribly wounded twice as many men. All of the British warships were captured, and the troops who had followed the ships in their advance into the United States hastily retreated back into Canada.

MacDonough's squadron battles the British on Lake Champlain during the War of 1812. Lake Champlain Maritime Museum

EAGLE

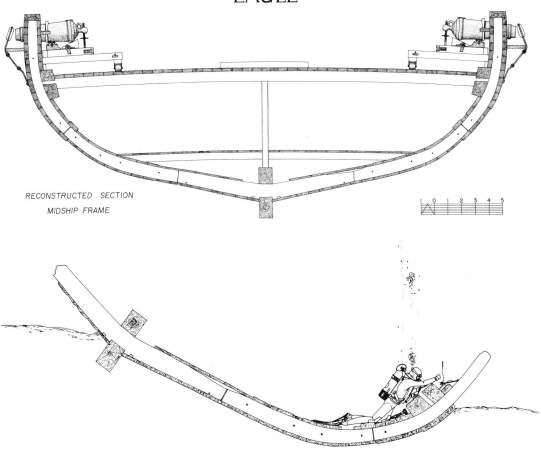

Excavation of the remains of *Eagle* allowed archaeologists to reconstruct the ship's form on paper (top), showing the thick clamps that supported the deck instead of the traditional wooden knees usually found on ship. Kevin Crisman

RECONSTRUCTED SECTION
MIDSHIP FRAME

The victory at Plattsburgh ended British plans to invade the United States from the north and left all the lakes bordering Canada with superior American naval forces. The situation was a deciding factor in Britain's agreement to end hostilities and sign the Treaty of Ghent on December 24, 1814. Under the terms of the peace, the lakes were demilitarized, and MacDonough's painstakingly assembled squadron was laid up at Whitehall, New York. The navy sold some of the converted merchant vessels and sank the six row galleys in the cold, fresh water to preserve them. The remaining ships, many of them rotting and half-sunk, were finally sold in 1825 to salvagers.

Archaeologists Kevin Crisman and Art Cohn surveyed the Whitehall area in 1982, locating the remains of *Eagle*, the row galley *Allen*, the captured Royal Navy brig *Linnet* and the armed schooner *Ticonderoga*. In 1995, they documented *Allen* and *Linnet*. Between 1983 and 1984, archaeological teams from the Lake Champlain Maritime Museum, working under Crisman and Cohn, excavated and studied *Eagle*. Although stripped and with only half its hull surviving, *Eagle* yielded much information about her hasty construction. Built of several different types of wood, some of them soft and ill-suited, like white pine and spruce for the frames, *Eagle* also had no reinforcing wooden or iron knees to support the decks. The deck beams were clamped between two thick timbers—a shelf of sorts—that would have allowed the beams to pull free and the decks to fail in rough seas. As Kevin Crisman has pointed out, MacDonough did not need a durable ship; he needed a platform for more guns. Time was of the essence, and the wreck of *Eagle* shows that this imperfect warship was completed just in time, thanks to shortcuts, to balance the scales of naval power and win the battle.

CHAPTER 6

Steel, Iron and Steam

THE INDUSTRIAL REVOLUTION resulted in tremendous changes to ships. Iron and steel replaced wood. More powerful weapons and steam power gave rise to new ways to fight. These changes were at first slow and often resisted by naval officers. Although the first steam-powered warship was launched in 1815, it took decades before the new technology was fully trusted and adopted. It was not until mid-century that most of the world's new warships were steam-driven. Wooden-hulled, these warships arrived on the scene just as shell-firing guns (an 1824 invention) did, occasioning a return to the ancient technique of armouring. The ironclad was introduced in 1858, though it was not until 1861 that two ironclads engaged in combat. That action changed the face of naval warfare. Over the next few decades, many naval powers built armoured warships with turrets and shell guns, each successive generation growing larger in calibre of the guns, the thickness of the armour, the power of the engines and the size of the ship itself.

The nineteenth century began with battles between wooden ships of the line at Trafalgar and the naval actions of the War of 1812. The last battles between wooden ships under sail came with the war for Greek independence at the Battle of Navarino in 1827. Harbingers of change were apparent in Russia's battles with Ottoman Turkey in 1856, when a Russian fleet, armed with shell-firing guns, destroyed a Turkish squadron. The use of new technologies, particularly against weaker powers, was readily apparent in the 1840s, as Britain used steam and shell guns to push aside Chinese resistance during the Opium Wars, and the United States began to flex its muscles in the expansionist war of 1846–48 against Mexico.

Considerable change was evident during the American Civil War of 1861–65, as both sides of

FACING PAGE **The Battle of Navarino, as depicted by Russian artist Ivan Konstantinovich Aivazovsky (1846).** Marine College, St. Petersburg/Bridgeman Art Library

RIGHT **The Battle of Trafalgar, 21st October 1805, The British Breaking the French and Spanish Line.** Bridgeman Art Library

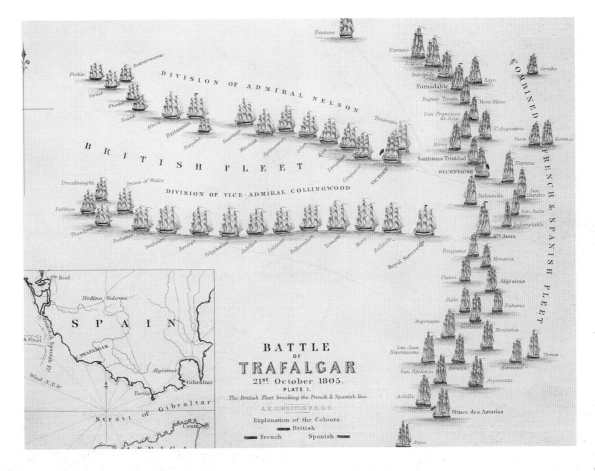

**Wrecks and battles of the
American Civil War and the
late nineteenth century.**

James P. Delgado, Eric Leinberger

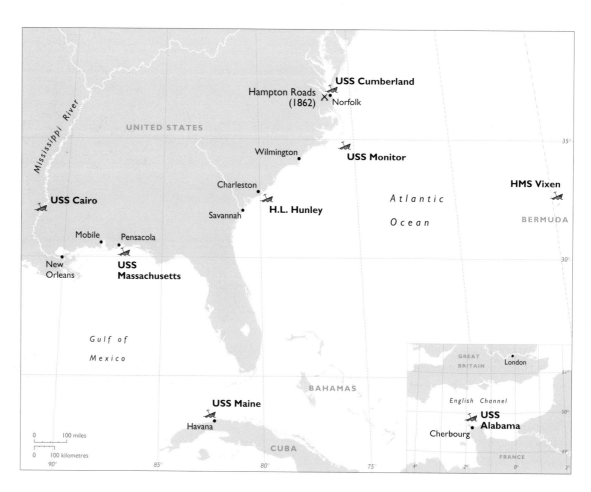

the conflict demonstrated the efficiency of steam, ironclads, turrets, mines and submarines. The innovations in the American Civil War were adopted by other countries in wars of their own, many of them unequal contests of colonial expansion in Africa, the Indian Ocean and the Pacific. The rise of the armoured ship was seized upon by Britain, which retained control of the seas throughout the century.

Archaeologists have documented the wrecks of a number of nineteenth-century warships, finding evidence of adherence to "tried and true" technologies and strategies in the face of new developments, as well as navies embracing the wrong new technologies and innovations, including following some evolutionary dead ends, such as late-nineteenth-century experiments with ramming.

uss *Cumberland*

The sloop of war uss *Cumberland* is best remembered as a symbol of an end of an era. A member of the last generation of wooden warships built to fight under sail, *Cumberland* was the first victim of a steam-powered, ironclad ship of war. *Cumberland*, launched in 1842 at the Boston Navy Yard, was a 1726-ton, wooden steam frigate that served for twenty years in American, Mediterranean and African waters. The U.S. Navy cut down the frigate to a sloop of war, mounting fewer guns in 1856. With the outbreak of civil war in 1861, *Cumberland* was one of several American warships at Gosport Navy Yard in Portsmouth, Virginia. The yard and its ships were caught behind enemy lines when Virginia seceded from the Union and demanded the surrender of all federal property, arms and warships within its territory. The commanding officer of the yard decided to destroy what he could of the facilities, ordnance and vessels that could not flee. *Cumberland* was one of the ships to clear the burning Gosport Navy Yard on April 20, but other ships were not so lucky, including the steam-powered frigate uss *Merrimack*, scuttled at the dock and set afire.

The two ships would meet again soon. On March 8, 1862, *Cumberland* and several other warships stood off Newport News, Virginia, blockading the James River. *Cumberland*, armed with a 70-pound rifle, two 10-inch Dahlgren pivot guns and twenty-two 9-inch Dahlgren guns, was a formidable opponent for any Confederate vessel that might challenge the blockade. But the Confederacy had adopted the latest technological innovations in naval warfare. Raising the sunken *Merrimack*, Confederate engineers cut the hull down, removed the masts, repaired the steam machinery and placed a battery of guns inside a sloping armoured casemate. Commissioned as css *Virginia*, the ironclad was not the world's first—France and Britain had already built ironclads—but *Virginia* would be the first to go into battle.

Steaming into view of the blockading ships, *Virginia* headed for the wooden frigate

uss *Cumberland*, c. 1856.
U.S. Naval Historical Center

uss *Congress*. Raking *Congress* with gunfire, *Virginia* continued on unscathed as cannon fire bounced off her armour. *Cumberland* was next. The captain was not aboard, and the executive officer, Lieutenant George Morris, was in command. As Franklin Buchanan, *Virginia*'s captain, called out for *Cumberland* to surrender, Morris yelled, "Never! I'll sink alongside!" *Virginia* lined up to sink *Cumberland*, with a 6-foot armoured ram projecting from her bow. *Cumberland* sank within minutes, taking about 120 of the crew with her as she settled in 21 metres (69 feet) of water. The age of the wooden walls had effectively ended decades earlier, but *Virginia*'s onslaught and *Cumberland*'s sinking were definitive illustrations of the point.

Archaeologists working with author and explorer Clive Cussler rediscovered *Cumberland* off Newport News in 1980. Intact decking, an anchor, the exposed remains of the bilge pumps and artifacts including the ship's bell, cannon fuses, a gunlock cover and calipers were visible to the divers who first visited the wreck.

But after the discovery, archaeologists and the U.S. Navy virtually ignored *Cumberland*, designating it as historic but not pursuing further study or excavation. The wreck remains on the bottom of the James River to this day, heavily looted by souvenir-selling relic hunters who plundered the site. After learning about the despoliation of USS *Cumberland* from the Confederate Naval Historical Society, the FBI arrested the looters, and the U.S. Navy and the State of Virginia accepted responsibility for working to study and preserve what was left. An archaeological survey of *Cumberland* in 1993 revealed extensive damage to the wreck. The second destruction of USS *Cumberland* is a striking example of what can happen to significant shipwrecks when insufficient resources to pursue an important find, or official indifference, leaves the door open for looters.

In this Currier and Ives lithograph, CSS *Virginia* rams USS *Cumberland* as the wooden ship vainly fires her guns. U.S. Naval Historical Center

uss *Monitor*

Another participant in the naval actions on the James River in March 1862 was a vessel that demonstrated, along with css *Virginia*, that the day of the wooden warship was done. News of the Confederacy's work on the raised hulk of uss *Merrimack* led Union officials to seek proposals for their own ironclad. On September 15, 1861, Swedish-American inventor John Ericcson presented the plans for a small steam-powered ironclad with a single rotating turret on its deck. The American government skeptically accepted Ericcson's proposal, and the race was on to see which ironclad—css *Virginia* or Ericcson's *Monitor*—would be finished first. Ericcson launched *Monitor* on January 30, 1862, whereas *Virginia* slid off the ways on February 17. Both ironclads then steamed for the mouth of the James and the blockading fleet.

Virginia won the race, hitting the blockading fleet hard on March 8 and sinking uss *Cumberland*. But the following morning, as *Virginia* readied for her next attack, *Monitor*, described as a "cheesebox on a raft," stood between the Confederate ironclad and the Union fleet. For four hours, the two warships hammered away at each other, firing point-blank. The battle ended in a stalemate that changed naval warfare forever. The 58-metre-long (190-foot-long), 11-metre-wide (36-foot-wide) *Monitor* mounted only two 11-inch Dahlgren smooth-bore guns in her rotating, armoured turret. But as the *London Times* later editorialized, the arrival of *Monitor* shifted the balance of naval power. The Royal Navy was effectively reduced in number from 149 "first-class warships" to only two "armoured vessels."

The success of *Monitor* was a profound revelation. And yet the vessel, though copied by the

uss *Monitor* and css *Virginia* battle each other to a standstill on March 9, 1862. From Charles Mackay's *The History of the United States*, vol. II, Private collection/Bridgeman Art Library

Sinking of uss Monitor.
Harper's Weekly, **December 6,**
1863. Author's collection

United States and other powers, was not a lasting success. With her shallow draft and low freeboard, *Monitor* was not a seaworthy vessel. Its short life is proof of that. After several months on station at Hampton Roads, the entrance to the James River and the site of her famous battle with *Virginia*, with a brief layover in Washington, D.C., for repairs and public tours, *Monitor* departed for Beaufort, North Carolina, towed by uss *Rhode Island* into the open ocean. She did not last long. Heavy seas washing over the deck began to fill the ship just a day out, and by the late evening of December 30, 1862, *Monitor* had lost her tow and was wallowing in the waves off Cape Hatteras. Boats from *Rhode Island* took off most of *Monitor*'s crew, and around 1:00 A.M. on December 31, the ironclad, with a red distress lantern hanging from a flag staff, slipped beneath the waves with thirty-five or more of the crew.

In 1973, archaeologists and other scientists located the wreck of *Monitor* in 75 metres (246 feet) of water off the North Carolina coast. A detailed photographic mapping of the wreck by the U.S. Navy in 1974 showed that the ironclad had rolled over while sinking. The heavy turret pulled free of the hull, and the overturned hull landed on top of the turret. The upside-down hull nearly obscured the turret, revealing only a small curved section as it protruded from the starboard quarter. The American government designated the wreck and the surrounding area as a National Marine Sanctuary in 1975, and since then, several archaeological expeditions have dived to examine *Monitor* and recover artifacts. The first dive to the wreck, in the submersible *Johnson Sea Link*, in August 1977, was an amazing moment for archaeologist Gordon P. Watts Jr. As the submersible landed on the sandy bottom and moved forward, the divers discovered a small brass marine lantern lying 13 metres (43 feet) away from the wreck. It was probably the same signal light flying from *Monitor*'s masthead atop her turret that "provided rescuers their last contact with the *Monitor* 115 years earlier."

Divers recovered the lantern and a loose, iron hull plate in 1977. This discovery was followed in 1979 by a test excavation inside a 2-metre-square (about 6-foot-square) grid near the starboard side of the bow. "Locking out" of a dive chamber from the submersible *Johnson Sea Link*, archaeologists Gordon Watts and John Broadwater used a water dredge to remove sediments and sand from what proved to be the collapsed remains of Captain John Bankshead's cabin. The archaeologists also examined the exposed remains of the wardroom and the engine room, where the intact machinery included the forced-air blowers that had pressurized that space, creating a forced draft for the boilers. The blowers were an amazing Ericcson innovation—and yet they, like the other machinery, relied on leather belts to run. As *Monitor* took on water, the wet leather belts had slipped off their shafts, stopping the fans, the boilers and the ship's pumps. Powerless to stop the incoming water, the ironclad had wallowed on the seas until she flooded.

The National Oceanic and Atmospheric Administration (NOAA) sponsored a 1983 expedition to recover *Monitor*'s unique four-fluke anchor, which Ericcson developed to fit inside a hollow anchor well below the deck and inside the bow. A steam-powered windlass inside the ship raised and lowered the anchor without exposing the crew to enemy fire. Later expeditions have recovered loose artifacts, more hull plating and most recently, the four-bladed propeller. The wreck is rapidly deteriorating, and within the next few years, NOAA and the U.S. Navy plan to raise more of the ironclad, including the turret and engines. These features were perhaps the more revolutionary features of *Monitor*, and when recovered, conserved and placed on display at the wreck's permanent dryland home, the Mariner's Museum, in Newport News, Virginia, they will offer visitors a first-hand look at a ship that signalled the most dramatic change in the way wars were fought at sea since the introduction of the gun.

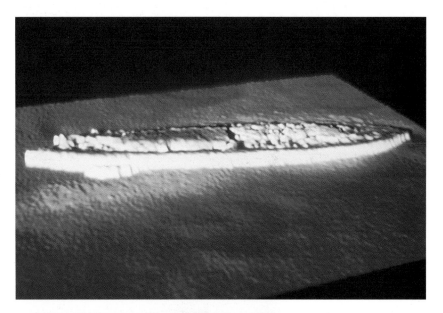

Computer images of wreck of *Monitor.* NOAA

Plan view, wreck of *Monitor*, as found in **1977.** NOAA

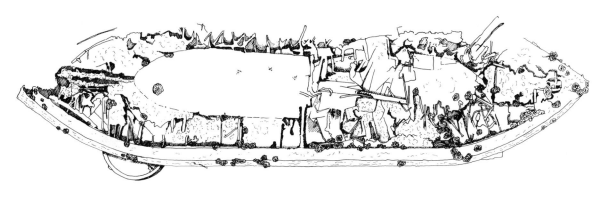

H.L. Hunley

The first battle between two ironclads during the American Civil War was just one significant demonstration of the changing face of war at sea. Another was the first use of a submarine to sink a warship. This time, the technological advantage lay with the beleaguered Confederacy. The small submarine *H.L. Hunley* was not the first submersible warship. Proposals for, and experiments with, submarines date back to the Spanish Armada. The first submarine used in time of war is said to have been a wooden-hulled, one-man craft invented by David Bushnell and taken into combat off Staten Island in September 1776 by Sergeant Ezra Lee to sink HMS *Eagle*, flagship of a British fleet that had escorted an expeditionary force to take New York. Some historians do not believe that this early submarine, which Bushnell named *Turtle*, was ever completed or taken into combat. Whether it did perhaps does not matter. Patriotic American tales of this ingenious Yankee craft inspired others to follow Bushnell's example.

Among those inspired was fellow American Robert Fulton. In 1800, Fulton built a small

submersible, *Nautilus*, for the Revolutionary French government, as well as floating mines that he called "torpedoes" after the North Atlantic ray *Torpedo nobiliana*, which uses electric shocks to stun its prey. Although Fulton's submarine did not participate in any actions, his "torpedoes" did, with mixed results. News of Fulton's inventions, inflated by hype, led British, French, Spanish and German inventors to experiment with submarines. German artillery officer Wilhelm Bauer built a working, all-iron submarine in late 1850, following it with another in 1855 for the Imperial Russian Navy.

The Submarine Torpedo Boat **H.L. Hunley.** Painting by Conrad Wise Chapman, Museum of the Confederacy, Richmond, Virginia

BELOW This plan of *H.L. Hunley* was prepared by Simon Lake, pioneering submarine inventor. It was based on a description of the Confederate sub provided by Charles Hasker, a former member of *Hunley*'s crew. From *McLure's* magazine, January 1899

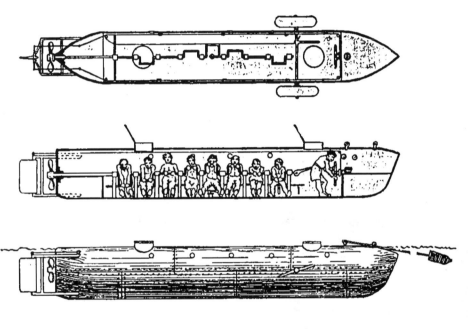

Edouard Manet's view
of the battle between
uss *Kearsarge* and
css *Alabama*, off
Cherbourg, France.
Philadelphia Museum of
Art/Bridgeman Art Library

css *Alabama*

Although the wrecks of several Civil War naval vessels lie on the ocean floor and riverbeds of the southern United States, a significant wreck that exemplifies the desperation and the prowess of the Confederate States Navy lies off the coast of France at the bottom of the English Channel. The Confederate States Navy, though confined to the coast and rivers of the southern United States to wage a desperate war against superior Federal forces, sent secret agents to sympathetic Britain to raise funds, purchase arms and outfit British-built vessels as Confederate warships. Operating under subterfuge to circumvent British neutrality, the Confederates built a number

of blockade-runners and raiders. The most famous was css *Alabama*.

Built at John Laird's shipyard in Birkenhead, England, near Liverpool, *Alabama* was a 64-metre-long (209-foot-long), 1023-ton, three-masted steam and sail-powered barkentine. Sailing from Liverpool and entering active service in August 1862, *Alabama* cruised under the command of Raphael Semmes, on a twenty-two—month voyage into the Indian Ocean, China Sea and the Atlantic. In that time, *Alabama* captured and then sank or ransomed sixty-four American merchant vessels. The actions of *Alabama* and other Confederate raiders on the high seas devastated the United States' shipping

industry, which never fully recovered.

Alabama engaged the steamer uss *Hatteras* off Galveston, Texas, on January 11, 1863, in a twenty-minute battle that sank *Hatteras*. The U.S. Navy dispatched ships to hunt down the Confederate raider. In June 1864, after Semmes slipped into the French port of Cherbourg to land prisoners and dry dock his ship, the sloop of war uss *Kearsarge* entered the harbour. Rather than flee, Semmes decided to fight. The two ships met in the English Channel off Cherbourg on June 19. Circling each other and firing, the two ships fought until *Alabama*, outgunned and not as staunchly built as the Union warship, sank.

Semmes surrendered, but he was saved from capture, along with several of his officers and crew, by an English yacht that had stood by and watched the battle.

Years of searching for the wreck paid off on October 30, 1984, when a French navy minesweeper discovered *Alabama* lying in 58 metres (190 feet) of water seven nautical miles off Cherbourg. Since then, a joint French-American team, led by archaeologists Max Guérout and Gordon P. Watts Jr., has explored and documented the wreck. Many details of the hull, which rests at a 20-degree angle along her starboard side, have been mapped, including the steam machinery. The priorities for

archaeological work have been studying the ship's technology, discovering the living conditions aboard and finding any evidence of *Alabama*'s twenty-two—month career as a raider. The team has recovered more than a hundred artifacts. These include one of the ship's Blakely guns, its loading interrupted by the order to abandon ship, leaving a live shell in the barrel, and the remains of *Alabama*'s wheel, with its brass bindings inscribed with *Alabama*'s motto: "Aide-toi et Dieu t'aidera" (God helps those who help themselves).

A modern computer graphic
accurately depicts *H.L. Hunley*
on the sub's final mission,
spar-mounted "torpedo" at
the bow. © Daniel Dowdey

Bauer's ideas and materials were sound, but both his submarines sank in operational accidents.

Most naval officers and government officials viewed with distaste the various experiments with submarines in the first half of the nineteenth century. The submarine and the torpedo were seen as evil weapons; one British officer, Vice Admiral Sir George Berkeley, wrote about "the Baseness & Cowardice of this species of Warfare." It took another conflict, and the desperation of a weaker naval power to take the risks to reputation and pocketbook, to build the next generation of submarines. The outbreak of the American Civil War and the limited resources of the Confederacy, when compared to the larger naval forces of the Union, led Confederate leaders to pursue risky and expensive new technologies. The Confederacy's first submarine, a small iron craft named *Pioneer*, lasted for a few months at New Orleans between her February launch and April scuttling in 1862 after the city fell to the Union. The builders of the submarine retreated to Mobile, Alabama, and in early 1863 built a second boat, *American Diver* (also known as *Pioneer II*), only to lose her when she

flooded and sank without her crew aboard while under tow to attack Union ships.

The next attempt by this same coalition of machinists and businessmen (the Singer Submarine Corps) was made in Charleston, South Carolina. An important Confederate port, Charleston was surrounded by a large fleet of Union ships that blockaded the harbour to prevent ships with supplies and munitions from supplying the Confederacy. A submarine's stealth, and the power of a "torpedo" delivered by it to unsuspecting Union ships, could disrupt the blockade.

But the technological wonder had its faults. The sub sank twice while on manoeuvres, killing five of the first and all of the second crew. The first accident, in August 1863, happened on the surface. The captain, Lieutenant John A. Payne, foolishly approached the submarine's berth with both hatches open. It is possible that the crew had not completely pumped out the fore and aft ballast tanks used to make the sub dive. With a low freeboard and very little buoyancy, the sub sank when Payne stepped on or bumped the diving plane and the bow dipped, sending water inside.

Payne and three other men managed to scramble free of the hatches before the submarine sank in about 13 metres (42 feet) of water.

The second accident, on October 15, 1863, with another crew, this time commanded by Horace L. Hunley, one of the financial backers, also ended badly. The submarine dived at too sharp an angle because the crew mistakenly flooded the bow ballast tank too quickly, sending the sub slamming into the muddy bed of the Cooper River. Half-buried in the river bottom, with the stern rising out of the mud at a 35-degree angle, the submarine was trapped, and the crew slowly suffocated. Three weeks later, when the Confederates were able to raise the submarine, the scene inside when the hatches were opened was "indescribably ghastly; the unfortunate men were distorted into all kinds of horrible attitudes ... the blackened faces of all presented the expression of their despair and agony."

Yet another submarine crew was readied for an attack on the Union fleet off Charleston Harbor. On February 17, 1864, the submarine, now formally named for its dead backer and captain as *H.L. Hunley*, moved out to sea under the command of Lieutenant George Dixon. Instead of towing a torpedo, *Hunley* carried a charge attached to a 5.75-metre-long (19-foot-long) metal spar attached to the sub's bow. Heading into the night and towards the sloop of war USS *Housatonic*, Dixon brought his submarine and crew right up the starboard side of the Union warship, just aft of the mizzen mast. Lookouts spotted the sub and raised the alarm. As the crew of the *Housatonic* beat to quarters, sentries opened fire, hitting the exposed upper works of the sub with musket fire. Captain Charles Pickering, *Housatonic*'s commander, fired his double-barrelled shotgun into the conning towers.

Then, just as *Housatonic* started to back away from the attacking sub, the spar torpedo exploded. *Housatonic* sank in about six minutes. *H.L. Hunley* slowly backed away from the sinking vessel, and then disappeared, not to be seen for over 130 years.

In May 1995, archaeologists Ralph Wilbanks, Wes Hall and Harry Pecorelli, working under contract for the National Underwater and Maritime Agency, in partnership with the South Carolina Institute of Archaeology and Anthropology (SCIAA), discovered the wreck of *H.L. Hunley* in 10 metres (33 feet) of water, buried in sediment.

This National Park Service drawing shows *H.L. Hunley* after test excavation in 1996 exposed the buried submarine for the first time since its 1995 rediscovery. Drawing by Matthew Russell, David L. Conlin and Larry V. Nordby, Submerged Cultural Resources Unit, National Park Service

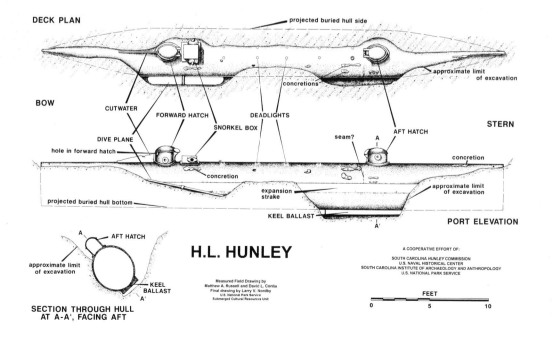

H.L. HUNLEY

Dixon and his crew had not gotten far from *Housatonic*; the two wrecks lay about 300 metres (1000 feet) apart. Wilbanks, Hall and Pecorelli removed enough sediment to expose a diving plane, the forward hatch and snorkel box, verifying that the wreck was in fact the lost submarine. The discovery sparked a number of controversies, principally between South Carolina and the American government over who would own and control the wreck, but these conflicts did not stop work on the site. In 1996, archaeologists from sciaa and the Submerged Cultural Resources Unit of the U.S. National Park Service returned to the site and did a more extensive test excavation of portions of *H.L. Hunley* as well as a detailed study of the wreck and its environment. Under the direction of the two archaeologists, Christopher Amer of sciaa and Larry Murphy of the NPS, the team exposed both hatches, the top of the submarine, the port-side diving plane and a section of the side down to the solid-iron bar keel.

The excavation of the submarine provided the first detailed look at a vessel that had never been documented during its brief career. Since the Civil War, a number of people had provided various descriptions and estimates of the submarine's size, the placement of the spar torpedo and the form or lines of the hull. But no plans or photographs existed for the vessel. The archaeologists discovered that most conclusions about the submarine's appearance and manufacture had been wrong. What they found was a sophisticated design and a well-constructed vessel. *Hunley*'s hull is hydrodynamic, with a sharp, knifelike bow, shaped to move through the water with minimal resistance. Instead of being fastened with thick rivets projecting from the hull plates, which would create drag in the water, the submarine is instead flush-riveted and smooth. This level of craftsmanship surprised the archaeologists, some of whom were expecting this rushed, wartime project to have construction shortcuts, much like those found with earlier warship wrecks like *Defence* or *Eagle*.

This view of the stern of *H.L. Hunley* shows the propeller and its damaged guard.
sciaa, Christopher Amer

The sharp, knifelike bow of
H.L. Hunley. The Confederate
sub, when excavated, proved
to be a sophisticated and
well-engineered craft. SCIAA,
Christopher Amer

H.L. Hunley is about 12 metres (39 feet, 5 inches) long, excluding the propeller and rudder, which add another metre (about 3 feet) to its length. Its inside was cramped for the crew. The hull is only about 1.2 metres (3 feet, 10 inches) wide, meaning that the crew had to sit, hunched over, as they turned the cranks to drive the propeller. Five pairs of glass deadlights, to let in light, were set into the top of the submarine, but they only worked during the day. Without electrical power, the crew of *Hunley* worked in near darkness, by candlelight in a crowded iron cylinder where they could not stand or stretch out, the air thick and hot in summer, and cold and damp in winter. It becomes easier to understand why they would run on the surface whenever possible with the hatches open. There was nothing glamorous about serving aboard *Hunley*, particularly after two other crews had drowned or suffocated inside what some were calling the "peripatetic coffin." It takes a special type of courage to get inside something like that submarine, and with the strength of your body fight the ocean to reach a warship, and then, at close range, set off an explosive charge that hits your vessel almost as hard as it hits the target.

The 1996 excavation was followed by a complete excavation and recovery of *H.L. Hunley*, culminating on August 8, 2000, when a 300-ton crane raised the submarine from the sea to begin a multiyear project to conserve and curate it. This work carefully removed hull plates to excavate the sand that had completely filled *Hunley*. Archaeologists discovered the remains of the sub's crew still at their posts.

The archaeological examination of *Hunley* also included a look at *Housatonic*. Even though major portions of the wreck were scrapped in 1872, and then again in 1909 to clear the harbour of obstructions, several feet of the lower hull remains buried. The most recent examination suggests that *Hunley*'s spar torpedo detonated close to a powder magazine near *Housatonic*'s stern. The powder—as much as four tons of it—exploded, ripping off much of *Housatonic*'s aft end, below the water, which would help explain why the Union warship sank so quickly. It may also help explain what happened to *Hunley*. When raised, the submarine had holes: one in the forward conning tower, and one near the bow on the starboard side.

But a larger hole in the stern could be explosion damage. The submarine's hull, originally a steam boiler, was built to withstand pressures of between 150 and 225 pounds per square inch. The 90-pound charge in the spar torpedo, when it exploded, would have generated 2383 pounds per square inch at a 20-foot distance, 953 psi at a 50-foot distance and 238 psi at a 200-foot distance. The underwater pressure wave from the spar torpedo alone could have cracked the hull or opened seams. Add the pressure wave from the magazine exploding, and *Hunley* and its crew could have been overwhelmed by the blast. Stunned, perhaps hurt with broken bones and ruptured eardrums, and with water leaking in through cracks or popped rivets, the submarine's crew may well have drifted off or slowly retreated until the sub settled on the bottom not far from its victim.

This computer graphic depicts *H.L. Hunley*'s second (of three) sinkings.
© Daniel Dowdey

Resurgam Will Rise Again

In 1995, the intact wreck of the short-lived *Resurgam*, the world's first mechanically powered submarine, was discovered in 12 to 18 metres (40 to 60 feet) of water of Rhyl, North Wales, after searchers spent twenty years trying to locate her. The wreck, snagged by a fisherman's net, was identified by sport divers who tried to sell the location. Rather than pay for the information, Britain's Archaeological Diving Unit (ADU) conducted its own search of the area and found *Resurgam* in 1996. Ongoing dives by the ADU, aided by volunteers, document the submarine while planning continues to raise and preserve the wreck, which is being damaged by trawlers hitting it.

This Currier and Ives litho-graph shows Union Ironclads like *Cairo* bombarding Fort Henry on the Tennessee River on February 6, 1862. U.S. Naval Historical Center

USS *Cairo*

Another American Civil War wreck, USS *Cairo*, is also a reminder of the increasingly technological nature of naval warfare in the nineteenth century. The ill-fated *Cairo* was one of many steam-powered ironclads built for service on the rivers of the south. *Cairo*'s greatest claim to fame is that she was the first warship sunk by an electrically detonated mine—an "infernal device," in the colourful language of her time. Like *H.L. Hunley* and CSS *Virginia*, the mine that sank USS *Cairo* was a cornerstone of the Confederacy's naval strategy to effect a "techni-cal surprise" by adopting innovations like ironclad warships, rifled and shell-firing guns, submarines and mines.

During the American Civil War, though the Union's naval strategy against the Confederacy was primarily devoted to a blockade of Southern ports and harbors, it also included seizing control of the Mississippi River. Controlling the river and

isolating the rebellious southern states would "strangle" the Confederacy. To wage war on the Mississippi and its tributaries, the Union built spe-cialized ironclads based on the design of western river steamboats. Known as the city-class gun-boats, these riverine warships were shallow-draft craft with sloping, armoured casemated sides. Inclined, reciprocating steam engines drove a pad-dlewheel recessed in the hull behind the armour. This armour, made from railroad iron, also pro-tected the crew and the ship's armament.

USS *Cairo*, named for Cairo, Illinois, was built in 1862 at Mound City, Illinois. Displacing 888 tons, the 53-metre-long (175-foot-long) vessel was extremely broad, with a 15-metre (51-foot) beam and a shallow, 1.8-metre (6-foot) draft. She did not enjoy a long career. The gunboat was lost on December 12, 1862, during naval operations in support of General U. S. Grant's siege of Vicksburg, Mississippi.

uss *Cairo* today.
James P. Delgado

The Confederates, using the technological advantage of electrically detonated "torpedoes," had mined the river. As *Cairo* slowly steamed up the muddy waters of the Yazoo to engage a Confederate shore battery, she passed over a minefield. Two sharp explosions rocked the ship, tearing two holes in the hull. As the water poured in "like the roar of Niagara," Captain Thomas Oliver Selfridge ran the sinking ironclad against the river's muddy banks. As the crew scrambled to safety, *Cairo* slid off, sinking in twelve minutes. Only the tops of the stacks and the flag staff rose above the swirling brown water. To thwart Confederate salvage, the crew pulled down these landmarks, leaving *Cairo* to the river.

Edwin C. Bearss, research historian at Vicksburg National Military Park, and local historian Warren Grabau rediscovered the wreck of *Cairo* in 1956. Plotting the ironclad's location with naval records and old maps, and working from a

Damaged area of *Cairo* with gun. James P. Delgado

archaeological site filled with the ship's ordnance, equipment, tackle and the personal items of the crew. Bearss and friends formed a private non-profit group, Operation Cairo, Inc., to bring up the ironclad. Dollars to raise *Cairo* came in, but there was just enough to do the job. No funds would be left to preserve the wreck or its contents. To compound the problems, when the lift finally happened in October 1964, it was an archaeological disaster. The marine salvors hired to raise the wreck underestimated the ironclad's weight. Using crane barges to pull on wire cables passed under the hull, the salvors broke the ship apart, cutting her into three pieces. Only the bow came up relatively intact. The wires crushed the midships portion of *Cairo*, and the stern collapsed and fell back into the river. Most of the material that fell into the river, such as armour, the wheelhouse, entire sections of the casemates and smaller artifacts, was never recovered.

The state of Mississippi barged the surviving pieces of the ship downriver to a shipyard in Pascagoula, Mississippi, to be cleaned and reassembled. Unfortunately, out of sight, they slowly began to rot and fall apart. The smaller artifacts from inside the wreck fared better: they were cleaned, restored and catalogued by volunteers led by Margie Bearss. Many of the artifacts were evocative, personal reminders of the crew, who, despite the difference of a few centuries, did not live that differently from the crew of *Vasa* or *Defence*.

The National Park Service restored and reassembled the remains of *Cairo*'s hull between 1977 and 1984. Only 15 per cent of the original vessel survived, but architects were able to support the hull fragments, armour and machinery on a laminated wooden framework that creates a "ghost" of the original ironclad. Displayed outdoors under an open shelter, *Cairo* and the nearby museum that houses her artifacts tell the story of how quickly a "new" technology—the torpedo—was deployed to counter the threat of another technology—the ironclad—in the rapidly changing nineteenth century.

rowboat, the two historians found the wreck with a handheld compass that swung wildly because of the huge mass of iron on the hull. Balancing over the side of the boat, they probed with an iron bar and were rewarded with the sound of iron. In 1959–60, local divers surveyed the exterior of the wreck, and in September 1960, Bearss and Grabau hired a salvage crane to pull the armoured pilot-house free of the hull and raise it to the surface. They were also able to grapple an 8-inch naval gun and yank it from the casemate, only to discover it was still loaded.

Cairo lay buried in the silt of the Yazoo, filled with mud, as a perfectly preserved, encapsulated

HMS *Vixen*

The last quarter of the nineteenth century was marked by competition among various European powers. Although the Royal Navy remained the world's most powerful naval force, Britain's hegemony on the seas was challenged not only by other European nations, but by the rising sea power of Japan and the United States. The rapid development and adoption of the ironclad was a signal of the increasing pace of the Industrial Revolution and its impact on the world's warships. The combination of the Industrial Revolution and a period of growing nationalism and imperialism around the world led to a four-decade-long naval arms race that finally brought global war in the early twentieth century.

The naval arms race began in the 1860s just as the United States was locked in bloody civil war. The American conflict demonstrated the technological advantages of rifled guns, submarines and torpedoes to the world, but its most potent lesson was the end of the wooden warship and the rise of the armoured ship. The United States was not the first nation to build ironclads, but the American experiences with monitors and other ironclads in combat during the Civil War inspired other powers to embrace the "ironclad revolution." Although some naval powers such as Russia and Sweden copied John Ericcson's design for monitors, the poor sea-keeping abilities of these essentially coastal craft meant that they were ill-suited for serious naval use. Architects in Britain, realizing this defect in the monitors, and working from their own experiments with armoured warships and turret-mounted guns, gradually developed seagoing ironclads that evolved into powerful battleships.

The evolution of the battleship was not a smooth progression, and the wreck of an early British ironclad in Bermuda is a striking example of what one prominent naval historian, David K. Brown, calls the "Age of Uncertainty." HMS *Vixen*, built in 1864 and scuttled to help block a channel in 1896, rests in 10.7 metres (35 feet) of water, her bow rising above the surface at the west end of Bermuda. Although built with iron frames and an iron hull as an "armoured gunboat," *Vixen* was covered with teak cladding because early iron hulls were easily fouled by marine growth. The hull below the waterline was also sheathed in copper to keep marine organisms from eating the wood.

Bow of HMS *Vixen* breaks the surface. James P. Delgado

The Royal Navy did not consider *Vixen*'s iron hull to be the ship's armour; instead, an armoured box at the heart of the ship protected the machinery. Iron plate used in shipbuilding in the nineteenth century was not as strong as modern metal. Brittle when cold, it had a tendency to shatter. This weakness was serious. During the age of the wooden walls, warships often blasted each other, even at point-blank range, without sinking because the thick wooden hulls had flexibility and wood is buoyant. But an iron ship, in a new age with the more powerful punch of rifled guns and exploding shells, would sink quickly once buoyancy was lost when the hull was shot through. The answer was armour, but the thick plate needed to protect a ship's machinery, guns and crew was incredibly heavy. Not only did the weight affect buoyancy, it could also overwhelm early, more inefficient steam engines. *Vixen*, therefore, is an embodiment of compromise, with just enough armour to protect her engines and boilers without making her too heavy.

Another compromise is seen in the ship's machinery. Powered by two 160-horsepower, direct-acting four-cylinder steam engines that drove a set of propellers, *Vixen* and her sister ships were the Royal Navy's first twin-screw warships. But *Vixen* was slow. The ship carried only enough coal to fuel the boilers for twelve days' operation, and so the Royal Navy compromised by equipping *Vixen* with masts and sails. Other than using her engines to manoeuvre in and out of harbour, or into battle, *Vixen* usually operated under sail. Apparatus at the stern allowed the crew to hoist the propellers out of the water, while a collapsible funnel dropped closer to the deck to allow the ship to work better with the wind. Inefficient, *Vixen* had a short life as a warship on the open seas. By 1868, she was sent to Bermuda to serve as a guard ship for the naval dockyard. With her decks cleared of superstructure and masts, she remained afloat for another twenty-three years, when she was scuttled.

Archaeologists from Brown University and Earthwatch, in cooperation with the Bermuda Maritime Museum, studied the wreck of *Vixen* between 1986 and 1988. Directed by archaeologist Richard A. Gould, the divers documented features not fully shown on the vessel's plans, such as a projecting, armoured ram at the bow. This anachronistic feature seemed to be a strange emphasis for the Royal Navy when the ship was equipped with modern, breech-loading guns that were not protected by armour. These construction choices are evidence of a period of uncertainty, or, as Gould terms it, "tactical indecision" as the Royal Navy grappled with the benefits of the new technology.

uss *Massachusetts*

By the 1890s, the various naval powers had settled into a pattern of building increasingly larger, more heavily armed warships. As experimentation and tactical indecision gave way to a school of thought that advocated classes of ships built to standard designs, the naval arms race also focussed on launching large numbers of each type, ranging from first- and second-class battleships, to armoured, protected, and unarmoured cruisers, to torpedo boats to torpedo-boat destroyers. The principal naval powers were Britain, France, Russia and Germany, but other nations, like Japan and the United States, were building more of the "modern" warships as part of a global development of naval power.

Archaeologists have studied only one warship from this period, uss *Massachusetts*. Part of the expansion of the U.S. Navy after decades of inactivity and decline following the Civil War, *Massachusetts* was an all-steel battleship laid down in 1890 as one of three sister ships along with uss *Indiana* and uss *Oregon*. These ships were the first heavy-calibre, heavily armoured warships built by the United States. The construction and fitting out of the 107-metre-long (350-foot-long), 21-metre-wide (69-foot-wide), 10,000-ton battleship took six years. Powered by vertical triple-expansion steam engines rated at 10,000 horsepower, and protected by armour as much as a

This early twentieth-century colourized postcard captures uss *Massachusetts* **in her pre-target ship glory.** Florida Department of State, Division of Historical Resources

Massachusetts **sinking after other navy ships bombarded her as a target ship.** Florida Department of State, Division of Historical Resources

half-metre (18 inches) thick, *Massachusetts* was armed with four 13-inch guns, twin-mounted in two turrets, and a secondary battery of eight 8-inch guns, mounted in pairs in turrets.

Massachusetts and her sister battleships, as well as new, smaller cruisers like USS *Olympia*, were the mainstay of American naval power as the United States attempted its own program of imperial expansion at the end of the nineteenth century. These ships fought against the Spanish navy in Cuba and the Philippines during the Spanish-American War of 1898, after the press of the day, a war-ready president and Congress reacted to the destruction of the battleship USS *Maine* in Spanish-controlled Havana Harbor on February 15, 1898. After the war, which added Puerto Rico and the Philippines to the United States as "overseas territories," the U.S. Navy continued to grow as the nation fully joined in the naval arms race, particularly under President Theodore Roosevelt, who sent the "Great White Fleet" around the world on a naval tour in 1908–1909.

By that time, the rapid pace of the naval arms race had left *Massachusetts* behind. The British all-big-gun battleship *Dreadnought*, launched in 1906, with her ten 12-inch guns and steam turbines driving the ship at a maximum speed of 21 knots, outclassed every other battleship in the world,

leading to the next phase of the race as the world's naval powers, the United States included, scrambled to build "dreadnoughts." The U.S. Navy laid up *Massachusetts* in 1906, but in 1910, the refitted and modernized battleship returned to service. Laid up again in 1914, *Massachusetts* returned to active duty in 1917 as a gunnery practice ship during World War I. She was then the oldest battleship in service for the U.S. Navy.

In 1919, the navy loaned the obsolete *Massachusetts* to the War Department for use as a target ship for coastal artillery practice. In January 1921, the navy scuttled the battleship in shallow water off Pensacola, Florida, after stripping the ship of her guns. Once the latest word in warship design, *Massachusetts*'s armour and decks shook with the impact of more than a hundred shells. A striking physical reminder of the nature of the naval arms race before World War I, *Massachusetts* is the last surviving battleship of her period. Archaeologists and volunteer divers, under the direction of Florida State underwater archaeologist Roger C. Smith, mapped the wreck in its shallow grave in 1990. Their efforts resulted in 1993 in the wreck's designation as a State Underwater Archaeological Preserve on the centennial of *Massachusetts*'s launch.

The Torpedo's Triumph

Perhaps the greatest irony of USS *Massachusetts* is that the race to build more, larger and heavily armed battleships that quickly made her obsolete was a wasted effort. The all-big-gun battleship's heyday was brief. The combination of two other late-nineteenth-century inventions would pose the greatest threat to the world's navies by the start of World War I. Those inventions were the submarine and the self-propelled torpedo. Designed in 1866 by British engineer Robert Whitehead, the new torpedoes were about 4-metre-long (14-foot-long), cigar-shaped devices driven by a compressed air engine at a speed of about 7 knots. Carrying an 8.16-kilogram (18-pound) explosive charge made from gun cotton, Whitehead's torpedoes had a range of about 600 metres (1968 feet).

The advantages of this new weapon took a few years to catch on. Whitehead sold his first two torpedoes to the Royal Navy in 1870. But the potential of the weapon and Britain's adoption of it inspired the navies of the world to follow suit. By the 1890s, flotillas of torpedo boats carrying the new weapon had joined the fleets of Great Britain and other nations. Perceptive naval officers, like French admiral Theophile Aube, argued that torpedo boats could swoop in, under the big guns of the battleships, and sink the huge ships with successive hits. Between 1890 and 1905, France built 435 first- and second-class torpedo boats, whereas Britain built 174. In response to this threat, navies adopted smaller-calibre, rapid-firing guns as part of a warship's armament and a specific class of warship: smaller, faster and highly manoeuvrable "torpedo boat destroyers," which in time became known simply as "destroyers."

The ultimate success of the self-propelled torpedo came with its marriage with the submarine. Following the success of *H.L. Hunley*, various experiments with submarines resulted in a

Holland I cuts through the waves, not under them, in this early twentieth-century view. Vancouver Maritime Museum

Holland I, now undergoing restoration, retains many original features, such as her gasoline engine, shown here.
James P. Delgado

number of craft, among them the privately built *Resurgam* (the name means "I shall rise again"), a 30-ton, steam-powered submarine invented by a British curate and launched in late November 1879. The short-lived *Resurgam* sank while under tow on February 26, 1880. Although *Resurgam* was unsuccessful, Irish-American inventor John Philip Holland was busy perfecting his submarine design. In 1876, Holland launched his first submarine, a 14-by-2-foot midget, with funding from Irish rebels living in the United States. The success of the small submarine in trials convinced the rebels of the "Fenian Brotherhood" to raise funds for a larger boat, *Fenian Ram*.

Launched in 1881, *Fenian Ram* was never used in combat; a falling-out between Holland and his backers in the Fenian Brotherhood laid her up. Other inventors in Europe tried various designs and propulsion systems, including electrically powered submarines, and successfully developed a torpedo-firing tube, merging the two weapons into a deadly instrument of war. But Holland persisted in developing his own submarine. The U.S. Navy, meanwhile, alarmed at the progress of the various foreign submarine initiatives, held three open competitions for an American submarine design that could outperform any European submarine. By 1895, Holland beat out his competitors, signing a contract to build a submarine for the U.S. Navy. Not entirely satisfied with the government's specifications, Holland raised private support to build another submarine to his own design.

That boat, "Holland VI," when launched in 1897, was the world's first completely successful submarine, armed with a single 18-inch-diameter torpedo tube, and powered by 45-horsepower gasoline engine for running on the surface and a 50-horsepower, battery-powered motor to manoeuvre when submerged. The 74-ton boat was 53 feet, 10 inches in length and 10 feet, 3 inches in diameter. "Holland VI" went on her sea trials in March 1898, just as the United States went to war with Spain. The performance of the submarine impressed observers, including Assistant Secretary of the Navy (and future president) Theodore Roosevelt. Nonetheless, navy officials insisted on a number of changes to the submarine before they accepted "Holland VI." It was not until April 11, 1900, that the navy purchased what newspapers called the "Monster War Fish" and commissioned her as uss *Holland* (ss-1).

The commissioning of uss *Holland* was more than the beginning of an American submarine fleet; it inspired the Royal Navy to follow suit. Although British admirals fumed about the submarine as "damned un-English" and a weapon "of a weaker power," they realized the threat and the need for their own fleet. Negotiating with Holland, the Royal Navy purchased the rights to build five Holland boats, and in October 1901, the first, "HM Submarine Boat No. 1," slid down the ways of the Vickers Yard at Barrow-in-Furness. *No. 1*, also known as *Holland 1*, was followed, first by other Holland boats, and later by other designs that gradually saw the submarine's size, number of torpedoes and range of operations expand. Even as the various nations competed in a naval arms race to build larger, more powerful battleships, they also raced to build more and better subs. Germany launched its first, u-1, in 1906, following the lead of France, the United States and Britain.

Ironically, it was the late-coming Germans who demonstrated the potential of the submarine in warfare during World War I. By 1914, as German U-boats hit the Royal Navy along England's shores, the pioneering Holland boats were gone. *Holland 1* was already obsolete by 1913, and in November of that year, it was sold for scrap. Partially stripped, *Holland 1* sank off Plymouth while under tow to the scrapyard.

In April 1981, a Royal Navy minesweeper rediscovered the wreck of *Holland 1* in the Solent, not far from where *Mary Rose* lay. No other Holland boat had survived, and so the Royal Navy Submarine Museum, under the direction of submarine expert Commander Richard Compton-Hall, raised *Holland 1* in September 1981. The boat was cleaned and treated to stop corrosion and

View of engine controls of *Holland I.* James P. Delgado

placed on display at the museum, but it began to suffer from additional corrosion and decay. Placed inside a tank and gradually soaked to free the steel of salt and to stop the rusting, *Holland 1* rests in her tank, now dry, awaiting final restoration.

The recovery of the submarine did not add much to our knowledge of the Holland boats, but it does provide a first-hand opportunity to appreciate the sophisticated engineering and construction—and the cramped, awful conditions—of something otherwise only imagined. Like the wreck of *H.L. Hunley*, *Holland 1* is a legacy of the beginnings of submarine warfare. The results of the nineteenth-century invention of the successful submarine and the torpedo, as seen in *Holland 1*, would be demonstrated before the world just a year after *Holland 1* was lost. The children of *Holland 1* would dramatically alter war at sea.

View forward in *Holland I*, showing the bow and torpedo tube. James P. Delgado

Gun from uss *Maine*, now at
the Washington Navy Yard,
Washington, D.C., and
the uss *Maine* Memorial,
Arlington National Cemetery.
James P. Delgado

Relics of uss *Maine*

The most famous American naval wreck of the Spanish-American War of 1898 is uss *Maine*. When the battleship sank in Havana Harbor on February 15, 1898, along with 260 of her crew, American suspicions that a Spanish mine had destroyed her precipitated a war. It was not until 1911 that an inspection of the wreck was possible. Salvagers built a cofferdam around the wreck's shallow grave and pumped it free of water. Covered with barnacles, and with human bones scattered on the decks, *Maine* was a pitiful sight. As workers cut apart the damaged portions

of the ship and stripped off the guns and hardware, an inspection board examined the wreck and decided that an internal explosion, probably from a magazine, had accidentally sunk the battleship. A 1976 reinvestigation by a team headed by Admiral Hyman Rickover determined that a coal-bunker fire had ignited the magazine. That conclusion remains controversial. Recent studies suggest that perhaps it was a Spanish mine, after all.

The cut-up portions and the intact stern section of uss *Maine* were taken out to sea for disposal. Floating

again on her own keel, the pumped-out stern section was towed and scuttled, flag flying, in deep water on March 16, 1912. The wreck site, in Havana Harbor, was dredged to remove any trace of the ship in an effort to thwart souvenir hunters. Resting off Havana, the stern of uss *Maine* has never been revisited. But other portions and relics of *Maine* can be found in Havana and in the United States. The ship's foremast, anchors and the ship's bell form a memorial to the ship and her dead crew at the U.S. National Cemetery at Arlington, outside Washington, D.C. The guns

from *Maine*'s forward turret are part of the battleship's memorial in Havana. Memorial plaques commemorating *Maine* and cast from metal taken from the wreck are found in cities throughout the United States, and a deck gun from *Maine* rests at the Washington Navy Yard in Washington, D.C. Poignant and powerful, these artifacts from the lost battleship add nothing to understanding how and why *Maine* was destroyed. But they do evoke an appreciation of how the loss of a battleship, invested with money and national pride, could start a war.

CHAPTER 7

Global Wars

THE NAVAL ARMS RACE that began at the end of the nineteenth century accelerated in the early twentieth century. The competition between Britain and France grew to include other European nations and the United States. The U.S. built a strong navy and went to war with weak Spain to seize the former colonial power's overseas possessions. Germany, Italy and Japan also built powerful navies to challenge Britain for the domination of the sea and colonial power.

The rapidly evolving technology of the period strongly influenced the naval arms race. Historian Clark G. Reynolds points out that this was a time of technological determinism, with each new weapon changing strategy. The emphasis was on size: bigger, faster battleships, with thicker armour and guns with greater range, better accuracy and bigger shells. Rival nations constantly "improved" their ships by alterations and with building programs to replace their fleets.

Quantity, rather than quality, defined naval policy. The big battleships of the early twentieth century supplanted the old wooden ships of the line as potent national symbols, but these nationalistic icons also characterized an intense international competition that would lead to war.

The end of the nineteenth century was a time of overseas expansion by nations using their industries and technologies to build navies and seize colonies and dominate nonindustrial peoples. The United States seized Puerto Rico, the Philippines and then Hawaii. France occupied Tunisia in Africa as well as the Pacific islands, Indochina (Vietnam), Cambodia and Laos. Italy annexed Eritrea. Britain established a "protectorate" over India, Egypt, Zanzibar, Bahrain and Palestine, seized the Malay Peninsula and fought a three-year war to retain South Africa. Belgium conquered the Congo. Germany built up colonies in Africa and the South Pacific. Japan, forcibly "opened" to the world in July 1853 by a squadron of U.S. Navy

FACING PAGE Constructed during Kaiser Wilhelm II's naval build-up, the panzerschiff *Odin* was the epitome of prewar German naval power. From the lithograph by H. Graf, *Odin* im Salut [*Odin* in Salute], 1899. Private collection/Bridgeman Art Library

RIGHT The Japanese were fascinated by the technological and naval prowess of the outside world. Within four decades of the arrival of the *gaijin* (foreigners) shown here at Nagasaki, Japan was one of the world's great naval powers. British Library/ Bridgeman Art Library

Japan consolidated its power through the naval defeat of China and the subjugation of the Korean Peninsula. Woodblock prints of the Sino-Japanese War depict the Japanese view of themselves as a technologically superior, British-trained Imperial Navy defeating a weaker Chinese Navy. Author's collection

warships demanding trading rights, burst into the Pacific between the 1870s and 1890s by seizing the Kurile and Bonin Islands, the Ryukyus (including Okinawa) and the Volcano Islands (including Iwo Jima). The stage was set for global conflict.

The Rise of Japan

The U.S. Navy first arrived at Tokyo Bay in 1853. At the time, Japan was a nonindustrial, feudal power. But within a decade, it fought a civil war that ended the dictatorship of the Shogunate in favour of the Meiji emperor. After 1868, Japan had an industrial base, along with an army and navy. These were used to support a program of overseas expansion and to assert Japanese control in Asian

waters, then largely dominated by European colonial powers. Japan borrowed liberally from its European rivals, both in technology and in ideas, including purchasing English warships and training its officers in Royal Navy strategies and tactics, before openly challenging them.

Japan decided to strengthen its position by conquering neighbouring Korea, nominally a vassal state of China. In turn, China, belatedly modernizing its navy with the purchase of German-built warships, was weak and an ineffective match for Japan's forces. A series of conflicts, on land and on sea, ensued, resulting in several defeats for the Chinese army and navy. Japan's thrust into Mongolia alarmed the European powers, particu-

larly Russia, which had designs of its own for that Chinese region. At the insistence of the West, Japan ended the war and its drive into China. The Treaty of Shimonoseki, signed in China and Japan in April 1895, however, forced China out of Korea, which was recognized as "independent," but in fact viewed by Japan as a vassal state, and also ceded Taiwan and the Pescadores Islands to Japan.

Now the principal Asian power in the region, Japan faced a challenge from Russia. Eager to expand its Far Eastern and Pacific power, Russia extorted a lease of the naval base at Port Arthur from China after the Sino-Japanese War and occupied portions of Manchuria. Japan countered by forging alliances with Britain and the United

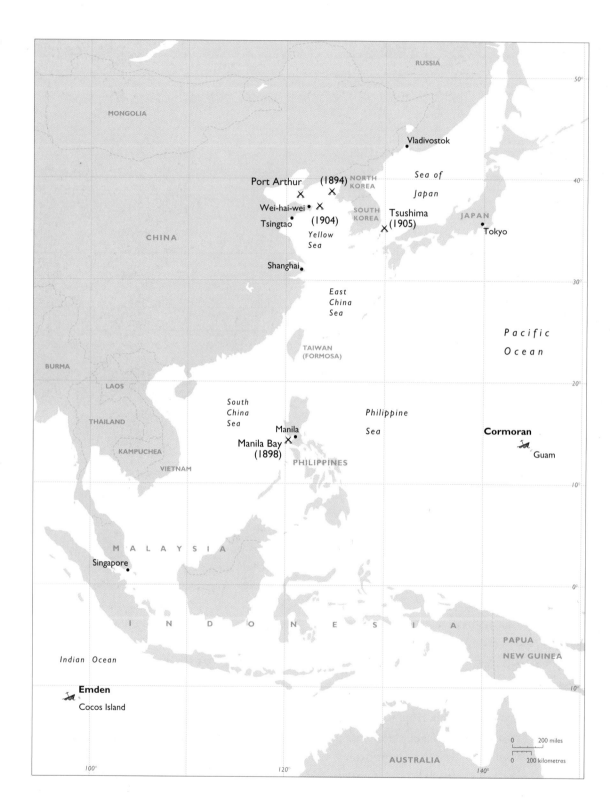

Wrecks and battles of the Far East. James P. Delgado, Eric Leinberger

戦闘艦レ
アレキサンル三世
スウオーロフ
ボロジノ
アリヨール
オスラビヤ
シソイウエリーキー
ナワリン
ナキモフ
ウシヤコフ
セニヤウィン
アプラキシン
モノマフ
ドミトリー
ドンスコイ
巡洋艦オレーグ
アウロラ
ジエムチューグ
イズムルード
スウェトラナ
海防艦アドミラル
装甲巡洋艦
スコットリント
水雷艦ブイヌイ
ルイザ
ボードイ
プロンキー
ベズウプレキ
ラ威壊沈没
ラ井ザ
ルダ
チンス

States, jointly patrolling China's Yangtze River to "assist" the Chinese government and encouraging British and American warships to use Japanese naval bases.

The naval buildup of Port Arthur and Vladivostok, Russia's naval base on Siberia's Pacific coast, and fear of a Russian advance into Korea finally induced the Japanese to attack the Russians. The Russo-Japanese War began with another surprise attack. Late in the evening of February 8, 1904, Japanese destroyers swept into Port Arthur, attacking the anchored Russian fleet with torpedoes. The next morning, the Japanese fleet bombarded the harbour, landed troops in Korea and, finally, on February 10, declared war on Russia. World opinion did not necessarily support the view that the Japanese would prevail against the power of the Russia, but in an amazingly adept display of strategy and tactics, the Imperial Japanese Navy defeated the Russians in two battles. The first, on the Yellow Sea in August 1904, defeated Russia's Pacific Squadron. The more decisive fight, in May 1905, was the first naval battle fought by "modern" big-gun battleships and cruisers.

To reinforce their fleet, the Russians dispatched warships from the Baltic. After a difficult six-month voyage of about 27,000 kilometres (17,000 miles), the Russian fleet—a collection of old and new warships—entered the Tsushima Straits between Japan and Korea on May 27. A Japanese fleet, commanded by Admiral Heihachiro Togo, was waiting. Togo's ships engaged the Russians, cutting them off as they tried to flee north. When the battle ended the following morning, eighteen Russian ships had sunk, with 4830 casualties. Togo lost three of his torpedo boats and just over a hundred men. The defeat of the Russians and the Treaty of Portsmouth in September 1905 confirmed Japan's new place as the pre-eminent Far Eastern power.

Togo's fleet smashes the Russians at Tsushima, 1905.
Author's collection

The shell-riddled wreck of the German raider *Emden* after her battle with HMAS *Sydney*.
Vancouver Maritime Museum

World War

The creation of the German empire in 1871, at the end of the Franco-Prussian War, had brought together a vast territory in the heart of Europe. It concentrated industrial resources under the control of the kaiser and his "iron chancellor," Otto von Bismarck. Bismarck's military strategy relied on the creation of a strong army. A large navy was not needed, because Germany's potential enemies were its neighbours. This policy changed after 1888 when a new kaiser, Wilhelm II, ascended the throne. Under Wilhelm's influence, the German navy expanded but without a consistent direction.

Germany's acquisition of far-flung colonies in the Pacific included the forced lease of the

Chinese harbour of Tsingtao as a naval base. The presence of the Germans in the region was a problem for the Japanese as well as the Chinese. When World War I commenced, Japan allied itself with the European powers opposed to Germany. Germany's naval forces in the Pacific were small, antiquated and no match for Japan's. With the coming of war in 1914 and Japan's entry into the conflict, German officials realized that the Pacific colonies would be lost, and the more effective battle to be fought was not in those waters. The German East Asiatic Squadron, under the command of Admiral Maximilian Reichsgraf von Spee, consisted of two heavy cruisers, three light cruisers and a few armed merchant ships.

Leaving the light cruiser *Emden* and the converted merchant cruiser *Cormoran* behind to harass British shipping—and avoid the Japanese—von Spee headed for the west coast of South America. *Emden* waged a successful, but brief campaign in the Indian Ocean, sinking twenty-three ships and bombarding Madras, India, before the Australian light cruiser HMAS *Sydney* caught up with her on November 9, 1914. In a brief, bloody engagement, *Sydney* stood out of range of *Emden*'s guns and blasted the German raider until she was a complete wreck and the captain surrendered.

As for *Cormoran*, she engaged in a short cruise, hiding from the Japanese, until finally, low on coal and provisions, she put in to Guam on December 14, 1914. An American territory, Guam was a neutral port because the United States had not yet entered the war. Unable to gain enough coal or food for a voyage to German East Africa, the captain of *Cormoran* agreed to intern his ship in Guam, a virtual prisoner, unable to fight and out of the war. By this time, German sea power in the Pacific was no more, because von Spee was dead and his fleet on the bottom of the ocean.

After leaving the Far East, von Spee had steamed west, alarming officials in Canada who thought the Germans were headed for Esquimalt, near Victoria, British Columbia. But Esquimalt, the British Empire's principal naval base on the

Pacific coast, was not the target. The Germans headed for South America. At Valparaiso, Chile, von Spee learned that a smaller, weaker British squadron was some 320 kilometres (200 miles) away. Steaming to intercept the squadron, von Spee's ships sank the cruisers *Good Hope* and *Monmouth* on November 1, 1914. There were no survivors. Aware that the British would seek revenge, von Spee headed into the Atlantic and back home to Germany. But a British fleet caught the Germans off the Falkland Islands on December 8. In the battle that followed, British fire sank four of von Spee's ships—the cruisers *Gneisenau* and *Scharnhorst* and the light cruisers *Leipzig* and *Nurnberg*. Only one ship, the light cruiser *Dresden*, escaped. Three months later, cornered by British warships in the small harbour of Juan Fernandez Island in the South Pacific, *Dresden*'s crew scuttled the ship.

With only *Cormoran* left afloat, but imprisoned on Guam's Apra Harbor, Germany's Pacific

LEFT *Emden's* **decks after the battle.** Vancouver Maritime Museum

BOTTOM *Emden* **settles on the reef at Cocos Island. Widely reported as scrapped,** *Emden* **still lies where she was destroyed in 1914. Wreckage from the raider lies in the shallows off Cocos.** Vancouver Maritime Museum

colonies were left unprotected. Japan used its superior navy—the largest in the Pacific—to seize Germany's colonies in Micronesia, including the Palaus, Marianas, Carolines and the Marshalls. The Treaty of Versailles confirmed Japan's seizures at the end of the war, expanding the Japanese empire well out into the Pacific. Now a major industrial and naval power, Japan was in a position to dominate the Pacific and Asia, much to the chagrin of its wartime allies who were eager to retain their own Far Eastern and Pacific possessions.

The war that erupted in Europe in 1914 spread not only to the Pacific, but to the Middle East, the Mediterranean, East Africa, the Indian Ocean, the North Atlantic and finally to the eastern shores of North America. On land and sea, the four-year conflict was a bloody stalemate, marked on land by horrific trench warfare, machine guns, tanks, barbed war and poison gas, and at sea by the Kaiser's navy remaining out of reach of the Royal Navy except for a few encounters.

A Royal Navy raid with two light cruisers and two flotillas of destroyers struck the Germans at Heligoland Bight, off the German coast in the North Sea, on August 28, 1914. The raiders sank two German torpedo boats, but they were then surprised, chased and repeatedly hit by fire from reinforcing German ships, including six light cruisers. The British commander called for help from the Royal Navy's First Battlecruiser Squadron, which was 64 kilometres (40 miles) away. Racing to the scene, the British battle cruisers sank three of the German ships.

The next fight, also in the North Sea at Dogger Bank, 96 kilometres (60 miles) off Britain's northeast coast, took place on January 24, 1915. A German force of four battle cruisers and a number of light cruisers and torpedo boats sortied on the evening of January 23 to sink British patrols off Dogger Bank. Instead, thanks to naval intelligence, the Royal Navy ambushed the Germans, who turned and ran for home with the Royal Navy in pursuit. The German ships were hit repeatedly, with the big guns on the battle cruisers striking their targets at incredible ranges. For example, HMS *Lion*, the British flagship, made her first hit on the German battle cruiser *Blücher* at a range of 16 kilometres (10 miles). *Blücher* was finally overwhelmed and sunk, but the other German ships escaped.

Heligoland Bight, Dogger Bank, Coronel and the Falklands battles of late 1914 and early 1915 did little to change the balance of naval power. Both the British and the German fleets remained strong and capable. They met once more in combat at the Battle of Jutland, the only full-scale encounter between the two navies. Lasting from May 31 to June 1, 1916, Jutland saw fifty-nine German ships engage ninety-nine British ships off the west coast of Denmark. The two fleets hit each other hard: the British lost fourteen ships and 6784 men, and the Germans lost twelve ships and 3099 men. A tactical draw, Jutland was a strategic victory for the Royal Navy, as the High Seas Fleet never again sailed to challenge British sea power.

Germany's principal success at sea during the war was the demonstration of the submarine as a potent new force in naval warfare. In the fifty years since *H.L. Hunley* sank USS *Housatonic* during the American Civil War, no other submarine had been successful in combat. Initial German sorties with their U-boats were not successful. The first submarine war patrol in history, by ten German submarines, sailed from Heligoland on August 6, 1914. Two of the subs were lost, one in a minefield, the other rammed and sunk by the British cruiser *Birmingham* after it was caught on the surface, unable to dive because of mechanical problems. Success came on September 5, 1914, when U-21, under the command of Lieutenant Otto Hersing, caught the light cruiser HMS *Pathfinder* about 50 kilometres (30 miles) off the Scottish coast and sank her. *Pathfinder* went down with 259 of her crew in four minutes.

The abilities of the submarine in warfare were again demonstrated, this time by the obsolete U-9, three weeks later on September 22. U-9's commander, Lieutenant Otto Weddigen, encountered the light cruisers *Aboukir*, *Hogue* and *Cressy* in the North Sea. Hitting *Aboukir* with a single torpedo, Weddigen was delighted to see the other two British ships come to her aid in the mistaken belief *Aboukir* had struck a mine. Firing two more torpedoes, U-9 hit *Hogue* and then *Cressy*, as belatedly her captain tried to flee. With five torpedoes and in less than an hour, Weddigen and U-9 sank three light

One of the most amazing propaganda pieces of the war is this British-struck medal. Ostensibly German, and celebrating the destruction of *Lusitania*, the medal was distributed to stir up anti-German sentiment.
Vancouver Maritime Museum, Michael Paris

cruisers, killing 1460 British seamen. Three weeks later, Weddigen repeated his feat when he ambushed and sank the cruiser *Hawke* on October 15. The submarine was definitely a weapon to be feared, a lesson that was demonstrated to the world when U-20 sank the liner *Lusitania* in May 1915.

German submarine successes were the major naval demonstration of the war, inspiring other nations to send increasing numbers of submarines into combat. British submarines in the Mediterranean and the Black Sea were able to challenge the Germans and their allies, the Ottoman Turks, but the submarine successes in the Mediterranean were German and Austrian, as a number of ships, including many older British battle cruisers, were lost to torpedoes and submarine-laid mines. The sinking of old warships had less effect, though, than the sinking of many merchant ships carrying valuable supplies, ordnance, armament and troops. Between May 1916 and January 1917, for example, German submarines sank 1152 ships. In the end, Germany's war against its enemies' commerce proved to be as effective as the beleaguered Confederacy's raids against Yankee shipping, striking economic blows as opposed to

The wreck of the German battle cruiser *Hindenburg* at Scapa Flow, just after the interned crew scuttled their ship along with the rest of the fleet. Vancouver Maritime Museum

The Wrecks of Scapa Flow

A concerted salvage effort after World War I scrapped nearly every one of the scuttled German High Seas Fleet from Scapa Flow. Starting in 1923 and continuing until 1939, divers raised the wrecks, which were towed away to ship-breaking yards. Today, only seven of the scuttled fleet remain on the bottom. The battleships *Konig*, *Kronprinz Wilhelm* and *Markgraf*, and the cruisers *Brummer*, *Karlsruhe*, *Koln* and *Dresden*, many of them veterans of Jutland, are also one of the last great collections of pre-dreadnought warships and a popular dive site. Other wrecks lie at Scapa Flow, including the British battleship *Royal Oak*. In a daring raid, the German submarine U-47, under the command of Lieutenant Gunther Prien, penetrated Scapa Flow and torpedoed *Royal Oak* on the evening of October 13–14, 1939. The ship sank quickly, taking 833 of her crew. British war graves laws do not allow divers to visit *Royal Oak*, which lies just 10 metres (33 feet) beneath the surface.

warship-to-warship encounters. The lessons of the submarine war of 1914–18 would be remembered and carried to greater lengths by both sides in the next world conflict.

When the war ended in November 1918, Germany's navy was intact, but bottled up not only by the Royal Navy but also by mutiny. The sailors rebelled against the orders of the High Seas Fleet commander, Admiral Franz von Hipper, who called for a last desperate, perhaps suicidal sortie against the British. Allied successes on land and sea, and a Communist revolution in Germany, forced the kaiser to abdicate on November 9, and two days later Germany signed an armistice. Under its terms, the High Seas Fleet was ordered to disarm and turn itself over to the Royal Navy. Rendezvousing on November 21, 1918, with the British Grand Fleet, the still-powerful German navy steamed into Scapa Flow in the Orkney Islands for internment, its crews virtually imprisoned aboard, as negotiators thrashed out a treaty to conclude hostilities. On June 21, 1919, responding to rumours that the British would seize his ships, the German commander, Rear Admiral Ludwig von Reuter, gave the command to scuttle the fleet. Although the British managed to beach some of the ships, fifty-nine of seventy-four German warships sank that morning.

The results of the war's end—a ravaged Europe, the increased Pacific empire of Japan, the failure of the battleship to contribute to the naval war, the success of the submarine and the development of aircraft as weapons—were portents of a terrible future. Germany's humiliation and anger would lead to the rise of Hitler and a new war within two decades. A continued emphasis on the battleship and a renewed naval arms race, Japan's fortification of its new Pacific empire, and the failure of politicians and some military leaders to assess the potential of the submarine and the airplane led to a difficult, if not near-disastrous start to World War II when Germany and Japan struck their first blows.

Wrecks and battles of the
early twentieth century in the
North Sea. James P. Delgado,
Eric Leinberger

NORWAY

Orkney Islands
Scapa Flow
**Scuttled
German
Fleet**

Jutland
(1916)

**Jutland
wrecks**

Atlantic

Ocean

SCOTLAND

DENMARK

North   Sea

HMS Pathfinder

Dogger Bank
(1915)

Blücher

Heligoland
(1914)

Wilhelmshaven

IRELAND

**HMS Aboukir
HMS Hogue
HMS Cressy**

NETHERLANDS

ENGLAND

GERMANY

BELGIUM

Holland 1

Calais

English
Channel

FRANCE

0   40 miles

0   40 kilometres

The Naval Wrecks of World War I

Although archaeologists have not studied many
warship losses from World War I, some ships are
available for examination. The survey crews of
adventure author and explorer Clive Cussler's
National Underwater and Maritime Agency have
found many World War I wrecks, including the
German cruiser *Blücher*, lost at Dogger Bank; HMS
Pathfinder, which lies in 47 metres (155 feet) of
water in the North Sea, broken into three pieces;
HMS *Hawke*, one of U-9's victims; several wrecks
from the Battle of Jutland; the British battle cruisers HMS *Invincible* and HMS *Indefatigable*; the heavy
cruiser HMS *Defence*; the destroyer HMS *Shark*; the
German heavy cruiser *Wiesbaden* and destroyers

V-48 and S-35, and several U-boats, including U-20
(which sank *Lusitania*), U-21, U-12 and UB-74.

The only World War I submarine studied by
archaeologists is the Australian AE2, lost in the
Black Sea as part of the British effort to thwart
German-Ottoman naval control at the time of the
disastrous Gallipoli Campaign. An early British-
built type "E" submarine, AE2 had a brief career,
against superior odds. Accidentally surfacing near
a Turkish gunboat on April 20, 1915, AE2 was
holed by enemy gunfire and could not dive to
escape, so her commander ordered the crew over
the side and scuttled the submarine in deep water.
Following rediscovery of the wreck by naval
enthusiast Selcuk Kolay, director of Istanbul's

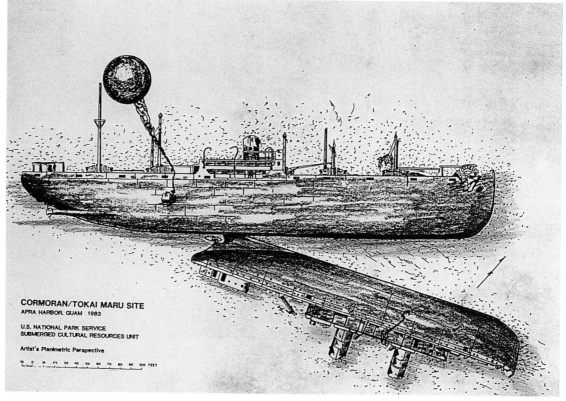

The wreck of *Cormoran* lies where the crew scuttled her in 1917. Next to the German raider is the Japanese armed transport *Tokai Maru*, a World War II loss. National Park Service

CORMORAN/TOKAI MARU SITE
APRA HARBOR, GUAM 1983

U.S. NATIONAL PARK SERVICE
SUBMERGED CULTURAL RESOURCES UNIT

Artist's Planimetric Perspective

In March 1988, Royal Navy divers working off the coast of Holland recovered the conning tower from the wreck of the British submarine E-17. The tower is identical to that of AE2, recently discovered in the Black Sea. James P. Delgado

Rahmi Koc Museum, Australian and Turkish divers, supported by the Turkish navy, dived on the wreck, which lies in 72 metres (236 feet) of water, and surveyed it in October 1998.

Another World War I wreck documented by archaeologists, in this case from the U.S. National Park Service's Submerged Cultural Resources Unit, is the armed merchant cruiser *Cormoran*. Lying on her side in 40 metres (130 feet) of water on the bottom of Apra Harbor in Guam, *Cormoran* is intact and a spectacular dive, with her open corridors and dark openings that beckon the adventurous—though lives have been lost penetrating the ship. The wreck's greater significance rests less with her allure; lying directly next to *Cormoran*, with her sternpost practically touching the German raider's keel is the Japanese merchant ship *Tokai Maru*. Sunk by an American submarine attack on January 26, 1943, *Tokai Maru* struck *Cormoran* on the way down. Divers have the unique experience, when they reach the spot where the wrecks come within a metre of each other, to reach out and rest their hands on ships lost in two world wars.

The battleship *Arkansas*, a veteran of two world wars, epitomized the battleship mentality of the world's naval powers. U.S. Naval Historical Center

Between the Wars: Battleships versus Carriers

The twenty-one years between the wars witnessed a denial by some powers, notably the United States and Japan, of the failure of the battleship to deliver on its promise as an effective weapon. The battles between the German and British fleets had not altered the progress or the outcome of the war. The United States and Japan, the two clear winners of the war, were in a position to jockey for domination of their respective spheres—in the case of Japan, the western Pacific and the Far East, and in the case of the United States, the Pacific, Atlantic and Caribbean shores of the country. Both nations built many battleships, with the Japanese outpacing American forces in the Pacific. At the same time, the Japanese introduced heavier armour and bigger guns. In 1920–21, they launched the battleships *Nagato* and *Mutsu*, the first battleships to carry 16-inch naval guns, capable of firing a shell well over the horizon at approaching ships.

The far more significant development of the period, however, was the steady adoption of submarines and aircraft into the naval arsenal. Although condemning the German U-boat war, the victorious powers built up their submarine forces. At the same time, the world's navies began to experiment with landing aircraft on ships. Naval strategists considered the airplane an auxiliary at best, with the capital ships—the strength of any navy—to be battleships. That view was challenged, as early as the end of the war, by U.S. Army Brigadier-General William "Billy" Mitchell. In 1921, using captured German warships as targets to demonstrate the vulnerability of the battleship, Mitchell sent squadrons of aircraft to attack. They quickly sank the cruiser *Frankfurt* and the battleship *Ostfriesland*, the latter in twenty-two minutes.

Although American naval officers were furious with Mitchell's staged tests, the U.S. Navy launched its first aircraft carrier, the converted collier uss *Langley*, in 1922. The next two American carriers, and their Japanese counterparts, were the result of naval arms limitation

In the space of a decade, carrier warfare adapted to combat. The principal weapon of a carrier was its aircraft. USS *Saratoga*, shown here in the 1930s and in 1944, switched from biplanes to high-performance torpedo bombers, dive bombers and fighters as a new type of naval warfare sought control of the Pacific. United States Naval Institute/Naval Historical Center

treaties. Laid down as cruisers, the carriers *Lexington* and *Saratoga*, the battle cruiser *Akagi* and the battleship *Kaga* were all completed as aircraft carriers between 1927 and 1928. Over the next decade, both countries, as well as Britain, built more carriers, though when the war in the Pacific started in 1941, Japan held the lead.

But even with these developments, the battleship reigned supreme. When the naval arms treaties negotiated between the world's naval powers expired and were not renewed in 1934, each country placed most of its assets into building more battleships. The United States took the lead, though most of its ships were not ready when it entered the war in 1941. The Germans and the Japanese built some of the world's most powerful ships of their time in the late 1930s, launching the powerful *Bismarck* in 1940, *Scharnhorst* and *Yamato* in 1941 and *Musashi* in 1942. The Japanese battleships were, on paper at least, the most powerful warships, mounting huge 18-inch naval guns, the largest ever carried on a ship and the culmination of the age of the gun afloat. But each of these ships, as well as many other battleships and cruisers, fell victim to the scorned submarine and airplane in the conflict between 1939 and 1941.

World War II

When war erupted in September 1939, following Hitler's invasion of Poland, Britain and its allies were ill-equipped to deal with the well-prepared Nazi military juggernaut that swept across Europe, taking most of the continent, including France. British expeditionary forces, trapped at Dunkirk, were saved only by a massive evacuation, under fire, by a flotilla of hastily assembled craft, including private yachts. By 1940, Britain was an island nation besieged, its continental allies gone, and its tenuous positions in the Mediterranean under attack from the Germans and their Italian allies. The situation was not good at sea; although the Royal Navy still possessed a better navy than its enemies, the German navy once again turned to its best naval weapon—the submarine—to strike at British warships and merchant shipping.

The naval ensign of the Kaiser was modified by the Nazis to become the flag of the Deutsches Kriegsmarine. This U-boat flag was captured at Kiel by a Canadian officer at the end of World War II. Vancouver Maritime Museum, Michael Paris

BOTTOM The launch of the cruiser *Prinz Eugen* was part of Hitler's prewar buildup of his naval forces. United States Naval Institute

Forced to the surface, the crew of a German U-boat surrenders during the Battle of the Atlantic. The U-boat war in the Atlantic left more wrecks on the seabed than any other action of the war.
Painting by Eric Riordan, Vancouver Maritime Museum, Mary and William Everett Family Collection,

Assisted by its colonial allies, particularly Canada, as well as the United States, which while officially neutral "loaned" warships and supplies, Britain grimly held on. The war expanded globally at the end of 1941, when Japan entered the conflict, striking at American, British and Dutch holdings and military bases in the Far East and the Pacific. During the next four years, as war raged on nearly every continent and every sea, the scale of the fighting was unprecedented in human history. Never before had so many ships fought on the water. By war's end, more warships had been lost in the six years between 1939 and 1945 than in the preceding four centuries of naval combat.

In all, 1454 warships were lost in World War II. The greatest number—402—were Japanese, followed by the ships of the Royal Navies (359),

Germany (244) and the United States (167). The greatest number of ships lost were destroyers: 545 were lost, followed by 110 cruisers, 78 battleships and battle cruisers, and 47 aircraft carriers. The global nature, and the ferocity of the conflict in some theatres is illustrated by where most of these lost warships went down: 332 sank in the Mediterranean, 227 were lost in Southeast Asia, 163 went down off Japan. In the South Pacific, 105 warships were lost, and 108 sank in the Atlantic. The greatest number of lost warships in history, these rusting hulks hold the bones of over a hundred thousand drowned sailors and marines. Although underwater explorers have found some of them, and divers regularly visit many World War II wrecks, archaeologists have studied only a handful of them.

The Wrecks of *Graf Spee* and *Bismarck*

Laid down at Wilhelmshaven in 1932, the pocket battleship *Admiral Graf Spee* was named for the heroic German admiral who had died at the Falklands in December 1914. Part of a new German naval strategy that emphasized a fast, movable force that could strike an enemy's commerce and outrun heavy battleships, *Graf Spee* was known as a *panzerschiff*, or "panther ship." Launched in June 1934, *Graf Spee* was a unique result of the naval arms limitation treaties and the German navy's desire to secretly circumvent the terms of those agreements. Limited to just 10,000 tons in weight by the treaties, the new panzerschiff actually displaced 12,000 tons. The 186-metre-long (610-foot-long), sleek hull was welded, not riveted, which saved weight, as did

aluminum in the ship's interior and superstructure. Instead of heavy steam turbines, *Graf Spee*'s engines were four diesels that gave her a speed of 28.5 knots. The weight saved by these changes allowed the Germans to add more armour to protect the ship. She also packed quite a punch: six 280-mm guns, mounted in two turrets, eight 150-mm guns, six 105-mm heavy anti-aircraft guns, eight 37-mm light anti-aircraft guns, and twelve 20-mm guns, as well as eight torpedo tubes.

With the outbreak of war, Germany's navy, the *Kriegsmarine,* was not as prepared as the *Wermacht* on land or the *Luftwaffe* in the air. The commander of the Kriegsmarine, Admiral Erich Raeder, had a force of two battleships, six cruisers, seventeen destroyers and fifty-seven U-boats in 1939—not enough to challenge Britain and France on the sea

Scuttled by her crew, *Graf Spee* **burns off the River Plate. Her shattered hulk still rests in the muddy waters.** United States Naval Institute

Nearly three miles down, the decks of *Bismarck* still bear the scars where shells ploughed through the teak. Quest Group, Ltd.

BOTTOM This wooden model of *Bismarck*, carved by a German prisoner of war at a POW camp in Lethbridge, Alberta, Canada, captures the lines and form of the famous battleship. Vancouver Maritime Museum, Michael Paris

and win a decisive battle. Instead, as Germany prepared for war, Raeder stepped up the construction of more U-boats and dispatched *Graf Spee*, under the command of *Kapitan zur See* Hans Langsdorff, to the South Atlantic, where she took up station as a commerce raider just as Hitler's troops crossed into Poland. On August 26, Langsdorff received instructions from Berlin to attack. Four days later, *Graf Spee* made her first of nine kills, sinking all those British merchant ships without a single casualty. Langsdorff was a honourable warrior of the old school.

Alarmed by the depredations of the raider, the British Admiralty ultimately dispatched twenty-three capital ships to find and sink *Graf Spee*. On December 13, 1939, the cruisers *Exeter*, *Ajax* and *Achilles* found the Germans off the mouth of the River Plate on the Uruguayan coast as she waited to attack a British convoy. Commodore Henry Harwood, in command of the three British cruisers, had gambled on Langsdorff attacking the convoy. The running fight began early in the morning. *Graf Spee*'s guns hit *Exeter* hard, killing scores of men, smashing the bridge and knocking one turret out of action. As her captain and crew fought to return fire and keep moving, more shells hit them, putting *Exeter* out of the fight with more than fifty casualties and the ship listing and on fire. Shells also hit *Ajax*, and it looked as if *Graf Spee* would finish off her attackers.

But British shells had also hit the German raider, damaging her. Nineteen British shells rained down and into *Graf Spee*, and Langsdorff decided to run for neutral Montevideo for repairs. Far from home, he could not risk further damage. The decision proved fatal for both captain and ship. Blockaded in port by the wounded, but still capable British cruisers, and with more ships arriving to reinforce Harwood, Langsdorff buried his dead, rushed through some emergency repairs and faced the reality of being trapped in a port that while neutral had no desire to shelter him except as an interned near-prisoner. Instead, on December 17, Langsdorff sailed at 6:30 P.M. and,

Anti-aircraft gun near the bow of *Bismarck*, a reminder of the futile battle the ship's crew fought against the British Swordfish that crippled her. Quest Group, Ltd.

when just three miles out of Uruguayan waters, scuttled his ship. As explosions ripped through *Graf Spee*, she sank into the shallows, burning through the night. Three days later, in his hotel room in Buenos Aires, Langsdorff lay down on his bed, on top of the flag of the old German Imperial Navy, lifted his revolver to his head and fired.

Archaeologists under the direction of Mensun Bound surveyed the wreck of *Admiral Graf Spee* in 1997, feeling their way around the shattered hulk in near-zero visibility in the muddy waters. Bound's survey documented a number of holes and missing portions of the ship, which he believes were not caused by battle damage or the scuttling, but from a clandestine British salvage of the wreck that recovered 50 tons of material—including rangefinders and the ship's primitive radar—on a mission that is still classified. Bound, working with the Uruguayan navy, raised one of *Graf Spee*'s 150-mm guns, which has been restored and now rests on display in a park.

The heavy battleship *Bismarck* lies far deeper than the shallow grave of *Admiral Graf Spee*. Laid down in 1936 to counter the threat of France's battleships, *Bismarck* was one of the first post–naval arms treaty battleships to break the 35,000-ton limit for a battleship. When launched in February 1939, the massive *Bismarck* displaced 44,734 tons. Armed with eight 330-mm turret-mounted guns, twelve 150-mm guns and sixteen 105-mm guns, *Bismarck* was a formidable—and much feared—foe. Commissioned in August 1940, *Bismarck* finally sortied in May 1941 with her smaller "little brother," the heavy cruiser *Prinz Eugen*, a near-copy of the huge battleship. Sent into the North Sea to attack British convoys, the two ships were spotted "breaking out" of the Baltic and intercepted by a British battle force off Iceland on May 24, 1941.

As the cruisers *Suffolk* and *Norfolk* spotted the German ships, the veteran battle cruiser *Hood* and the newer *Prince of Wales* moved to intercept them. *Prinz Eugen* opened fire, followed by *Bismarck*. Shells from *Prinz Eugen* hit *Hood*, and as she turned to port to bring more of her own guns to bear, a shell from *Bismarck* came in high and plunged through the

decks, deep into the British battle cruiser. The shell exploded inside a magazine, and then, in an instant, *Hood* exploded, breaking in two, her bow and stern rising out of the sea before she sank in a fireball and pillar of black smoke. Only three of the 1418 crew members survived.

Prince of Wales, hit several times by the Germans, withdrew with heavy damage. *Bismarck*, also hit and partially flooded, did not pursue. Instead, Admiral Gunther Lutjens and Kapitan Ernst Lindemann decided to run to Nazi-occupied St. Nazaire, France, for repairs and to separate from *Prinz Eugen*. The vengeful Royal Navy, however, had other plans. The brief sixteen-minute battle and the loss of *Hood* that followed was a stunning blow to British morale and pride. Prime Minister Winston Churchill, an astute politician, decided that the Royal Navy had to sink *Bismarck* at any cost. The Admiralty dispatched more ships, including the battleship *King George V*, the battle cruiser *Repulse* and the aircraft carrier *Victorious* to pursue the Germans.

While the heavy gun ships stayed clear, shadowing *Bismarck*, *Victorious* launched eight torpedo-carrying Swordfish aircraft in a late-afternoon attack on May 24. A hit from a torpedo jarred open temporarily patched holes, but *Bismarck*

shook off her pursuers and continued on. Thirty-two hours later, on May 26, a patrolling seaplane spotted the German battleship and the Royal Navy again raced to the scene to pick up the fight. Another torpedo bomber attack, from the carrier *Ark Royal*, hit *Bismarck*'s stern, damaging her steering gear and jamming the rudders. Not fully manoeuvrable and leaking oil, *Bismarck* continued to race for France.

The Royal Navy caught up with *Bismarck* on the morning of May 27. *King George V*, the battleship *Rodney*, and a force of cruisers and destroyers engaged the German battleship and within an hour had blasted *Bismarck* so heavily that the ship was a blazing shambles. Closing and firing almost point-blank into *Bismarck*, the British warships shot off 2876 rounds. As many as four hundred of these shells hit *Bismarck*. Then, burning fiercely as the crew abandoned ship, *Bismarck* began to roll over as the cruiser *Dorsetshire* fired a torpedo into her. *Bismarck* slipped beneath the waves at 10:36 A.M. Her crew, struggling in the cold, oil-thick water, called for help as the British ships closed in to pull them out of the sea. But a submarine alarm called off the rescue, and with just 110 German sailors on their decks, the British pulled away to leave

The British battle cruiser *Hood*, shown here entering Vancouver harbour, was destroyed during her battle with *Bismarck* when a shell apparently hit her magazines. Only two of her crew survived. The wreck of *Hood* lies undiscovered in the icy seas of the North Atlantic.
Vancouver Maritime Museum

Bismarck's survivors to the Atlantic. Only three of them reached home, plucked off a raft by a passing U-boat after drifting on a now-empty sea.

In June 1989, Dr. Robert D. Ballard and his team of scientists discovered the wreck of *Bismarck* some 650 kilometres (400 miles) off Brest, France, in 4600 metres (15,000 feet) of water. Using cameras towed over the wreck, Ballard's team extensively photographed and surveyed the battered hulk, which capsized as it sank. The heavy turrets, with the 330-mm guns, tore free of the ship and sank as *Bismarck* righted and then hit the slopes of an undersea mountain. An avalanche of mud carried the sunken battleship and her turrets deeper, where the ship now lies, half-buried, with any battle wounds below the waterline obscured by the mud. The survey allowed naval architects and battleship historians William H. Garzke Jr. and Robert O. Dulin Jr. to conduct a forensic analysis of *Bismarck*'s battle damage: punched holes and ploughed furrows in armoured deck steel where huge shells hit, the near-complete destruction of the battleship's superstructure. When she sank, *Bismarck* was heavily damaged, yet she demonstrates to Garzke and Dulin her "damage-resistant" construction as she "absorbed a remarkable amount of punishment before succumbing to overwhelming damage."

The discovery team was surprised, given the accounts of how many shells hit *Bismarck*, to find her relatively intact. Although British shellfire started *Bismarck* on her way to the bottom, German scuttling charges had finished the job. The testimony of *Bismarck* survivors that they had set off the charges is supported by the fact that when the ship went under, she was completely flooded. Otherwise, the pressure of the depths would have crushed a partially flooded hull and perhaps broken up the ship. Instead, she glided down to rest in darkness, her secondary armament still pointing out and up at long-gone foes, traces of her painted swastika deck identification marks symbols of the resurgent German militarism as well as the Nazi regime that sent her to sea to die.

Robotic exploration of the wreck of *Bismarck* by a team led by Dr. Robert Ballard picked out the armoured fire-control station manned during the ship's final battle by the Baron von Mullenheim-Rechburg, Third Gunnery Officer and highest-ranking survivor of *Bismarck*'s crew. Quest Group, Ltd.

uss *Arizona* cruises off
Diamond Head, Oahu,
in late 1941. Painting by
Tom Freeman. Courtesy of uss
Arizona Memorial Museum
Association

uss *Arizona*

World War II witnessed the death of the battleship. The war was a triumph for both the submarine and the aircraft carrier. There were plenty of
hints from before the war, like Billy Mitchell's
aerial bombing demonstrations. Early in the war,
on the evening of November 11–12, 1940,
Swordfish torpedo bombers from HMS *Illustrious*
swept in from the Mediterranean to attack the
Italian fleet at Taranto, sinking three battleships,
Littorio, *Conte de Cavour* and *Caio Duilio*, as well as
two fleet auxiliaries. The lesson of Taranto was
not lost on some officers in the Imperial Japanese
Navy, particularly Isoroku Yamamoto, the newly
appointed commander-in-chief of the Combined
Fleet. Yamamoto and his staff officers, particularly a
talented young commander, Minoru Genda, began
to plan for a surprise attack on the United States
Pacific Fleet at its base at Pearl Harbor, Hawaii.

Tensions between the United States and Japan
had grown in the 1930s, particularly following
Japan's invasion of China in 1937. When, in

December 1937, Japanese aircraft "accidentally"
sank the gunboat uss *Panay*, part of the international patrol on the Yalu River, both sides avoided
war. But the United States' outrage grew as the
Japanese occupied Hainan Island in the Gulf of
Tonkin and signed a pact with Nazi Germany and
fascist Italy to form the Axis powers. American
president Franklin D. Roosevelt relocated the
United States Pacific Fleet from its base at San
Diego to Pearl Harbor to counter Japanese plans.
The Japanese felt the implicit threat and accelerated their war plans. In the summer of 1941, they
seized French Indochina. When Roosevelt halted
oil sales to Japan in response, Japan's war cabinet
decided to strike throughout Southeast Asia. The
army and navy made preparations to seize the
Dutch East Indies, British Malaya and the
American Philippines after neutralizing the U.S.
Pacific Fleet.

To sink the American fleet's battleships and
carriers, Yamamoto and Genda planned to send in
waves of carrier-launched torpedo, dive-bombers

and high-altitude bombers. Even as negotiations with the American government continued, the Japanese task force of thirty-three ships sailed from northern Japan in late November. The carriers *Akagi*, *Hiryu*, *Soryu*, *Kaga*, *Zuikaku* and *Shokaku* reached their launch position, 320 kilometres (200 miles) north of Oahu, early on December 7, 1941. Two waves of fighters, dive-bombers and high-altitude bombers, took off just before dawn. At 7:55 A.M., Hawaii Time, the first wave, under Commander Mitsuo Fuchida, hit Pearl Harbor and surrounding Army, Navy and Marine Corps bases, destroying aircraft on the ground. A second wave, under Lieutenant Commander Shigekazu Shimazaki, struck again an hour later. Japanese torpedoes, bombs and projectiles slammed into ships, aircraft and men, wreaking a terrible toll. When the attack ended, eight battleships, three light cruisers, three destroyers and four auxiliary craft were sunk, capsized or damaged, 188 aircraft lost and 159 damaged, and 2403 killed or missing and 1178 wounded.

In a morning filled with explosions, fire and death, the most traumatic event was the destruction of the battleship *Arizona*. By 8:10, the ship was on fire from several hits as the crew fought the flames and incoming aircraft. Then, in a sudden blast, the ship exploded. The blast from *Arizona* blew men off the decks of surrounding ships and threw tons of debris, including parts of bodies, all over the harbour. The fury of the attack continued unabated, with *Arizona* reportedly receiving eight bomb hits as she sank. Abandoned at 10:32 A.M., *Arizona*'s burning superstructure and canted masts loomed through the smoke. Of the approximately 1177 men aboard, fewer than 200 of *Arizona*'s crew survived.

The battle-scarred and submerged remains of *Arizona* sixty years later are the focal point of a shrine erected by the people of the United States

Fires out, the bombed and burned wreck of *Arizona* settles into the mud of Pearl Harbor. National Park Service/ USS *Arizona* Memorial

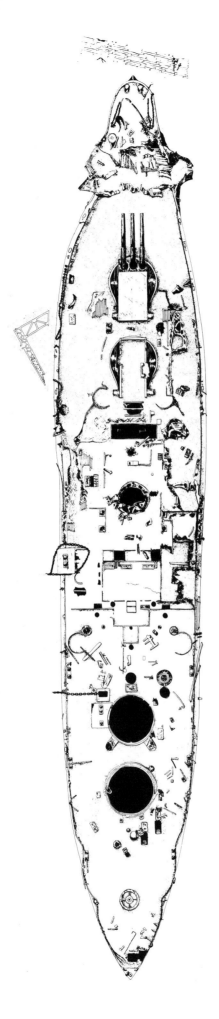

Thousands of hours of dives in the murky waters of Pearl Harbor by a joint U.S. Navy/ National Park Service team produced detailed plans of the wreck of USS Arizona.
National Park Service/Submerged Cultural Resources Unit

to honour and commemorate all American servicemen killed on December 7, 1941, particularly *Arizona*'s crew. *Arizona*'s burning bridge, listing masts and superstructure, photographed in the aftermath of the attack and her sinking, which were emblazoned on the front pages of newspapers across the land, epitomized "Pearl Harbor" to the nation and form one of the best-known images of World War II in the Pacific. *Arizona* and the *Arizona* Memorial have become the major shrine and point of remembrance for both Americans and foreign visitors, including large numbers of Japanese.

National Park Service archaeologists from the Submerged Cultural Resources Unit began to survey and study the wreck of *Arizona* in 1983, which lies intact, unsalvaged and resting in the silt of Pearl Harbor. Work since then has examined the exterior of the sunken battleship and most recently the interior compartments in the aft sections. Slightly listed to port, *Arizona*'s decks lie just beneath the surface, with portions of the ship rising above the water. The hull just aft of the bow is distorted and cracked from gunwale to keel on the port side and nearly so on the starboard side, indicating the bow either was nearly blown off or has since settled and cracked. The armoured deck forward was blown both upward and forward by the force of the blast—tons of powder blasting from deep within the battleship's twisted portions of the deck, folding it together near the bow. But the wooden decks in this area are intact, with snaking lines of fire hoses still in place. They lie where they were dropped when the blast swept the decks and killed the ship's crew.

Near here, the ship's No. 1 turret, with its gun barrels pointed down, rests inside a collapsed crater formed by the explosion. Archaeologists were surprised to find it when they made the first dives in 1983, because historical accounts suggested that every bit of *Arizona*'s armament was salvaged in 1942. Popular belief, beginning during the war, also suggested that a bomb going down her stack and into the boilers sank *Arizona*. But

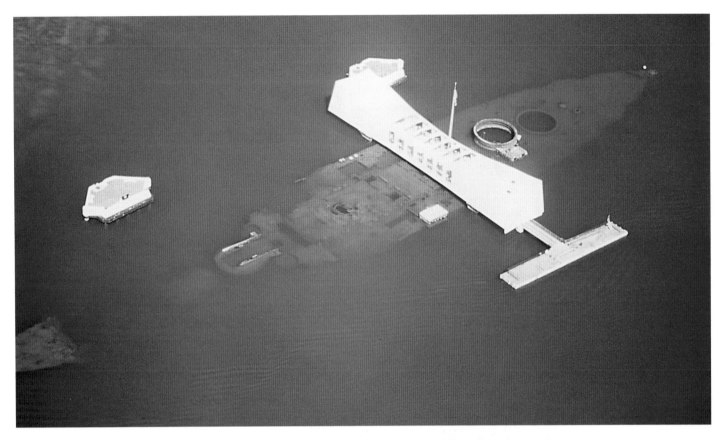

the stack gratings are intact. The fatal shell, like *Bismarck*'s hit on *Hood*, went through the deck. Based on the archaeological analysis and historical research in Japan, it is now clear that a huge aerial bomb, modified from a Japanese 16-inch shell, hit the deck near the No. 2 turret and plunged down to erupt in the forward magazine.

Perhaps the most amazing discovery on *Arizona* is not the extent of the destruction, but what remains. Along the hull, a number of portholes are intact, with the glass and the interior blast covers in place, trapping air, water and oil inside them. Dives inside the wreck, moving through silt-clogged corridors and into compartments and cabins discovered furniture lying on decks, clothes hangars in lockers, and unbroken light bulbs. And yet in the midst of all this, the steel of the wreck is crumbling on the inside, and a casual brush against a bulkhead sends pieces of it falling into the silt.

ABOVE This aerial view of the wreck of *Arizona* shows the sunken ship's relationship to the *Arizona* Memorial. National Park Service/USS *Arizona* Memorial

LEFT Air and oily water trapped inside a deadlight on the hull of USS *Arizona*. National Park Service/Submerged Cultural Resources Unit

The super battleships *Yamato*, *Musashi* and others were rushed to completion by the Imperial Japanese Navy as the war progressed. Most of them, as well as Japan's merchant fleet, ended up at the bottom of the sea by **August 1945.** U.S. Naval Historical Center

The Wrecks of Guadalcanal and Midway

The end of the battleship was underscored again when Japanese aircraft sinking the British battle cruisers *Repulse* and *Prince of Wales* off Malaya on December 10, 1941. Japan's early victories in the Pacific War, including Pearl Harbor, the fall of the Philippines and the fall of Hong Kong and Singapore expanded the Japanese empire to what proved to be untenable limits. The high-water mark was reached by mid-1942. In June that year, Japanese troops began construction of an airfield on Guadalcanal, in the recently occupied British Solomon Islands Protectorate in what would be Japan's farthest southeastward expansion in the Pacific. The Japanese thrust was met by the United States, Australia and New Zealand in a bloody six-month campaign on the island, in the skies and on the sea.

A number of naval engagements, skirmishes and battles sank nearly fifty ships off Guadalcanal and nearby islands. The two most famous engagements took place on August 8–9, 1942, the Battle of Savo Island, and November 12–16, 1942, the Battle of Guadalcanal. The waters surrounding the islands were named "Ironbottom Sound" because of the many ships sent to the bottom during these battles.

The naval battle on the evening of November 13, 1942, was one of the most ferocious. American cruisers and Japanese battleships, joined by destroyers, pounded each other, with tremendous cost in lives. In all, over twenty-one hundred sailors and marines were killed, and nearly forty-five hundred tons of steel sent to the depths of Ironbottom Sound. The fighting was wild and in some ways, according to historian James Grace, reminiscent of an earlier age as technological advantages, such as radar, were abandoned. A planned American ambush of the Japanese force went awry as both fleets stumbled into each other in the dark. The battle that followed, argues Grace, exemplified Nelson's adage that "No captain can do

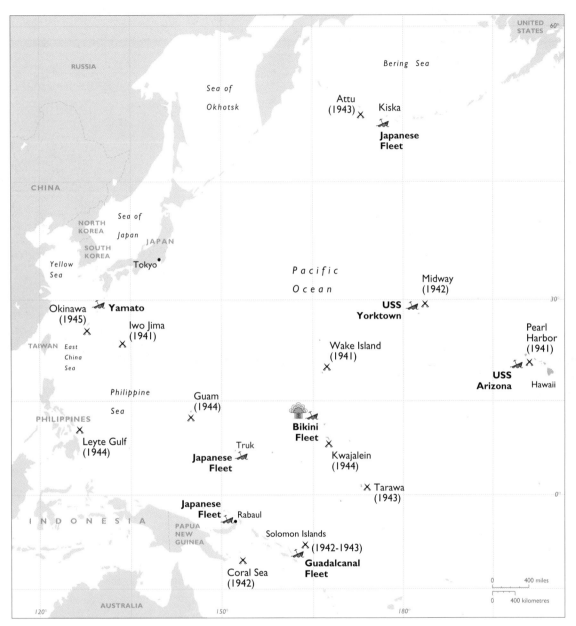

Wrecks and battles of the Pacific, 1941 to 1946.
James P. Delgado, Eric Leinberger

very wrong if he places his ship alongside that of an enemy." Facing battleships that outgunned them, and at considerable cost, the captains of the American cruisers and destroyers forced the Japanese to withdraw by engaging the enemy at point-blank range. In this way, says Grace, "the Americans won a fight that, by all odds, they should have lost."

In the fall of 1991, a team led by Robert D. Ballard led a team of scientists, U.S. Navy technicians and specialists, and American, Japanese and Australian veterans of the battles to survey the waters of Ironbottom Sound. They found ten wrecks and returned in the summer of 1992, to look for more and photographically document them with robotic cameras and the submersible *Sea Cliff*. Warship specialist Charles Haberlein of the U.S. Naval Historical Center in Washington, D.C., made the identifications of the sunken ships.

In all, thirteen wrecks were studied. They included the Australian heavy cruiser HMAS *Canberra*, and the U.S. cruiser *Quincy*, both sunk in

uss *Yorktown*, intact and nearly three miles below where she sank during the Battle of Midway. Illustration by Ken Marschall, © Madison Publishing Inc. from *Return to Midway*, a National Geographic Society/Madison Press Book

the Battle of Savo Island, and the Japanese battleship *Kirishima*, the U.S. cruiser *Atlanta*, the Japanese destroyers *Ayanami* and *Yudachi*, and the U.S. destroyers *Laffey*, *Cushing*, *Barton*, *Monssen* and a wreck that was either the destroyer *Little* or *Gregory*, still unidentified, all sunk during the Battle of Guadalcanal. Ballard also rediscovered the wreck of the U.S. cruiser *Northampton*, sunk during the Battle of Tassafaronga on November 30, 1942, and the U.S. destroyer *DeHaven*, sunk by Japanese bombers on February 1, 1943, as the campaign for Guadalcanal ended.

The survey pinpointed where the lost warships had sunk, often at great distances from where naval records had placed the ships, as would be expected when ships sink in fierce

battle, at times in the dark and with great confusion. The Guadalcanal surveys also provided a more detailed understanding of battle damage, including shell hits, torpedo damage and evidence of magazine explosions that tore some huge ships apart. uss *Quincy* had its bow blown off, and its stern area has partially collapsed. uss *Monssen*, hit by at least thirty-three shells, lost its superstructure, and uss *Barton* was blown in half by a torpedo hit. The survey only discovered the destroyer's bow. The Japanese *Kirishima* lies in pieces and upside down, the bow torn apart by a catastrophic magazine explosion.

The majority of the wrecks lay in waters ranging from 300 to 1110 metres (about 1000 to 3600 feet) deep. Other wrecks lie in shallower waters, like the cruiser *Atlanta* in 130 metres (425 feet). A joint American and Australian technical dive team led by Terrence Tysall and Kevin Denlay photographed several wrecks in November 1995, focussing on *Atlanta* and the U.S. destroyer *Aaron Ward*, which was sunk on April 7, 1943, in 74 metres (240 feet) of water and rediscovered by diver Brian Bailey in September 1994. They also visited the U.S. oiler *Kanawa*, the bow of the U.S. battleship *Minneapolis*, blown off by a torpedo (the battleship survived), the U.S. attack transports *Calhoun* and *John Penn*, the Japanese transports *Asumassan Maru, Sasako Maru, Ruaniu*, the Japanese submarine I-123, the New Zealand corvette *Moa*, the U.S. tug *Seminole*, landing barges and submerged aircraft, including a B-17 "Flying Fortress," and Japanese and American fighters and Kawanishi flying boats.

Their discoveries, along with those of Ballard's team, show that Ironbottom Sound is an untouched underwater battlefield where lost warriors lie exactly where they fell. For Ballard, it is "the literal evidence of war—shell holes in blasted metal, guns and torpedo tubes still trained as if to fire or pointing crazily askew, the wrecked bridge where a captain or an admiral breathed his last" that makes these lost warships so special. This is a theme Ballard returned to in 1998, when his team searched the depths off Midway Island to find the lost ships from the pivotal battle of the war in the Pacific. Surveying in waters more than 4,000 metres (13,000 feet) deep, Ballard sought the carriers *Yorktown, Kaga, Akagi, Hiryu* and *Soryu* and the destroyer *Hammann*. The two-day clash between the Japanese and American fleets, on June 4–6, 1942, was a clear demonstration of the ultimate triumph of the aircraft carrier. U.S. carrier aircraft sank the Japanese carriers, avenging Pearl Harbor, while Japanese aircraft crippled *Yorktown* and allowed the submarine I-168 to find and sink her and one of her escorting destroyers.

The robotic exploration of *Yorktown* revealed her lying intact, listing to starboard. Anti-aircraft guns still point skyward, and torpedo-blast holes,

Yamato explodes and sinks on April 7, 1945. Forty years later, deep ocean submersibles rediscovered the shattered wreck in 335 metres (1100 feet) of water. Most recently, salvors recovered artifacts from the wreck for the Yokohama Maritime Museum. U.S. Naval Historical Center.

The Japanese submarine
RO-65's blasted hulk rests deep
in the dark Aleutian waters
off Kiska. National Park Service,
Larry Murphy

probably from aerial torpedoes sent into her by
planes from the carrier *Kaga*, join bomb holes in
the decks as reminders of the Battle of Midway.
Amazingly well preserved, the lost carrier's
wooden decks are intact, and the paint on her hull,
except where it was scarred by fire, looks fresh.
Examining images of *Yorktown*, it is easy to imagine
that she sank yesterday, not six decades ago.

The Lost Ships of World War II

The defeat of Japan, Italy and Germany on land
and sea left a number of battlefields. Monuments
and cemeteries mark those on land. Those on the
sea—the Battle of the Atlantic, the Coral Sea,
Leyte, the waters off Okinawa and Iwo Jima, for
example—are unmarked patches of ocean. In
many ways, the scale of World War II at sea is so
vast, and the losses so great, that a separate volume just on the lost warships of that conflict could
be written.

Divers and underwater explorers, not archaeologists, have discovered many of those lost warships. Archaeologists and diver-historians have
surveyed some of them. They include lost
Japanese warships and transports in the Marshalls,
particularly at Kwajalein, in Palau, Rabaul, Saipan
and Guam. In the Pacific, a great deal of this work
has been accomplished by the U.S. National Park

Service's Submerged Cultural Resources Unit,
including the examination of the sunken wrecks
off Kiska and Attu in Alaska's Aleutians, a distant
and bitterly cold battlefield in 1942.

Divers have also explored some of the lost
ships from the Normandy landings off the French
coast, the beginning of the end for Hitler's *Festung
Europa*, or "Fortress Europe," while others have
discovered wartime wrecks off the Mediterranean
coasts of France, Italy, Greece and Malta. The
allure of these wrecks lies not only in their rela-
tive intactness, but also in the immediacy of the
events of the war. Many of these lost warships are
graves of men whose wives, children and siblings
are still among us to lament their loss. Veterans
still live among us. Perhaps it is too soon to sci-
entifically examine these lost warships. The pas-
sions of the war echo through the years and, in
many ways, remain with us still.

The Wrecks of Truk

Truk Lagoon, a 64-kilometre (40-mile) diameter atoll comprising 245 islands in the central Pacific, is an exceptional natural anchorage. Truk, a German colony, was ceded to Japan after World War I and developed as a base for the Imperial Japanese Navy's Fourth Fleet. Known as the Japanese Pearl Harbor, Truk was fortified after 1940, when small repair and refuelling facilities and a seaplane base were built. Fortifications were added after January 1944 in anticipation of an Allied invasion, and Imperial Japanese Army troops arrived to garrison the islands. During the war, American radio broadcasts referred to Truk as the "impregnable bastion of the Pacific."

Truk was attacked on February 16–17 and April 29–30, 1944, by the U.S. Navy, and on June 16, 1945, by the Royal Navy. As well, American bombing raids, by B-24 and B-29 aircraft, also hit Truk. In 1944, American military planners considered dropping the atomic bomb, then under development, on Truk's anchorage, but the plan was never acted on. After the war, the U.S. Strategic Bombing Survey concluded that the strikes against Truk had destroyed more than 416 aircraft and sunk at least forty-three major ships, including three light cruisers, four destroyers, a seaplane tender, a patrol vessel and numerous small craft. Many of the atoll's airstrips and naval facilities were crippled or destroyed. Truk had been neutralized as an extension of Japanese military power in the Pacific.

The carrier raids and bombing of Truk left a substantial submerged material record in the form of sunken vessels, aircraft and equipment. Truk Lagoon is today considered one of the world's top diving attractions because of its large number of World War II shipwrecks. Some wrecks protrude above the water, while others lie deep in the lagoon. The deep-water wrecks have an incredible array of untouched material, including cargoes, armament, ordnance and human remains, though a concerted effort by Japanese groups has recovered many remains for cremation in funeral services ashore.

Surveys and photographic documentation of the wrecks at Truk have been undertaken by diving researchers and historians, and in 1992, the U.S. National Park Service's Submerged Cultural Resources Unit, at the request of the government of Truk, documented the impact of dynamite fishing and sport diving on a number of sites. A number of documentary films, books and magazine articles have greatly contributed to Truk's fame and popularity.

Howitzers on the deck of Nippo Maru. Dan E. Bailey

The Nuclear Age

THE AFTERMATH OF World War II left the United States as the world's major naval power. The era of the battleship was over, even though the United States had built a group of powerful *Iowa*-class battleships armed with 16-inch guns—and accepted the Japanese surrender on the deck of one of them, the battleship *Missouri*. But as the new global power, the United States faced a series of challenges. The first was the role of nuclear weapons. Did the atomic bomb make navies obsolete? Was there a role for the navy in the age of aircraft and missile-delivered nuclear weapons?

The second challenge came from a wartime ally, the Soviet Union. The Cold War that lasted from 1946 until 1990 witnessed a new naval arms race and regional conflicts throughout the world. The development of the nuclear-powered submarine in the late 1950s, and the capability of those submarines to deliver massive nuclear strikes, made them the ultimate naval weapon, surpassing even the aircraft carrier as the new capital ships.

Lost warships from the last half of the twentieth century now join other naval wrecks of the past four millennia. They include Korean War,

Vietnam and Arab-Israeli conflict wrecks, and British and Argentine combat losses, including the Exocet missile–devastated HMS *Sheffield* and the former American cruiser *Admiral Belgrano*, lost to submarine attack. There are also a handful of nuclear submarine losses, ranging from early American fleet boats like USS *Thresher* and *Scorpion*, the Soviet *Komsomolets* and the recently lost Russian submarine *Kursk*. They are all reminders that the sea remains our greatest battlefield and our largest graveyard.

Archaeologists are just beginning to study World War II wrecks, and as part of those studies, they have examined the first wrecks of the nuclear age and the beginnings of the Cold War.

The Sunken Fleet of Bikini Atoll

In July 1946, the United States conducted the first nuclear weapons tests in the world in the middle of the Pacific Ocean. Bikini Atoll, about 7200 kilometres (4500 miles) west of San Francisco, was the setting for "Operation Crossroads," a massive military effort to assess the effects of the atomic bomb on warships. In all, a fleet of 242 ships, 95 of them atomic targets, 220 tons of test equipment, several thousand test animals, and 43,000 military personnel and scientists were assembled within a matter of months and at a cost of hundreds of millions of dollars. In a spectacular display, two bombs were detonated at Bikini, sinking twenty-two ships, and irradiating seventy-three others. Bikini, with its 167-person native population evacuated for the tests, was contaminated with fallout. The United States used the atoll between 1946 and 1958 for dozens of more-powerful nuclear tests, including a 15-megaton surface blast, "Bravo," in March 1954. Bikini is now abandoned, its shores littered with rusting machinery and cables, its islands covered by thick concrete bunkers. The bottom of Bikini's lagoon is pocked with nuclear blast craters and the sunken ships of Operation Crossroads.

In 1989 and 1990, archaeologists from the National Park Service's Submerged Cultural

FACING PAGE The massive carrier *Saratoga*, her 270-metre (888-foot) length covered with test equipment, sails from San Francisco for Bikini Atoll in 1946. San Francisco Maritime National Historic Park

RIGHT The 20-kiloton Baker blast erupts from Bikini Lagoon on July 25, 1946, dwarfing *Saratoga* as she is swamped by a nuclear tidal wave. U.S. Naval Historical Center

The crew of USS *Shangri La* practise their drill for the first atomic bomb test at Bikini. Exposed on deck, miles away from the blast, sailors reported that they could see the bones in their arms through closed eyes when the Able test blast lit the skies on **July 1, 1946.** U.S. Naval Historical Center

RIGHT As the mushroom cloud from the Able test climbs into the sky, sailors aboard the cruiser USS *Fall River* witness the dawn of a new age in warfare. U.S. Naval Historical Center

Resources Unit returned to Bikini with the U.S. Navy to relocate the sunken fleet of Operation Crossroads and conduct a detailed study of the ships. The team surveyed eleven vessels during two field seasons, including the wreck of the former German cruiser *Prinz Eugen*, a Crossroads target vessel, at nearby Kwajalein Atoll. The majority of the fieldwork at Bikini focussed on the aircraft carrier *Saratoga*. Other vessels surveyed to varying degrees were the battleships *Arkansas* and *Nagato*, the attack transports *Gilliam* and *Carlisle*, the submarines *Apogon* and *Pilotfish*, the yard oiler YO-160, the floating dry dock ARDC-13 and the landing craft LCT-1175. A survey in 1999 focussed on the wreck of the destroyer *Anderson*.

The surveys documented extensive nuclear damage to the vessels. Formerly classified military accounts from 1946 report that the second atomic test, "Baker" (July 25, 1946), placed the target ships around a 20-kiloton bomb lowered 27 metres

(90 feet) below the surface. When Baker erupted from the lagoon, a mass of steam and water mounded up into a "spray dome" that climbed at a rate of 2500 feet per second into a gigantic column. The centre of the 975-foot-thick column was a nearly hollow void of superheated steam that rose faster than the more solid 300-foot-thick water sides, climbing 11,000 feet per second and acting as a chimney for the hot gases of the fireball. The gases, mixed with excavated lagoon bottom and radioactive materials, formed a cauliflower-shaped mushroom cloud atop the column. When the column collapsed, two million

tons of water and sand fell back on the target ships. The battleship *Arkansas*, caught in the upward blast, was crushed, capsized and sunk in less than a second. Archaeological dives in 1990 documented that two-thirds of the breadth of the hull was crushed nearly flat, leaving only a deformed, but intact port side. The superstructure and turrets above the main deck were hammered into the coral bottom, leaving a 1.8-metre (6-foot) gap between deck and seabed.

The Baker blast also created "atomic tidal waves" waves that smashed into the ships. The first wave, a 28.7-metre (94-foot) wall of radioactive water, lifted and smashed into *Saratoga*. The carrier's hull was twisted, the flight deck partially collapsed, and *Saratoga* sank within seven and a half hours, slowly settling by the stern. Archaeological dives documented a 20-foot-deep, 7-foot-wide and 200-foot-long dent in the flight deck; heavy "washboarding" along the starboard side, which faced the blast; and the rupture and twisting of every starboard hatch and deadlight. The attack transport *Gilliam*, lost in the first "Able" test (July 1, 1946), was caught in the incandescent fireball of a 20-kiloton airburst and battered down into the water by the shock wave and sank in seventy-nine seconds. *Gilliam*'s superstructure was swept away, and the intense heat softened and

LEFT The captured Japanese battleship *Nagato*, brought to Bikini by the U.S. Navy, was a bomb-ravaged hulk kept afloat by salvage ships as crews readied the vessel for sinking in the atomic bomb tests. Los Alamos National Laboratory

BOTTOM Bikinian divers, working with a U.S. National Park Service team, map test equipment scattered on the deck of uss *Saratoga*. National Park Service, Larry Murphy

Blasted by the bomb and sunk loaded with test equipment, ship's stores and armament, the ships of Bikini are a ghost fleet from the dawn of the nuclear age. The emergency radio room inside USS *Saratoga* is filled with equipment more than fifty years after the blast, while aircraft like this SB2C "Helldiver" (below) line the hangar. National Park Service, Larry Murphy

warped the hull into a collapsed, twisted shape that flows into the hull's interior.

In addition to documenting gross physical damage to the ships, the team also measured residual radiation, which was negligible (fewer than 10 microcuries), assessed unexploded convention (non-nuclear) ordnance left aboard the ships for the tests and documented the presence of test instruments for measuring blast, heat and radiation effects. Some instruments were found that had not previously been recovered, despite post-test salvage dives on the ships. The presence

of these instruments was ascribed to fears of radioactive contamination immediately after the tests.

During the Baker test, a boiling mass of radioactive water and steam penetrated nearly every target ship left afloat and contaminated the lagoon water. Radioactive material adhered to wooden decks and paint, rust and grease. For weeks after the tests, the U.S. Navy tried to wash off the fallout with water and lye, and sent crews aboard contaminated ships to scrub off paint, rust and scale with long-handled brushes, holystones and any other "available means," but they could not remove the radiation. In August, Bikini was abandoned, and badly damaged, contaminated ships were sunk. All but a handful of the Crossroads target ships were scuttled after being placed off-limits at various naval bases.

The sunken ships of Bikini Atoll are evocative artifacts of the world at a crossroads. The archaeological team's reason for diving the shipwrecks of Bikini Atoll was not merely to satisfy historical curiosity about these vessels and their fate. The

Past and present merge on the ocean floor. The 5-inch/51-calibre anti-aircraft guns on the port side of the battleship USS *Arkansas*, once the setting of a seagoing yarn session, now rest 55 metres (180 feet) beneath the sea. U.S. Naval Historical Center/National Park Service, Larry Murphy

team looked at the wrecks as artifacts, then applied an archaeological perspective not only to assess the historical record, but also to compare that record with the basic patterns of human behaviour.

The presence of two badly battered Japanese ships on the bottom are material statements of domination and power. The ships, seized by the United States at the end of World War II, were taken to Bikini for symbolic reasons and deliberately placed in proximity to each test detonation to ensure that they sank. The selection of the battleship *Nagato* was particularly significant: it had been the flagship of the Imperial Japanese Navy and the site of that navy's planning for the attack on Pearl Harbor.

Social anthropologist Hugh Gusterson argues that nuclear weapons tests were a rite of passage for the scientists who built the bombs. They were an important means by which the scientists simulated "human knowledge and control over events that otherwise seem mysterious and uncontrollable." The test instruments found aboard the ships in 1989 and 1990 reflect both the fear of contamination that brought about the decision to abandon the project and the fear of being unable to control what had happened. After thousands of years of war, we remain as driven by our technology and our aggression as we did when humans first took to the sea and fought with clubs and knives.

World War II and the dawn of the nuclear age finally ended the age of the big gun. As obsolete as the ram, Greek fire, the wooden walls and cannon, the massive 16-inch guns of the Japanese battleship *Nagato* serve as a perch for scientists preparing the ship for sinking at Bikini Atoll in 1946. Today, the silent guns, resting beneath the waves, are a reminder that the sea is our greatest museum of human sacrifice, bravery and folly. Los Alamos National Laboratory

List of Maps

Bibliography

A vast amount of published information is available on the archaeology of ships of war, most of it in articles in various professional journals such as the *International Journal of Nautical Archaeology*, *Historical Archaeology,* the annual underwater archaeology proceedings for the Society for Historical Archaeology, *British Archaeological Reports,* the newsletter of the Institute for Nautical Archaeology, *Dossiers d'Archéologie, Maritime Archaeology Newsletter from Roskilde, The Mariner's Mirror, The American Neptune, Archeologia Subaquea, Australian Institute for Maritime Archaeology Bulletin* and *Archaeonautica,* as well as more popular journals such as *Archaeology, Naval History, National Geographic* and *Sea Classics.*

A separate volume could be filled with citations for articles about the archaeology of guns, ships of war and technical treatises, particularly on the debate over the form and design of ancient warships. I strongly recommend John Sherwood Illsley's *An Indexed Bibliography of Underwater Archaeology and Related Topics* (Oswestry, Shropshire: Anthony Nelson, 1996), which unfortunately cuts off at 1994 but otherwise provides a comprehensive, 360-page bibliography. I provide this reference rather than fill pages with citations for the hundreds of articles consulted for this book. Similarly, I have only cited books here that were particularly helpful or were used in the preparation of *Lost Warships.*

Books

Ahlstrom, Christian. *Looking for Leads: Shipwrecks of the Past Revealed by Contemporary Documents and the Archaeological Record*. Helsinki: Finnish Academy of Science and Letters, 1997.

Akerlund, Harald. *Nydamskeppen: En Studie Tidig Skandinavisk Skeppsbyggnadskonst*. Goteborg: Elanders Boktryckeri Aktiebolag, 1963.

Bailey, Dan E. *WWII Wrecks of the Kwajalein and Truk Lagoons*. Redding, California: North Valley Diver Publications, 1989.

Bailey, Dan E. *WWII Wrecks of the Truk Lagoon*. Redding, California: North Valley Diver Publications, 2000.

Ballard, Robert D., and Rick Archbold. *The Discovery of the Bismarck*. New York: Madison Press, 1990.

Ballard, Robert D., and Rick Archbold. *The Lost Ships of Guadalcanal*. New York: Madison Press, 1993.

Ballard, Robert D., and Rick Archbold. *Return to Midway*. Washington and Toronto: National Geographic Books/Madison Press, 1999.

Bass, George F., ed. *A History of Seafaring Based on Underwater Archaeology*. New York: Walker and Company, 1972.

Bass, George F., ed. *Ships and Shipwrecks of the Americas*. London and New York: Thames and Hudson, 1988.

Bassi, Maria Teresa Parker de. *Kreuzer Dresden: Odyssee ohne Wiederkehr*. Herford: Koehlers Verlagsgesellschaft mbH, 1993.

Bearss, Edwin C. *Hardluck Ironclad: The Sinking and Salvage of the Cairo*. Rev. Baton Rouge: Louisiana University Press, 1980.

Bound, Mensun, ed. *The Archaeology of Ships of War*. Oswestry, Shropshire, England: Anthony Nelson, 1995.

Bound, Mensun, ed. *Excavating Ships of War*. Oswestry, Shropshire, England: Anthony Nelson, 1998.

Bound, Mensun. *Lost Ships: The Discovery and Exploration of the Ocean's Sunken Treasures*. New York: Simon & Schuster, 1998.

Brogger, A. W., and Haakon Shetelig. *The Viking Ships*. Oslo: Dreyers Forlag, 1971.

Brown, David. *Warship Losses of World War II*. London: Arms and Armour Press, 1990.

Bruce, Anthony, and William Cogar. *An Encyclopedia of Naval History*. New York: Checkmark Books, 1999.

Cain, Emily. *Ghost Ships: Hamilton and Scourge, Historical Treasures from the War of 1812*. New York and Toronto: Beaufort Books, 1983.

Casson, Lionel. *The Ancient Mariners: Seafarers and Seafighters of the Mediterranean in Ancient Times*. Princeton: Princeton University Press, 1991.

Casson, Lionel. *Ships and Seafaring in Ancient Times*. London: British Museum Press, 1994.

Casson, Lionel, and J. Richard Steffy. *The Athlit Ram*. College Station: Texas A & M University Press, 1991.

Christensen, Arne Emil, ed. *The Earliest Ships: The Evolution of Boats into Ships*. London: Conway Maritime Press, 1996.

Compton-Hall, Richard. *The Submarine Pioneers*. Phoenix Mill, Gloucestershire: Sutton Publishing, 1999.

Crisman, Kevin. *The Eagle: An American Brig on Lake Champlain During the War of 1812*. Annapolis and Shelburne, Vermont: Naval Institute Press, 1987.

Crumlin-Pedersen, Ole. *Viking Age Ships and Shipbuilding in Hedeby / Haithabu and Schleswig*. Shleswig and Roskilde: Viking Ship Museum, 1997.

Cussler, Clive, and Craig Dirgo. *The Sea Hunters: True Adventures with Famous Shipwrecks*. New York: Simon & Schuster, 1996.

Delgado, James P., ed. *British Museum Encyclopaedia of Underwater and Maritime Archaeology*. London: British Museum Press, 1997.

Delgado, James P. *Ghost Fleet: The Sunken Ships of Bikini Atoll*. Honolulu: University of Hawaii Press, 1997.

Delgado, James P., Daniel J. Lenihan, and Larry E. Murphy. *The Archaeology of the Atomic Bomb: A Submerged Cultural Resources Assessment of the Sunken Fleet of Operation Crossroads at Bikini and Kwajalein Lagoons*. Santa Fe: National Park Service, 1991.

Doumas, Christos. *The Wall-Paintings of Thera*. Athens: Thera Foundation–Petros M. Nomikos, 1992.

Forward, Laura, and Ellen Blue Phillips. *Napoleon's Lost Fleet: Bonaparte, Nelson and the Battle of the Nile*. New York: Roundtable Press, 1999.

Friel, Ian. *The Good Ship: Ships, Shipbuilding and Technology in England, 1200–1520*. Baltimore, Maryland: Johns Hopkins University Press, 1995.

Frost, Honor et al. *Lilybaeum: Atti Della Accademia Nazionale Dei Lincei, Anno CCCLXXXIII, Notizie Deglie Scavi Di Antichita*. Vol. 30, supp. Rome: Accademia Nazionale Dei Lincei, 1981.

Gardiner, Robert, ed. *The Line of Battle: The Sailing Warship, 1650–1840*. London: Conway Maritime Press, 1992.

George, James L. *History of Warships: From Ancient Times to the Twenty-First Century*. Annapolis: Naval Institute Press, 1998.

George, S. G. *Jutland to Junkyard*. Edinburgh: Birlinn Ltd., 1999.

Gesner, Peter. *Pandora: An Archaeological Perspective*. Queensland, South Brisbane: Queensland Museum, 1991.

Gould, Richard A. *Archaeology and the Social History of Ships*. Cambridge: Cambridge University Press, 2000.

Gould, Richard A., ed. *Shipwreck Anthropology*. Albuquerque: University of New Mexico Press / School of American Research, 1983.

Grace, James W. *The Naval Battle of Guadalcanal: Night Action, 13 November 1942*. Annapolis: Naval Institute Press, 1999.

Greenhill, Basil, and John Morrison. *The Archaeology of Boats and Ships: An Introduction*. London: Conway Maritime Press, 1995.

Griffith, Paddy. *The Viking Art of War*. London: Greenhill Books, 1998.

Guilmartin, John F. *Gunpowder and Galleys: Changing Technology and Mediterranean Warfare at*

Sea in the Sixteenth Century. Cambridge: Cambridge University Press, 1974.

Harding, Richard. *Seapower and Naval Warfare: 1650–1830*. London: UCL Press, 1999.

Haywood, John. *Dark Age Naval Power: A Reassessment of Frankish and Anglo-Saxon Seafaring Activity*. 2nd edition. Norfolk, England: Anglo-Saxon Books, 1999.

Hill, Richard. *War at Sea in the Ironclad Age*. London: Cassell & Co., 2000.

Hutchinson, Gillian. *Medieval Ships and Shipping*. London: Leicester University Press, 1994.

Johnston, Paul F. *Ships and Boat Models in Ancient Greece*. Annapolis: Naval Institute Press, 1985.

Johnstone, Paul. *The Sea-Craft of Prehistory*. London and Henley: Routledge & Kegan Paul Ltd., 1980.

Keegan, John. *Battle at Sea: From Man-of-War to Submarine*. London: Pimlico, 1993.

Kemp, Paul. *The Admiralty Regrets: British Warship Losses of the 20th Century*. Phoenix Mill: Sutton Publishing, 1999.

Kirsch, Peter. *The Galleon: The Great Ships of the Armada Era*. Annapolis: Naval Institute Press, 1990.

Kloeppel, J. E. *Danger Beneath the Waves: A History of the Confederate Submarine H. L. Hunley*. Orangeburg, South Carolina: Sandlapper Press, 1987.

Kvarning, Lars-Ake, and Bengt Ohrelius. *The Vasa: The Royal Ship*. Trans. Joan Tate. Stockholm: Bokforlaget Atlantis, 1998.

Lambert, Andrew. *War at Sea in the Age of Sail*. London: Cassell & Co., 2000.

Lavery, Brian. *The Arming and Fitting of English Ships of War, 1600–1815*. Annapolis: Naval Institute Press, 1987.

Lavery, Brian, ed. *Line of Battle: The Sailing Warship, 1650–1840*. London: Conway Maritime Press, 1992.

Lavery, Brian. *The Royal Navy's First Invincible*. Portsmouth: Invincible Conservation Ltd., 1988.

Lavery, Brian. *The Ship of the Line*. 2 vols. London: Conway Maritime Press, 1983.

Lenihan, Daniel J., ed. USS *Arizona Memorial and Pearl Harbor National Historic Landmark: Submerged Cultural Resources Assessment*. Santa Fe: National Park Service, 1989.

Levathes, Louise. *When China Ruled the Seas: The Treasure Fleet of the Dragon Throne, 1405–1433*. New York: Simon & Schuster, 1994.

Lewis, Archibald R. *Naval Power and Trade in the Mediterranean*, A.D. *500–1100*. Princeton: Princeton University Press, 1951.

Lindemann, Klaus P. *Hailstorm over Truk Lagoon*. Singapore: Maruzen Asia, 1982.

MacDonald, Rod. *Dive Scapa Flow*. Edinburgh: Mainstream Publishing Company, 1990.

McKee, Alexander. *King Henry VIII's Mary Rose*. London: Souvenir Press Ltd., 1972.

Marsden, E. W. *Greek and Roman Artillery: Historical Development*. London: Oxford University Press, 1969.

Marsden, Peter. *English Heritage Book of Ships and Shipwrecks*. London: B. T. Batsford Ltd. and English Heritage, 1997.

Martin, Colin. *Full Fathom Five: The Wrecks of the Spanish Armada*. New York: Viking Press, 1975.

Martin, Colin. *Scotland's Historic Shipwrecks*. London: B. T. Batsford Ltd. and Scottish Heritage, 1998.

Martin, Colin, and Geoffrey Parker. *The Spanish Armada*. Rev. Manchester: Mandolin, 1999.

Marvel, William, ed. *The Monitor Chronicles*. New York: Simon & Schuster, 2000.

Miller, Edward M. USS *Monitor: The Ship That Launched a Modern Navy*. Annapolis: Leeward Press, 1978.

Molaug, Svein, and Rolf Scheen. *Fregatan Lossen: Et Kulturhistorisk Skattkammer*. Oslo: Norsk Sjofartsmuseum, 1983.

Morrison, J. S., and J. F. Coates. *The Athenian Trireme: The History and Reconstruction of an Ancient Greek Warship*. Cambridge: Cambridge University Press, 1986.

Morrison, J. S., and J. F. Coates. *Greek and Roman Oared Warships: 339–30 B.C.* Oxford: Oxbow Books, 1996.

Muckelroy, Keith. *Maritime Archaeology*. Cambridge: Cambridge University Press, 1978.

Murphey, Rhoads. *Ottoman Warfare: 1500–1700.* New Brunswick, New Jersey: Rutgers University Press, 1999.

Musicant, Ivan. *Divided Waters: The Naval History of the Civil War*. New York: HarperCollins, 1995.

Needham, Joseph, Ho Ping-Yu, Lu Gwei-Djen, and Wang Ling. "The Gunpowder Epic." In *Science and Civilization in China*. Vol. 5. Part 7. Cambridge: Cambridge University Press, 1971.

Olsen, Olaf, and Ole Crumlin-Pederson. *Five Viking Ships from Roskilde Fjord*. Roskilde: Viking Ship Museum, 1987.

Ormerod, H. A. *Piracy in the Ancient World*. New York: Dorset Press, 1978.

Owen, Olwyn, and Magnar Dalland. *Scar: A Viking Boat Burial on Sanday, Orkney*. Phantassie, East Linton, Scotland: Tuckwell Press, 1999.

Palmer, Roy, ed. *The Oxford Book of Sea Songs*. Oxford and New York: Oxford University Press, 1986.

Partington, J. R. *A History of Greek Fire and Gunpowder*. Cambridge: 1960.

Plutarch. *The Rise and Fall of Athens: Nine Greek Lives*. Trans. Ian Scott-Kilvert. London: Penguin Books, 1960.

Redknap, Mark, ed. *Artefacts from Wrecks: Dated Assemblages from the Late Middle Ages to the Industrial Revolution*. Oxbow Monograph 84. Oxford: Oxbow Books, 1997.

Reynolds, Clark G. *Navies in History*. Annapolis: Naval Institute Press, 1998.

Rodgers, W. L. *Greek and Roman Naval Warfare: A Study of Strategy, Tactics, and Ship Design from Salamis (480 B.C.) to Actium (31 B.C.).* Annapolis: United States Naval Institute, 1937.

Rodgers, W. L. *Naval Warfare Under Oars, 4th to 16th Centuries: A Study of Strategy, Tactics, and Ship Design*. Annapolis: United States Naval Institute, 1940.

Rule, Margaret. *The Mary Rose: The Excavation and Raising of Henry VIII's Flagship*. Annapolis: Naval Institute Press, 1982.

Samuels, Peggy, and Harold Samuels. *Remembering the Maine*. Washington and London: Smithsonian Institution Press, 1995.

Sanderson, Michael. *Sea Battles: A Reference Guide*. Middletown, Connecticut: Wesleyan University Press, 1975.

Sands, John O. *Yorktown's Captive Fleet*. Charlottesville, Virginia: University Press of Virginia and the Mariner's Museum, 1983.

Shippen, Edward. *Naval Battles Ancient and Modern*. Philadelphia: J. C. McCurdy, 1883.

Shomette, Donald G. *Flotilla: The Battle for the Patuxent*. Solomons, Maryland, 1981.

Smith, Peter L. *The Naval Wrecks of Scapa Flow*. St. Ola, Kirkwall: Orkney Press, 1989.

Smith, Roger C. *Vanguard of Empire: Ships of Exploration in the Age of Columbus*. New York: Oxford University Press, 1993.

Starr, Chester G. *The Influence of Sea Power on Ancient History*. Oxford and New York: Oxford University Press, 1989.

Starr, Chester G. *The Roman Imperial Navy*. Cambridge: Heffer, 1960.

Steffy, J. Richard. *Wooden Ship Building and the Interpretation of Shipwrecks*. College Station: Texas A & M University Press, 1994.

Stenuit, Robert. *Treasures of the Armada*. Newton Abbot: Devon, 1972.

Stewart, William H. *Ghost Fleet of the Truk Lagoon*. Missoula, Montana: Pictorial Histories, 1985.

Stillwell, Paul. *Battleship Arizona: An Illustrated History*. Annapolis: Naval Institute Press, 1991.

Torr, Cecil. *Ancient Ships*. Cambridge: Cambridge University Press, 1895.

Tucker, Spencer C. *The Jeffersonian Gunboat Navy*. Columbia: University of South Carolina Press, 1993.

Unger, Richard W., ed. *Cogs, Caravels and Galleons: The Sailing Ship, 1000–1650*. London: Conway Maritime Press, 1994.

Unger, Richard W. *The Ship in the Medieval Economy, 600–1600.* London: Croom Helm, 1980.

Vat, Dan van der. *The Grand Scuttle: The Sinking of the German Fleet at Scapa Flow in 1919.* Annapolis: Naval Institute Press, 1986.

Vegetius, Publius Flavius. *Epitome of Military Science.* Trans. and ed. N. P. Milner. Liverpool: Liverpool University Press, 1993.

Wachsmann, Shelley. *Seagoing Ships and Seamanship in the Bronze Age Levant.* College Station: Texas A & M University Press, 1998.

Weisgall, Jonathan M. *Operation Crossroads: The Atomic Tests at Bikini Atoll.* Annapolis: Naval Institute Press, 1994.

Yoshida, Mitsuru. *Requiem for Battleship Yamato.* Annapolis: Naval Institute Press, 1999.

Articles

Brown, Ruth. "Arms and Armour from Wrecks: An Introduction." In *Artefacts from Wrecks: Dated Assemblages from the Late Middle Ages to the Industrial Revolution*, edited by Mark Redknap. Oxbow Monograph 84. Oxford: Oxbow Books, 1997.

Clarke, Richard, Martin Dean, Gillian Hutchinson, Sean McGrail, and Jane Squirrell. "Recent Work on the R. Hamble Wreck near Bursledon, Hampshire." *International Journal of Nautical Archaeology* 22.1 (1993): 21–44.

Delgado, James P. "Operation Crossroads." *American History Illustrated* 28, no. 3 (May/June 1993): 50–59.

Denlay, Kevin. "Solomon Islands/Guadalcanal." *Immersed: The International Technical Diving Magazine* 2 (Summer 1996): 44–51.

Eliot, John E. "Bikini's Nuclear Graveyard." *National Geographic* CLXXXI, no. 6 (June 1992): 70–83 .

Friel, Ian. "Henry V's *Grace Dieu* and the Wreck in the R. Hamble, near Bursledon, Hampshire." *International Journal of Nautical Archaeology* 22.1 (1993): 3–19.

Garzke, William H., Jr., and Robert O. Dulin Jr. "Who Sank the *Bismarck?*" United States

Naval Institute *Proceedings* 118, no. 6 (June 1991): 48–57.

Gould, Richard A. "The Archaeology of HMS *Vixen*, an Early Ironclad Ram in Bermuda." *International Journal of Nautical Archaeology* 20.2 (1991): 141–53.

Hockmann, Olaf. "Late Roman Rhine Vessels from Mainz, Germany." *International Journal of Nautical Archaeology* 22.2 (1993): 125–35.

Hockmann, Olaf. "The Liburnian: Some Observations and Insights." *International Journal of Nautical Archaeology* 26.3 (1997): 192–216.

Lo, Jung-Pang. "The Decline of the Early Ming Navy." *Oriens Extremus* 5 (1958): 149–68.

McGrath, H. Thomas, Jr. "The Eventual Preservation and Stabilization of the USS *Cairo*." *International Journal of Nautical Archaeology and Underwater Exploration* 10.2 (1981): 79–94.

Marsden, Peter. "A Hydrostatic Study of a Reconstruction of Mainz Roman Ship 9." *International Journal of Nautical Archaeology* 22 (1993): 137–41.

Morneau, Daniel. "The Punic Warship." *Aramco World Magazine* 37, no. 6 (November/December 1986): 2–9.

Mott, Lawrence V. "Ships of the 13th Century Catalan Navy." *International Journal of Nautical Archaeology* 19.2 (1990): 101–12.

Murray, W. M., and M. Petsas. "The Spoils of Actium." *Archaeology* 41, no. 5 (1988): 28–35.

Murray, W. M., and M. Petsas. "Octavian's Campsite Memorial for the Actian War." *Transactions of the American Philosophical Association* 79, no. 4 (1989).

Neyland, Robert S. "The Archaeology of Navies: Establishing a Theoretical Approach and Setting Goals." In *Underwater Archaeology, 1998*, edited by Lawrence E. Babits, Catherine Fach, and Ryan Harris. Tucson: Society for Historical Archaeology, 1998.

Watts, Gordon P. "The Location and Identification of the Ironclad USS *Monitor*." *International Journal of Nautical Archaeology* 4.2 (1975): 301–29.

Internet Resources

The Internet is a fast-growing tool for public and professional access to research as well as virtual tours of wreck sites and museums. Site addresses are current as of May 2001 and may change.

NAVIS I: A Database on Ancient Ships
Provides excellent and detailed information on sites, ships and museums, including the Skuldelev wrecks, Gokstad and Oseberg ships, Nydam ship, Mainz ships and Marsala Punic warships.
index.waterland.net/Navis/home/frames.htm

Underwater Archaeology Branch, U.S. Navy
Discusses U.S. Navy research and its policies on sunken ships and aircraft. Links to information about wrecks such as css *Alabama*, uss *Housatonic* and others not covered in *Lost Warships*.
www.history.navy.mil/branches/nhcorg12.htm

Underwater Archaeology in France
Offers information about sites on the French coast and abroad, including the wrecks of the Battle of La Hougue, css *Alabama*, *Lomellina* and *Slava Rossii*.
www.culture.fr/culture/archeosm/en/

U.S. National Park Service's Submerged Cultural Resources Unit
Provides reports for wreck sites such as uss *Arizona*, *Cormoran*, Bikini Atoll, and *H.L. Hunley*.
www.nps.gov/scru/home.htm

Institute of Nautical Archaeology
Presents the work of George F. Bass and his colleagues, including Kevin Crisman's research on *Eagle* and other wrecks from the War of 1812.
ina.tama.edu/

National Underwater and Marine Agency
Profiles Clive Cussler's not-for-profit organization dedicated to discovering such wrecks as *H.L. Hunley* and the ships sunk in the Battle of Jutland.
www.numa.net/

Ships of Discovery
Features archaeologists working in conjunction with the Corpus Christi Museum and others to find, study and interpret ships of the age of discovery, including the Molasses Reef wreck.
www.shipsofdiscovery.org/

Individual Wrecks

AE2
www.navy.gov.au/9_sites/AE2

uss *Cairo*
www.nps.gov/vick/cairo/cairo.htm

H.L. Hunley
www.hunley.org/

Hamilton and *Scourge*
www.hamilton-scourge.city.hamilton.on.ca/

Invincible
www.wgarrett.demon.co.uk/excavat.htm

Kronan
www.kalmarlansmuseum.se/kronan/english/

Mary and Elizabeth
www.mcc.gouv.qc.ca/pamu/champs/archeo/epaphips/wreck01.htm

Mary Rose
www.maryrose.org/

uss *Massachusetts*
dhr.dos.state.fl.us/bar/uap/

uss *Monitor*
monitor.nos.noaa.gov/

Swan
www.gillean.com/SIMS/

Vasa
www.vasamuseet.se/indexeng.html

uss *Yorktown*
www.nationalgeographic.com/midway/

Index